ARAB ROUTES

Stanford Studies in
COMPARATIVE RACE AND ETHNICITY

ARAB ROUTES

Pathways to Syrian California

Sarah M. A. Gualtieri

STANFORD UNIVERSITY PRESS
Stanford, California

STANFORD UNIVERSITY PRESS
Stanford, California

Printed in the United States of America on acid-free, archival-quality paper

Library of Congress Cataloging-in-Publication Data

Names: Gualtieri, Sarah M. A., 1967– author.
Title: Arab routes : pathways to Syrian California / Sarah M. A. Gualtieri.
Other titles: Stanford studies in comparative race and ethnicity.
Description: Stanford, California : Stanford University Press, 2019. |
    Series: Stanford studies in comparative race and ethnicity |
    Includes bibliographical references and index.
Identifiers: LCCN 2019007667 | ISBN 9781503606173 (cloth : alk. paper) |
    ISBN 9781503610859 (pbk.)
Subjects: LCSH: Syrian Americans—California, Southern—Ethnic identity. |
    Arab Americans—California, Southern—Ethnic identity. |
    Immigrants—Cultural assimilation—California, Southern. |
    Arab Americans—Relations with Hispanic Americans—History. |
    California, Southern—Emigration and immigration—History. |
    California, Southern—Ethnic relations—History.
Classification: LCC F870.S98 G83 2019 | DDC 305.8009794/9—dc23
    LC record available at https://lccn.loc.gov/2019007667

Cover design by Kevin Barrett Kane

Cover image: Four male gymnasts in acrobatic balancing stunt in front
of Khoury's Café at Muscle Beach, Santa Monica, CA. Courtesy of Santa
Monica History Museum, Santa Monica History Museum Collection.

Typeset by Kevin Barrett Kane in 10.5/15 Adobe Garamond Pro

For Anees
My Light and Sky

CONTENTS

ARAB ROUTES

ARAB AMAIRKA

WHEN KATRINA SA'ADE DIED in Long Beach, California, in 1989, at the age of eighty-nine, an intricate journey that had begun in Bethlehem, Palestine, came to a close. Born in 1900 into a family that produced and sold religious objects from the Holy Land, Katrina spent her childhood in tsarist Russia, only to be displaced by the political turmoil there. She returned to Palestine, where her family arranged a marriage to a fellow Palestinian whose family had established a clothing business in Mexico. In 1914 Katrina traveled to San Pedro de las Colonias, in the northeastern state of Coahuila, Mexico, to join her eighteen-year-old husband, Emilio Kabande, who had come to Mexico by way of Cuba. Two years later, she was a widow with two children, her young husband having died in a train crash allegedly orchestrated by the armies of Mexican revolutionary Pancho Villa.[1]

Relying on family connections, Katrina made her way to Long Beach, where she remarried and later worked alongside her second husband in a five-and-dime store that catered to immigrant workers primarily from Mexico, Italy, Greece, and the Philippines. By the age of thirty-seven she was a divorced single mother, providing for her children through several entrepreneurial activities that included making and selling women's and children's apparel. In addition to her mother tongue of Arabic, Katrina spoke Russian, Spanish, and English. She lived, as her granddaughter Kathy remarked, in "five worlds" that were shaped by major historical shifts of the twentieth century: the collapse of the Ottoman Empire, the Russian and Mexican revolutions, the Great Depression, and World War II.[2]

Katrina's movement, multiple homes, and expansive family networks are recurring motifs in the history of the Arab diaspora in Southern California. Ethnically diverse, economically vibrant, and connected to the Pacific and to Latin America, Los Angeles has attracted thousands of Syrian migrants, in particular, since the late nineteenth century.[3] A *Los Angeles Times* article in 1940 claimed that fifteen thousand people made up "the Southland's Syrian colony."[4] In the twenty-first century, as figures from the US Census Bureau's American Community Survey show, Los Angeles has the largest population of Middle Eastern origin and descent in the United States; and people from Lebanon, Palestine, Syria, and Jordan (areas once referred to as "*bilad al-Sham*" or the "lands of Syria") make up the largest percentage.[5] Often depicted as new arrivals, as emblems of a crisis-ridden Middle East, or as marginal actors in fields of study dominated by the histories of other immigrant groups, Syrians are deeply layered into the western United States. They have shaped communities from Calexico to Calabasas, and their voices speak through a rich and expansive archive—border-crossing cards, naturalization and census records, newspaper articles, photographs, novels, letters, and the retelling by migrants of their journeys to and through *Amairka*.[6]

This book reconstructs the lives of men and women whose personal relationships and civic engagements capture a different facet of the history of the peopling of Los Angeles. It weaves Syrians, the first Arabic-speaking immigrants to the United States, into the tapestry of

Southern California life. By placing migrations like that of Katrina at the center of a larger narrative about the mutability of the concept of home, the attachment to multiple national identities, and the processes of Arab-Latino/a interaction, it tells a new kind of transnational immigration history. Arabic-speaking migrants and their descendants in Southern California provide a crucial window into understanding migration as a hemispheric process that was sustained by the creative navigation of nation-state boundaries and the fashioning of inter-American imaginaries.[7] *Arab Routes* thus disrupts dominant narratives in the history of Arab American migrants, redresses their erasure from California history, and complicates understandings of Latin American migration and of *Mexicanidad.*[8]

BEYOND ELLIS ISLAND

The traditional Arab American historical narrative goes something like this: at the end of the nineteenth century, thousands of Arabic-speaking migrants, most from what became the Republic of Lebanon, made their way across the Atlantic to the shores of Ellis Island, relieved by the sight of the outstretched arm of Lady Liberty. They had left lives of poverty and in some cases persecution by their Ottoman overlords. Enticed by ship agents and the stories of wealth abroad, they joined the gigantic wave of people on the move, seeking to make America their home. Lower Manhattan soon became the site of a bustling Little Syria, a community of co-ethnics building lives together as Arabs in the *mahjar,* the land of emigration.[9] New York became the "mother colony," the staging ground for a vibrant institutional and economic life rooted in peddling and trade, a place out from which families moved to other locations, predominantly in the East and Midwest.[10]

Like other classic renderings of ethnic-group assimilation, the Arab American one is based on a bounty of evidence, with passenger lists and ship manifests being an especially popular way to access the moment of arrival. Yet the narrative has also been reproduced and remythologized due to the practices of historiography, to the way history is told. These practices involve the repeated use of archives and repositories situated in New York and in Washington; the use of personal papers of people connected to those places but whose papers are housed in other repositories; the allure of Ellis Island as monument, museum, and agent in the immigration industry; and a tendency to position early Arab American history in relation to white ethnics whose stories emanate from the eastern Atlantic.

In the field of immigration history, where Arabs have too often been marginalized or made invisible, the existence of these repositories and the insertion of Arab stories into the Ellis Island narrative speaks back to that silence. An overreliance upon them, however, skews popular and scholarly accounts of Arab American history in particular ways: they are oriented toward the East Coast; they are driven by assimilationist, up-by-their-bootstraps stories of immigrant success; they focus on in-group relations instead of contact with other racial or ethnic groups; and they are bounded within nation-state paradigms. The lives of the migrants at the center of this book were not easily contained within these categories.[11] They moved in and around the Southwest and came together in organizations celebrating their Pacific orientation. Some spoke Spanish and naturalized as Mexican, and then as US American; and they labored in varied economic niches including as seamstresses, grocery-store clerks, mechanics, merchants, growers, and peddlers. Importantly, they worked and lived alongside Latino/as and formed alliances with them. *Arab Routes* opens the narrative up to these Syrians of the Pacific not for the sake of finding exceptions or aberrations, but to ask how their stories help to reorient the field of Arab American studies. This endeavor encourages the posing of new questions and devising new methods to answer them. If we continue to think metaphorically of New York as the "mother colony," then *Arab Routes* is interested in other kinds of family idioms—her unacknowledged lovers, her forgotten half-sisters, her surrogate daughters, and her renegade sons. This book finds them in places like El Paso,

Pasadena, Los Angeles, Long Beach, and San Pedro de las Colonias. It tells the story of how they shaped a Syrian American culture that was Arabized and Latinized—a culture that was highly flexible and mobile, one that revolved around family networks, religious practices, work, and leisure. Whereas scholars of US migration once focused primarily on how immigrants "became American" by shedding ethnic ties and integrating into a dominant Anglo American culture, this book contributes to a rich body of work that demonstrates how migrants retained, adapted, and forged new solidarities in multiracial environments.[12]

ARAB LATINIDAD

It was in San Pedro de las Colonias, Mexico, that Katrina learned the Spanish she later used with her customers in a small grocery store in Arizona. When she first left Mexico for Long Beach, she left extended Palestinian family there that would become "the Mexican side of the family." Three generations later, Katrina's relatives form part of the large, heterogeneous community of Arab origin and descent in Mexico. They understand their Mexicanness to include Syrian expressive culture, Arabic food ways, and family networks that reaffirm the history of early migrants.

This sense of belonging to a panethnic Latin America, of *being* Latin American, and expressing this attachment in an Arabized register—what I call Arab *Latinidad*—is conveyed in the sources in multiple ways.[13] Elias Vitar, for example, came to Southern California as a Spanish-speaking migrant of "Syrian race" and Mexican nationality. He was born in Monterrey, Mexico, in 1916 and after crossing at Laredo, Texas, traveled west to Los Angeles to work as a lumber salesman. He took up residence east of downtown. His warm hazel eyes look out from the declaration of intention he filed to become an American citizen (see Figure 1), with the Arabic name Elias, rendered into Spanish as "Helias" (mistyped as "Heilas") and his nickname, "Leo," firmly signed at the bottom of his photo.[14] He is among the thousands of

Syrians in Southern California who formed part of a Latin American migration stream, and whose identities point to the multiethnic make-up of the Mexican nation. His story suggests that Mexicanness could be embodied by men and women who also carried with them the cultures of the Middle East.[15]

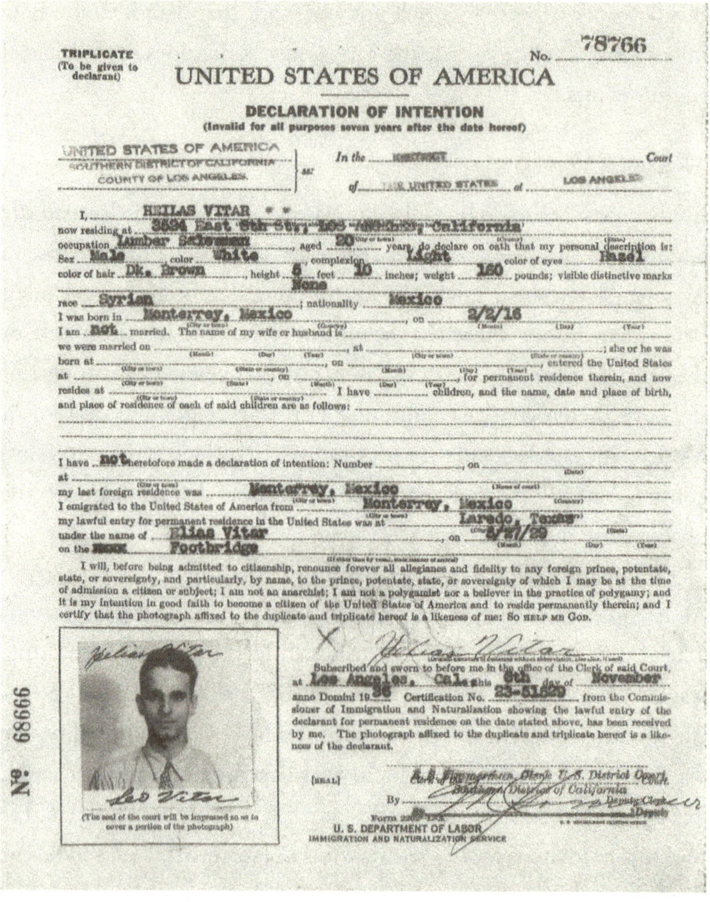

FIGURE 1. Declaration of Intention to Become an American Citizen of Heilas [sic] Vitar, 1936. Source: National Archives and Records Administration. *Naturalization Records of the US District Court for the Southern District of California, Central Division (Los Angeles), 1887–1940.* Ancestry.com.

Like Elias, most Syrian immigrants to Los Angeles were what historian Leslie Page Moch calls "step migrants"—their journey to Southern California involved multiple stops, stages, or "steps."[16] Los Angeles represented the second, third, or greater long-distance migration for them; and they came to the city for a multitude of reasons. Some had family members there, while others searched for years for the familial. They pursued a variety of trades and professions and lived in different locations. Although narratives of migration often assume a linear trajectory, the movement of the Syrian American diaspora was multilineal. Many families moved several times within the city itself and not infrequently back to places they had been before.

New York was a common point of entry to the United States for Syrians, but many came in from Mexico and Canada, having first lived in other parts of the Americas. Naturalization records for Southern California, for example, reveal three main pathways to Los Angeles: (1) Syria to France (through Cherbourg, Le Havre, or Marseilles) on to New York City and then to California; (2) Syria to France (again through Cherbourg, Le Havre, or Marseilles), to Canada, and then to California; or alternatively, (3) Syria to Mexico to El Paso and ultimately California. These government records capture only points along the journey. Augmented by other sources, they indicate the interstices of transatlantic and intrahemispheric travel, and the intricacies of the social worlds that migrants inhabited and shaped along the way.[17]

Scholars have argued that migrants used this last pathway (from Mexico) as a "back door" to the United States, particularly as a way to evade medical inspection after the passage of the Disease Act of 1891, which gave US immigration officials the right to turn away any migrant suspected of harboring a "loathsome and contagious" disease. To be sure, one disease, trachoma, an infection of the eye, was a major concern for Syrian migrants in the early twentieth century. Oral histories often reveal that the most dreaded part of the inspection process at Ellis Island was the flipping back of the eyelid with a "buttonhook" tool normally used to pull shoelaces tight. A diagnosis

of trachoma meant exclusion, separation from family, and in some
cases a decision to attempt entry into the United States via alternate
routes perceived to be more porous and less regulated. In 1907 the
US Immigration Bureau expressed concern with a so-called "smug-
gling ring" in El Paso orchestrated by a Syrian interpreter who was
allegedly demanding bribes from Syrians, some of whom were seeking
treatment for trachoma.[18]

Other records suggest that Syrians "dressed up" or performed as Mexicans in order to pass more easily across the border. The commissioner-
general of immigration and naturalization wrote to the inspector in
charge at El Paso to inform him that: "the inspectors, assigned to
bridge duty . . . are by no means vigilant in the performance of their
duties, since they apparently pay little attention to persons [who] have
the appearance of being Mexicans, which has led to that form of dis-
guise being adopted by aliens of other nationalities who are desirous
of finding an easy means of ingress to this country."[19]

These reports reveal more about the state's concern with policing
the border and producing a discourse around a "fit" citizenry, than they
do about the lives of Syrian migrants. Moreover, while the US government relied on systems of classification that favored homogeneity and
single categories, the lived experience of Syrians was far more complex
and liminal. Syrians who came into the United States from Mexico
were not just dressed up as Mexicans, and sojourns in Mexico or other
parts of the Americas were not merely way stations to the United States.
They were crucial chapters in the development of transnational families
and of diasporic identity, chapters that allow us to understand the ease
with which Katrina Sa'ade slipped into Spanish when relatives from
Mexico visited her in her Long Beach home.

Taking account of these different registers of identity, *Arab Routes*
builds on the critical turn in ethnic and American studies that moves
away from a focus on a single ethnic group often contained in a particular location (the Mexicans in Chicago, the Italians in New York City,
and so on), to demonstrate the importance of circulation over against

settlement, and of the existence of multiple ethnicities within a migrant group.[20] Many of the migrants whose life histories are at the center of this book were Syrian-born, Arabic- and Spanish-speaking individuals. They were both Syrian and Latin American, indicating the overlap of identities often thought of as discrete and bounded by rigid communal and national ties. This suggests the extent to which patterns of migration and identity—including ones typically thought of as exclusively Latino/a—have been Arabized in significant ways.

The archive of California's Syrian population is replete with evidence that speaks to the Latin Americanness of many families, yet because of scholarly conventions that tend to bind migrants in nation-state boundaries, these families are lost in the analysis. There are compelling books on the Lebanese in Brazil and Argentina, the Syrians and Palestinians in Mexico and in Colombia, and many other case studies of Arab communities in particular countries.[21] A newer body of scholarship in Middle Eastern migration studies addresses the bias in the historiography (one that deemed migrants lost to the nation), and argues for the centrality of migrant histories in shaping the economic, political, and social realities of the modern Middle East. It has also more recently demonstrated the significance of Arabic-speaking migrants from geographical Syria to the colonial tropes of progress and modernity.[22] All of these works tell important stories of migration and integration into sometimes fraught national projects.[23] Yet when people are on the move, the story becomes more complicated.[24]

A photo from the twentieth annual commencement ceremony of Flintridge Sacred Heart Academy in Pasadena, California, in 1951, for example, contains language that is instructive. Among the thirty graduates are three young women with Arab last names: Mary Ann Kuri, Agnes Necebia Haddad, and Bertha Marie Touche.[25] Bertha was born in Chihuahua, Mexico, to Palestinian parents with US citizenship. We find a link to California in her father's 1924 border-crossing card at El Paso, Texas, indicating that he was on his way to Venice, California, presumably to attend to the affairs of his recently deceased father.[26] Was Bertha Mexican, Palestinian, Syrian, or American? This book finds answers in the spaces and places in which these categories commingled, overlapped, and resonated. It *unbinds* migrants from national boundaries in order to identify the effects of multiple migrations and to recognize that many migrants embodied a kind of national simultaneity. Their stories remind us that "transnationalism challenges concepts of citizenship and of nationhood itself."[27]

To say that Syrians were part of the heterogeneity of the Mexican nation is not to say that they were Mexican in the same way that the Spanish-speaking migrants and their children who formed the backbone of a vibrant, yet often vilified, Latino/a community in Southern California were. Rather, it is to argue that understanding Syrian identifications with Mexicanness—as a product of having Mexican-born children, of having lived in Latin America, speaking Spanish, and of having relationships with Mexicans—pushes Arab American studies out of a US-centric framework and underscores the fruitful intersections with Latin American, Latino/a, and Asian American studies. These intersections, captured in the lives of those in the spaces in between national categories, can serve to unravel multiple discourses of exclusion. Jonathon Fox describes, for example, the ways that different groups, notably bilingual indigenous and immigrant populations, have been "culturally excluded from the [Mexican] national imaginary," a process that US-based scholarship has also documented in various ways.[28]

And while this book does not claim equal degrees of expertise across the archival terrain of the United States, Mexico, Syria, and Lebanon, it does propose a method for exploring the lives of those who moved across them. It builds on recent scholarship that pluralizes Mexicanidad, incorporating multiple ethnic groups within it, and by positioning Syrians within Latin American migration streams to California. Most especially, it conceptualizes Los Angeles and its surroundings as an "intersecting node for many journeys" and the historical ground on which were forged forgotten alliances, and connections between Middle Eastern American and Latino/a activist projects.[29]

Thus, the central narrative thread of the book is one of intercommunal, particularly Latino/a and Arab, solidarities and tensions.

A case in point, Syrian petitions for US citizenship reveal that those who served as witnesses (testifying that they knew the applicant and that she or he was in good standing) very often had Spanish surnames. That Syrians developed trusted friendships with people particularly of Mexican origin and descent is hardly surprising given the patterns of residential segregation in pre–World War II Los Angeles—patterns that drew non-Anglos into close contact with each other. However, these solidarities and "strange affinities" should also be connected to the Latinidad of the Syrian diaspora and to histories of community building, language acquisition, and identification that occurred prior to migration to Los Angeles, most notably in Latin America.[30] These connections were sustained by back-and-forth travel to Mexican towns like San Pedro de las Colonias and Monterrey, and help to explain Syrian racialization as relational and ethnic identity as flexible.[31]

ARCHIVAL ACTIVISM AND
SYRIAN RACIAL PALIMPSESTS

Arab Routes traces the interconnectedness of Syrian communities in diaspora and uses a transnational framework to capture the overlapping strands of Syrian American identity. It situates the project within a continental Amairka, a geographical descriptor as well as a place that exists in the realm of the imagination, and into which we can map the connections that Southern Californian Syrians had to multiple locations.

The research for this project is based on a rich and varied archival base from California, Texas, Syria, Lebanon, and Mexico. I am the first scholar to work extensively with the naturalization records of Syrians filed at the US District Court for the Southern District in Los Angeles between 1887 and 1940 (often reviewing multiple records for each of the approximately 1,140 persons I studied).

Containing information on birthplace, date of arrival in the United States, occupation, and other information necessary for the application for US citizenship, these records have been especially useful for developing a demographic profile of the early Arab community in Southern California.

Perhaps most significant, the naturalization records have allowed me to track the complex patterns of movement and remigration that characterized the experience of Syrians in Los Angeles. I follow the story of families like that of Nessim and Victoria Hoha, originally from Aleppo, Syria, whose nine children were born in three different countries (Egypt, Argentina, and the United States). The Hoha family lived in three of the principal nodes of the Syrian diaspora, acquiring knowledge of different languages, nationalities, and experience of highly cosmopolitan environments.[32] In addition, Nessim Hoha's petition for naturalization suggests the complex layers of Syrian racial identity as seen through the prism of US naturalization law. His 1937 declaration of intention to become an American citizen (see Figure 2) lists his color as "white," his complexion as "medium," his nationality as "Turkey," and his race as "Hebrew" (indicating a Syrian Jew). I use these records to explain both identifications with, and disassociations from, Arabness. Nessim was one of the founders of the first Sephardic synagogue in Los Angeles, and he took the family name Levy. This occlusion of Arabness (but not of Syrianness) is one of the threads this project narrates as it explores the origins, evolutions, and contradictions of social identities.

In addition to my review of naturalization and census records, my interviews with members of the extended families at the center of this project offer especially rich material to amplify the sections of the book that deal with connections to Syria, Lebanon, and Palestine across generational lines. I have also made use of family papers, letters to religious officials, records of organizations and churches, newspapers, and directories that allow me to explore a set of theoretical questions around fragmented archives, the erasure of Syrian Americans from California history, and of Arab Americans more generally from narratives of the

American West. This endeavor has involved revisiting, both literally and conceptually, established and heavily used archives in order to reposition them away from the Ellis Island trope. The Faris and Yamna Naff Arab American Collection at the Smithsonian Institution, for example, deposited by the indefatigable historian and daughter of Lebanese immigrants, Alixa Naff, yielded surprising western US origins.

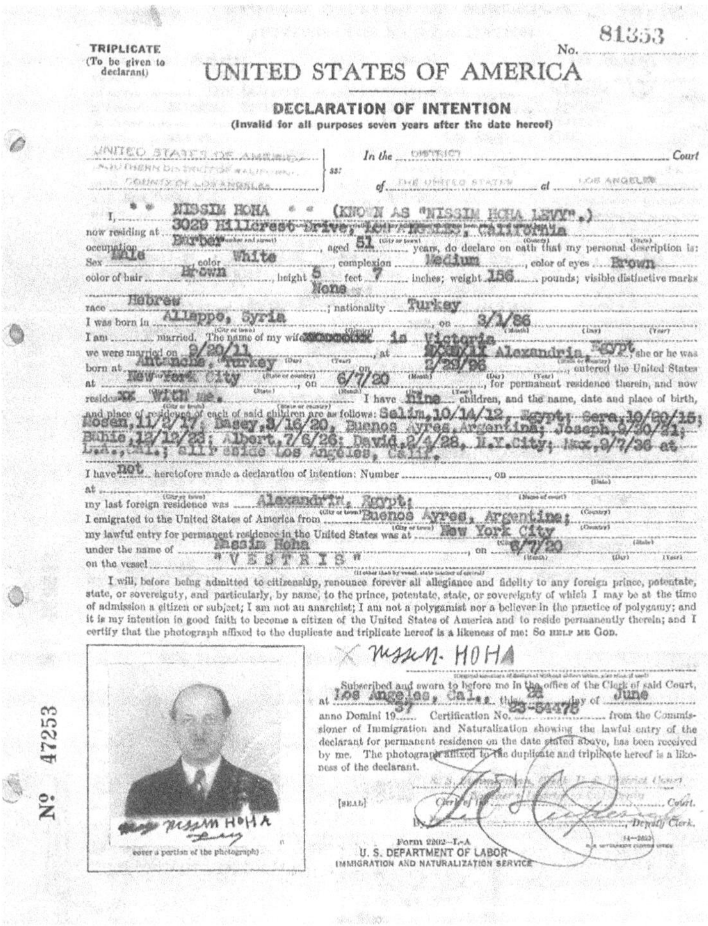

FIGURE 2. Declaration of Intention to Become an American Citizen of Nessim Hoha, 1937. Source: National Archives at Riverside, CA. *Records of District Courts of the United States, 1685–2009*. Ancestry.com.

Engaging with this Syrian American archive also revealed the slippage between categories of evidence: oral histories became sites for the gathering of photos, letters, and passports, which allowed me to supplant, augment, and reinterpret material found in national, state, and local archives, while the retrieval of documents from homes and libraries became occasions for interviews. Historian Alessandro Portelli has written that "Oral history . . . refers [to] what the source [that is, the narrator/interviewee] and the historian [that is, the interviewer] do together at the moment of their encounter in the interview." Portelli's emphasis on the "doing together," or what he calls the "dialogic exchange" in oral history, is an important corrective to stances that assume that the material provided by the narrator is the "stuff" to which the scholar applies her analysis. Rather, it is through the dynamic of listening, asking questions, and redirecting that the interviewer and the interviewee collaborate on the task of interpretation.[33]

Moreover, while we often associate the archive with repositories where material is held and cataloged, the oral history interview is often a place where *archival transactions* occur. In nearly all the interviews I conducted for this book, I have been shown material from family papers, given videos and photographs, copied things, returned things, and received things anew. There is a space in time, in other words, in which the archive is mobile, existing between a place where it is not yet cataloged and rendered classifiable. It exists in a set of entrusted transactions between the writer/researcher and the interviewee. While sitting at the dining room table with Vera Tamoush, for example, I noticed a weathered copy of a phone book called the *Pacific Syrian-American Guide* published in 1936. This guide allowed me to develop a richer demographic profile of the Syrian community in Southern California, including places of residence and occupations; while it also encouraged the probing of different imaginaries, notably the Syrian Pacific.

It bears reiterating that rather than just augment the archive, oral history helps produce it. And it is in this production that we find the fabric of the transnational, not as straight or fully ironed cloth, not as "chains, paths, threads, and conjunctions," but as frayed, knotted, and reknotted points where we identify the intensification of relationships to multiple homes.[34]

CHAPTER DESCRIPTIONS

Arab Routes uses a mixed-method approach and Arab American analytic to explore overlapping layers of Syrian identity in Southern California in five substantive chapters. Each chapter captures interethnic, relational, racial, and gendered formations in different ways. Chapter 1 traces the pathways through which Arabic-speaking migrants arrived in Los Angeles and describes how areas of the city served as steps toward further movement and consolidation of family networks that spanned the Americas. Drawing on James Clifford's theorization of routes, over against roots, the chapter uses the concept of routing, an active, ongoing process of travel and of the social contacts associated with it.[35] Specifically, it locates El Paso, Texas, as a central point in Syrian circuits of mobility and in the migrant imaginary—a place through which thousands of Syrians crossed, returned, and helped to forge a Spanish-speaking Syrian borderland culture. It explores the economic life of this migrant community, reaching beyond the peddler-to-proprietor paradigm, with a focus on disjunctures and ruptures, particularly those connected to the stresses of the Great Depression. Chapter 1, The Syrian Pacific, also probes the ways in which Syrians creatively navigated the US immigration regime and were pieces in what Alexandra Stern has called the "eugenic puzzle of the 1920s."[36]

Chapter 2 examines another site of interethnic contact: Syrian participation in the defense of sixteen Mexican American youth who were convicted, on weak circumstantial evidence, in the murder of José Díaz in 1942, near a popular Los Angeles meeting spot called the Sleepy Lagoon. The case fueled tensions that erupted in the Zoot Suit Riots in 1943. By homing in on the role that Syrian American defense attorney George Shibley played in the trial and acquittal of the accused (particularly his strategy to Americanize the defendants in the face of the prosecution's attempt to portray them as foreign and dangerous because of their "Oriental characteristics"), the chapter probes issues of interethnic and international solidarity that arose from the case. It further exposes the archival silences in the voluminous Sleepy Lagoon Defense Committee (SLDC) papers housed at University of California, Los Angeles, which were donated by activist and SLDC executive secretary Alice McGrath. Exploring the fragments of Shibley in this archive and his whitewashing in the memorialization of the case, including in Chicano playwright Luis Valdez's celebrated play, *Zoot Suit,* I discuss a broader paradox in contemporary ethnic studies—that post-9/11 critiques of profiling and racial "othering" of Middle Eastern migrants and refugees to the United States often obscure earlier layers of Arab American coalition-building.

Chapter 3 shifts to the register of self-representation to explore the Southern California *mahrajan* (outdoor festival) as an important space of Syrian community formation and image making. Building on scholarship about festival culture, this chapter discusses the adaptation of this "homeland" event to the California landscape, paying particular attention to the themes of institution building, the gendering of traditions considered emblematic of Syrian culture, such as food and music, and the marketing of the festivals to Syrian American youth.[37] Based on oral histories and newspaper and magazine coverage, including of mahrajan mainstay, actor Danny Thomas, Meeting at the Mahrajan counters the portrayal of the festivals as mere social events organized by the Syrian churches and considers them rather as spaces of incubation of an Arab American activist voice.[38]

Chapter 4 revisits the insights of the groundbreaking anthology, *Food for Our Grandmothers,* to map the spatial and affective ties to multiple homes.[39] It explores second- and third-generation Syrian American engagement with questions of identity through feminist activism, cultural production, and archiving. The chapter analyzes the oral histories shared with me by Arab American women, including the granddaughters of early twentieth-century migrants to Southern California.

Expanding upon literary critic Carol Fadda-Conrey's concept of "re-arrival" and Nadine Naber's concept of "diasporas of empire," I focus on how these women narrate their journey through highly assimilated Americanness toward Arabness.[40] Highlighting the importance of travel to Palestine and Lebanon to my interviewees, and of their reassessment of the racialized Californian terrain upon their return (or "rearrival"), the chapter posits a particular form of Arab American critique of US imperial ventures in the Middle East, while it also theorizes engagement with the documentary past as a form of activism.[41]

Chapter 5 extends the central themes of the book with an analysis of several texts to demonstrate how California has acquired an iconic dimension, in narratives of Syrian and Lebanese migration. It explores a set of photographs taken in the 1940s at the original Muscle Beach near the Santa Monica Pier that feature agile acrobats set against the backdrop of a Syrian-owned café. I again use the concept of the palimpsest, a layer of obscured detail lying underneath another more obvious one, to pull out the meanings of this Arab presence rendered oblique by the passage of time. The chapter also includes a discussion of Lebanese author Rabee Jaber's prize-winning novel in Arabic, *Amerika,* which narrates the experience of its central character, Marta Haddad, a turn-of-the-twentieth-century migrant, as she moves from the East Coast to Pasadena, routing first through New Orleans to track down her wayward husband.[42] Beyond Jaber's obvious interventions that include centering the story around the migration of a Lebanese woman, unsettling the rags-to-riches trope, and bringing Syrian characters into contact with other racialized groups, the novel is important because of the way it engages with, yet fictionalizes, Arab American archives.

Arab Routes ends with a return to origins by discussing interviews that "the mother of Arab American studies," Alixa Naff, conducted in Los Angeles after she moved from Detroit to the Southland in 1959. Her book, *Becoming American,* is the foundational text of the study of Arabs in the United States. Naff's work solidified the East Coast and

Midwest orientation in the field, but the lesser-explored California beginnings of her project reveal the importance of westward pathways, and of the people encountered along them, to the early migrants.

These literary, personal, and visual texts offer powerful examples to nonhistorians on how to reinscribe Syrians into Southern Californian history, while they also suggest new possibilities on how to orient Arab American studies within a Pacific space. By telling a story of how Arabic-speaking people of Syrian origin helped forge a global Los Angeles, this book counters a long history of portrayals of Arabs that rely on stereotypes of outsiderness, and it underscores their place in debates around interethnic solidarities, past and present.

CHAPTER I

THE SYRIAN PACIFIC

IN A 2011 interview conducted at her home in La Brea, California, Vera Tamoush, the daughter of Syro-Lebanese immigrants to Los
Angeles, related how her father, Mansur, had hired a young Mexican
woman named Sipriana to serve as a "mother's helper" in their Boyle
Heights home. The young woman spoke Spanish to the children and to
Mansur, who was fluent. When I remarked to Vera on her father's facility
with the Spanish language, she exclaimed: "Oh yes, he was Mexican!"[1]

How did Mansur Nahra, from the tiny village of Kobeh in Mount
Lebanon, become so identified with being Mexican that his own
daughter described him as such? Answering this question involves
tracing the physical movement of Mansur from Kobeh to Homs in
present-day Syria, to Monterrey, Mexico, where he worked for several
years before moving via Laredo, Texas, to Los Angeles in 1913.[2] In
one of the many government documents generated by this movement,
his border-crossing card lists his first names as "Mansur or Manuel,"
suggesting the Spanishization of his identity in Mexico.[3] Yet another,

his declaration of intention to become an American citizen, filed at
the Los Angeles Superior Court that same year, lists his US address as
3448 Opal Street in Boyle Heights.[4] Situated east of downtown Los
Angeles, Boyle Heights was home to a multiethnic, primarily working-class immigrant community; a community where, as Vera later
recollected, Syrian, Greek, Russian, and Mexican families shared their
respective holiday dishes, and where her Syrian neighbor was married
to a Mexican woman. The 1920 census finds Mansur and his wife,
Shafiqa, by then new parents, sharing a home on New Jersey Street,
also in Boyle Heights, with extended family. Mansur's brothers Antonio and Naoum, who had also lived in Mexico, were part of the
household, as was Shafiqa's brother, Saur Hallal.[5]

This movement to and within the Americas reveals Mansur to be a
quintessential step migrant, making several long journeys throughout
his lifetime in pursuit of stability and economic security for his family.[6]
He was not simply a Syrian immigrant who ended up in Los Angeles
but also a man who came to the City of Angels imprinted with experiences in revolutionary Mexico. He was a Spanish- and Arabic-speaking
merchant whose "Mexicanness" may help explain why he ended up
in East Los Angeles, the owner of a furniture store on First Street that
catered to a Spanish-, English-, and Arabic-speaking clientele; a man
who served as best man for his Mexican employee, Ysidoro, in 1929;
and who, after a move from Boyle Heights to suburban Downey at his
wife's urging, still longed for the rhythms of life in East LA.[7]

This chapter aims to unsettle the boundaries of Middle East migration studies and to extend the cultural and social history of Arab
America by more fully considering Mansur Nahra's, and that of others
like him with similar patterns of movement and connection to Mexico.
It tells a story not so much of interethnic relations between Syrians
and Latinos but of intracommunal heterogeneity that maps identification with Latin America and facility with the Spanish language onto
Arabic-speaking migrants in California. Put another way, this chapter
tries to understand what it meant for Mansur to move through the

world as a man from Mount Lebanon who, as his daughter Vera un-equivocally affirmed, "was at heart a Mexican."[8]

To do this, I resist the impulse to classify Southern California Syrian migrants using solely the categories of the US immigration and naturalization regime. Mansur's naturalization papers, for example, list him as "Syrian." However, when he filed his declaration to become a US citizen in 1913, he renounced "forever all allegiance and fidelity to any foreign prince, potentate, state, or sovereignty, and particularly to *The United States of Mexico*" [italics added]. To acquire US citizenship, Mansur had to renounce his Mexican citizenship, which had taken at least three years to acquire. In the time that he lived in Mexico, he was part of a well-established network of Syro-Lebanese communities clustered in Mexico City, and in various towns in the states of Coahuila, Chihuahua, Puebla, and Veracruz.[9]

The approach here embraces the complexities and fluidity of identity that are, ironically, found on closer scrutiny of the records of the state that are too often analyzed in linear and teleological ways. We can read Mansur's declaration of intention as a document that captures his process of becoming American, imbued with assimilatory ambitions and a desire to acquire the rights of citizenship in the United States. If, however, we categorize the document as one of renouncement, of losing a set of legal rights within Mexico, we are encouraged to ask different questions. How did his time in Mexico shape him? What were the implications of losing Mexican citizenship? As a speaker of Spanish, what kinds of relationships did he forge in Los Angeles?

Mansur Nahra maintained a connection to his Mexicanness after he crossed into the United States in 1913. That same year, Adela Rico Mazon crossed the border, and twelve years later she became the teenage bride of Ysidoro Organista (see Figure 3). Originally from Teocaltiche, in the state of Jalisco, Ysidoro had entered the US at El Paso in 1916.[10] The lives of all three would intersect in the polyglot neighborhood of Boyle Heights, and Mansur and Ysidoro, two Mexicans of different ethnicity, would end up working together in Mansur's furniture store, sharing not only their work life, but also, as the resplendent photo of Ysidoro and his young wife suggests, social and familial intimacies.

Marriage, and the communal ties associated with it, brought other Syrian Mexicans together too. In the same interview, Vera recalled the love affair between her uncle Rafiq (Rufie) Hallal and his young wife, Jennie, of the Khoury (Kuri) family. Rufie was a straitlaced, bow tie–wearing storeowner who poured his money into three stores near the Santa Monica Pier. Jennie was previously Juana Kuri, from Torreón, in the state of Coahuila, Mexico. She crossed into the United States with her brother, Emilio, in October of 1924. In the still-evolving and inconsistent categorizations of the US Department of Labor, which assessed her "head tax" (a tax imposed on noncitizens entering the US), her nationality is listed as "Mexican," her race as "Syrian," and her language read and spoken as "Spanish." When she petitioned to become an American citizen in 1943, she changed her name to Jennie "K" Hallal, effacing, at least in this documentary evidence, her Spanish first name.[11]

FIGURE 3. Marriage of Ysidoro Organista and Adela Rico in 1929, with Mansur Nahra (right, seated) serving as best man. Mansur's wife, Shafiqa, sits to the left. Courtesy of Vera Tamoush.

Of 1,136 petitions for naturalization that were filed in the California Southern District Court in Los Angeles between 1887 and 1949, forty-six show entry via Mexico.[12] While this is admittedly a small percentage, it is worth keeping in mind that these records consist only of those who intended to become citizens of the United States; they do not capture the movement of people who did not apply to naturalize.

These documents also, even in their numerical thinness, point to a thicker story around the place of El Paso in Syrian American history.[13] When scholars take account of the different kinds of records and remembrances generated by Syrian migrants in California, they should consider El Paso a node in the Syrian American imaginary—a space through which thousands of Syrians crossed, a place to which many returned and forged lives as Spanish-speaking, borderland Syrians. Mansour Farah, for example, founder of the famous Farah clothing company in El Paso, had first owned a dry goods store in Las Cruces, New Mexico, before moving to New York City to learn the garment trade (in what we might characterize as a reverse migration). Returning to El Paso, he expanded his small factory into a clothing empire, and members of the Farah family became scions among the Syro-Lebanese industrialists of the Southwest. Employing thousands of mostly Chicana seamstresses, the company has a history that captures the fraught relations between the worker's rights movement and immigrant entrepreneurship.[14]

While the story of the Farah family resonates with the arriviste trope in the narrative of Syrian migration, the most common Syrian niche in El Paso was in small-scale grocery and dry goods stores. So ubiquitous was the Syrian presence in the grocery niche in El Paso, according to Linda Gomez, whose first informal job was in a Syrian-owned store, that the words *grocer* and *Syrian* were practically synonymous.[15] More to the point, El Paso figured in the journey of thousands of ordinary Syrians, those whose stories, unlike the Farah

family's success narrative, are not captured in the historiography. The
US National Archives contain more than twenty-six thousand records
of border crossings from Mexico to the United States, the vast majority at El Paso, in which the race is listed as "Syrian."[16]

NORTH FROM MEXICO . . . AND OTHER
PARTS OF THE WESTERN HEMISPHERE

Syrians were moving in and around the borderlands from the late
nineteenth century on, but there were periods when migration north
from Mexico accelerated due to political upheaval. The events of the
Mexican Revolution (1910–1920) figure prominently in the recollections of early Syrian migrants to Southern California. Indeed, Syrians
of Mexican nationality were part of a more generalized movement related to the disruptions of the revolution. Katrina Sa'ade might have
stayed in what, by her own account, was a comfortable life in San
Pedro de las Colonias, Coahuila, but like thousands of other residents
of northern Mexico, her sense of security was shattered when her husband became a casualty of the clashes along key transportation lines.[17]
She thus embarked on yet another long-distance migration to Long
Beach, California, with her young daughter, Julia, and there married a
fellow Palestinian, Suleiman Farhat. If we unpack her movement even
further, we see that the disturbance of the revolution did not prevent
the new configuration of her family from returning to Mexico in 1921,
this time to Hermosillo in the state of Sonora. The family viewed the
move as opportune, given Katrina's facility with the Spanish language
and the deteriorating economic situation in the United States. Typical of the way state documents efface women's complex work lives,
Katrina's border-crossing card lists her occupation as "none," while
her oral history reveals her crucial involvement in the family store.
Because her second husband couldn't speak Spanish and didn't know
the business very well, she was left to manage it. She recalled:

> I was 21 when I remarried (Solomon [Suleiman]) Farhat. We came
> to Long Beach in 1919 and I met him. When we married, we went

to Mexico. Over there you make better money. I had to be in the store and take care of George [her son]. Every day, I am in the store at 8 a.m. One time I was giving him a bath; his uncle came to stay with us. He said, "Katrina, come and talk to these people, we can't understand them." You think he make the money?[18]

Within two years, the Farhats were back again in Southern California, and then tried their luck at a mining town in Jerome, Arizona. The relocations and displacements did not end there. Yearning to return to Palestine, Suleiman urged Katrina to move back ahead of him with three of their children while he tried to resolve their debts in San Francisco. Within a few months, she found herself in a bitter dispute with her husband's parents over money and the care of her children. In a gripping and often heartbreaking correspondence with Suleiman over the space of two years (1933–1934), Katrina beseeches him to intervene on her behalf, finally taking the decision to leave Palestine with her children and head back to the United States. In a scathing letter in Arabic to the Orthodox patriarch in the ecclesiastical court in Jerusalem, through whom the Farhat family initiated divorce proceedings (it was granted in 1937), she condemned her treatment: "I am in astonishment and pain. I cannot believe that this is happening to me. He is doing to me what he did to his [previous] woman . . . Are we women like old clothes, whenever a man chooses he would take off his clothes and put on a new suit?"[19] Not only did Katrina condemn the lack of financial support extended to her by her husband, but also the practice by men in the mahjar, the land of emigration, of taking more than one wife. Suleiman had claimed he was single when he married Katrina, but she later found out that he had a wife (the Arabic used in the letter is *hurma*) and daughter from whom he was estranged.[20] While his letters to Katrina after he returned to Palestine suggest that he was initially interested in reconciliation, the divorce made clear that he was moving on. He soon remarried to a woman from Gaza and had four children with her.[21]

Katrina settled for the third time in Long Beach (see Figure 4). The 1940 census shows her as the head of household to a family consisting of her two daughters, Julia and Mary, and son, Fred. According to her granddaughter, Kathy, she poured her life savings into the purchase of a commercial building with a storefront on the lower level and apartments on the upper. With her earnings, she purchased a three-bedroom home, where she lived the rest of her life. The connection to Mexico was maintained through family visits and through her daughter Julia's decision to take her own daughters there for visits.

FIGURE 4. Katrina (Katherine) Sa'ade Farhat, Long Beach, probably 1930s. Courtesy of Kathy Saade Kenny.

These connections fostered a distinctly Latin American Syrian imaginary that folded attachment to the Southwest and to Mexico into understandings of Arab America. Indeed, by the mid-1930s, Syrians had a new term for expressing their place of belonging: *the Syrian Pacific*.

AN ARAB WESTERN IMAGINARY

By 1937 Los Angeles had the largest Arab population in seven western and southwestern states, according to the *Pacific Syrian-American Guide*. Compiled by Reverend Methodios Shalhoob, archmissionary for the Orthodox Church in the western states, the guide included the names and addresses of Syrians in Arizona, California, New Mexico, Nevada, Oregon, Texas, and Washington. It shares many of the characteristics of Syrian immigrant texts in English, which aim to convey information on the Syrian American community in terms that resonate with assimilation discourses, yet it also captures the obverse, that is, the ways that members of the community rendered their American spaces "Syrian."[22]

The opening sections of the guide contain copies of speeches by Syrian immigrant leaders, as well as letters from state governors. Frank F. Merriam, then the governor of California, noted: "Throughout the years your people have responded to the high ideals of individual and social justice. They have always cooperated in movements planned for the benefit of mankind."[23] A short letter of support also came from Governor Sholtz of Florida, where in 1929, Syrian grocer Nola Romey had been lynched and his wife, Fannie, killed by the Lake City chief of police.[24] In the rosy words of a New Deal politician, Sholtz obfuscated the terror that the lynching had brought upon the Romey family and the fear that it had roused among other southern Syrians. He exclaimed: "The splendid accomplishments of the Syrians have not escaped the attention of our intelligent thinking people and we are proud of the contribution that they are making as American citizens in upholding our principles of government and in the various fields of industry and commerce. I number the Syrians of Florida among my friends and consider them upright, law-abiding citizens."[25]

The guide incorporates the patriotic rhetoric of the Syrian immigrant leadership.[26] Its published keynote address by Abraham M. Malouf, the presiding chairman of the Western Federation of Syrian-American Societies, an organization that served as the connective tissue for Syrians across the United States, celebrates Syrian assimilability.

Entitled "The Syrian People in the United States as a Cornerstone in American Life," Malouf's address notes that in Syria's "climate and physiographic formation it is almost the picture of the State of California; ocean on the west, mountains on the east, cold weather on the north, and tropical climate on the south; similar also in its agricultural products and climatic conditions."[27] The guide thus orients the Syrian American toward a western and Pacific focal point, not an eastern one. It makes sense of this space as one of consolidation and extension, and it claims affinity between Syria and California in geographical and topographical terms.

There is also a tone of relief in these assertions of affinity. Reverend Shalhoob's support of President Roosevelt's New Deal is palpable, his tribute casting the president as a "gallant leader" who has confronted the "most horrible and devastating enemies of mankind; hunger, pauperism, and loss of confidence and self-respect."[28] The 1930s had been lean years for many Syrian Americans as they confronted the ravages of the Great Depression. Those with corner grocery stores faced hungry clients unable to pay their accounts; others closed up shop and returned to peddling; and some returned to Syria. The French Ministry of Foreign Affairs, in its capacity as the mandatory power over Syria and Lebanon, began to note in its reports this phenomenon of return migration and of diminished emigration.[29] Attributing the reduction in the number of people leaving, and the return of many who had left, to restrictive immigration policies in countries of destination, the report covering the year 1931 also noted that "the economic crisis in Syria and Lebanon was far less serious than in the industrialized countries."[30] The authors of the subsequent 1932 report argued that more migrants would have returned—especially from the United

States—but because of unemployment, they did not have the funds to purchase the tickets to do so.[31] While perhaps containing the boastful rhetoric of a colonial power intent on propping up its accomplishments, the French ministry's report findings are echoed in records of Syrian benevolent societies; diary entries; press accounts of anti-Syrian backlash in Colombia, Mexico, Liberia, Cuba, and the United States; and recollections of sons and daughters remembering the anxious looks on their parents' faces.[32]

In 1933, for example, Syrians became the target of a nativist campaign in Nayarit, Mexico. The Union of Mexican Merchants distributed flyers that warned of the pernicious influence of foreigners but especially of the "Russians, Poles, Syrio-Lebanese, Arabs, Chinese," who were all compared to parasites. Drawing on language that cast women as the guardians of hearth and home, and of the products brought into it, the Union encouraged its readers not to buy from "Arab merchants," for doing so would risk the "desolation of your homeland."[33]

The decade of the 1930s was thus characterized by displacements, insecurities, and in some cases downward mobility. The numbers offered by the French Mandate authorities are revealing. In 1929 they registered only 635 persons emigrating from Syria and Lebanon to the United States, while the number of those leaving for Brazil and Argentina surpassed that by almost fourfold.[34]

The situation began to change by the end of the 1930s and most especially with the start of World War II. Reverend Shalhoob's 1942 guide adopted a more celebratory tone, comparing President Roosevelt to a "Prophet" "who is trying to save the world." Affinity between Syria and California was now cast as support of the war effort so that the "world may be liberated from the tyranny of Nazism, Fascism, and the Japanese." The trope of Eastern spirituality infusing Western materialism, found in the writings of the early mahjar poets, including Kahlil Gibran, now seemed to find a militarized purpose.[35] "East has met West," Shalhoob asserted "Through this combined knowledge we have become a great and powerful nation and we have only begun our progress toward ultimate greatness." The 1942–1943 guide expanded its purview, becoming the *Pacific Syrian-American Lebanese-Palestinian Guide*, recognizing that the inclusive term *Syrian* could no longer carry the divergent national aspirations that had accelerated under Mandate rule. Based on Shalhoob's eleven months of travel along the Southern Pacific and Northern Pacific railroad systems, the guide also expanded its reach, incorporating Vancouver, Canada; and Ensenada and Chihuahua, Mexico. In fact, the governor of Chihuahua, Alfredo Chávez, submitted a note of congratulations for the publication of the guide, noting that the well-established (*radicada*) "*Colonia Syria*" in his state was "*muy trabajadora y gente grata.*"[36]

Two subsequent directories published in Los Angeles capture the growth of the Syrian community, connected as it was to the post-World War II boom in entrepreneurship among its "western families." As had been the case for other ethnic groups, the war had propelled new stories of movement and relocation. Philip (Phil) Tamoush remembered that his brother, who had served in the Pacific theater during the war, returned to Boston at its close and told their mother that the California streets were paved with gold. So, Phil continued, "She sent my dad and her younger sister here to buy a house and to buy a grocery store." Leaving behind the depressed area of south Boston where the family had run a grocery store and "practically took care of the whole neighborhood" through "deferred billing" and by extending credit to those who could not pay, Phil's mother packed her five boys into a 1947 Plymouth and drove across the country to join her husband and sister in a house on Westlake Avenue. Phil recalls that they arrived in Los Angeles in August 1947. The family relocated to Silver Lake a year later, but continued to operate the grocery store on 9th Street and Valencia Avenue, where the younger Tamoush boys spent their after-school hours playing and tending to the store.[37]

For many Syrians, Route 66, which extended from Illinois, through Missouri, Kansas, Oklahoma, Texas, New Mexico, and Arizona before ending in Santa Monica, California, was an important pathway to postwar LA. They integrated into preexisting community structures and began to forge new ones. The *1948–1950 Syrian Directory of California,* compiled and published by Elias Sady, priest of St. George's Orthodox Church on Gramercy Place and 36th Street,[38] registered this expansion and the ways that Syrians resolved the fitful years of the 1930s. Heralding itself as a "channel of connection for American Arabic-speaking people," the 1948–1950 directory signaled, with new enthusiasm, Syrian participation in California's postwar posterity. This was conveyed visually and viscerally on the first page with a full-page advertisement for Mode O'Day, the clothing company owned by the Malouf brothers. The ad featured a photo of the eleven-story building on Washington Boulevard standing impressively on the corner, its spires reaching into the sky. The one-dollar dresses that were the hallmark of the company's modest beginnings were now supplanted by moderately priced fashion that was "young in line, fresh in color, crisp in feel." By the early 1950s, the Mode O'Day Corporation was operating on a franchise basis, firmly ensconced in the Southern California fashion scene, its marketing and advertising consistent with trends that promoted slim, idealized, feminine whiteness. The scion of the Malouf Corporation, Annis B. Malouf, was recognized in the first pages of the subsequent 1954 guide, not for his business acumen and the success of Mode O'Day, but for "his generosity, noble support and tireless effort to enhance the progress of our new church."[39]

Being a benefactor for the building of a place of worship was a longstanding tradition in the California Syrian community. It was one of the main ways to ensure ascendancy and recognition by co-ethnics. In 1929, for example, when Father Boulos Meouchi wrote to the Maronite patriarch in Bkerki (sometimes transliterated as Bkerke), Lebanon, about his congregation in Los Angeles, he spent a good deal of time describing the funeral of parishioner Mike George, which was attended by Syrians from "all over the United States and Mexico." He was particularly impressed by George's contributions to the building of a Maronite church and seemed chagrined that his untimely death at the age of forty-eight precluded following through on efforts to fund a school.[40] The *Los Angeles Times* was also impressed by George's ascent from "peddling vegetables," noting that he left behind an estate worth $100,000.[41] His widow, Maggie, made sure to honor him with a full-page "in memoriam" notice in the 1937 *Pacific Syrian-American Guide* directory.[42] In 1954 it was Malouf's turn to be recognized.

The "new church" to which Annis Malouf had devoted so much of his energy was St. Nicholas Antiochian Orthodox Christian Cathedral. Erected in 1950 the building represented the ambitious efforts of parishioners to establish a larger place of congregation for close to 350 Orthodox families in greater Los Angeles. The *Western Pacific Directory and Buyers Guide of 1954–1955*, published by St. Nicholas's board of directors, captured the rapid growth and consolidation of the community, as well as the establishment of "St. Nick's" as the preeminent Arab institution in the greater Los Angeles area.[43] Close to three hundred pages long, with 2,497 families listed, the 1954 guide was subtitled *A Directory of Americans of Lebanese, Syrian, and Arabic-Speaking Origin in the Eleven Western States*. It shows a highly diversified community, involved in multiple economic niches, including manufacturing, produce, dry goods, restaurants, and the service industry.

The new church also became a vehicle through which to form friendships and alliances with other members of the Orthodox faith, a kind of multiethnic Orthodox movement sustained by summer camps, a pan-Orthodox choir, and a youth council. Phil Tamoush's brother Ed married Mansur Nahra's daughter, Vera, and they became involved in St. Nicholas, where, according to Phil, "everybody was Arab."[44]

BEING ARAB IN SOUTHERN CALIFORNIA

When asked whether he faced discrimination as an Arab working in the field of arbitration, Phil responded "no." He even registered some surprise at the fact that he did not experience bias in the workplace because his name, Tamoush, "was some ethnic." However, other forms of documentary evidence as well as the recollections of fellow community members indicate that the Syrian encounter with race and racism in Southern California was varied. Syrians were variously racialized as nonwhite, as Asian, as black, and as white ethnics. Placing Syrians in a Pacific space allows for a different lens through which to study the racial formation process. The naturalization and census records, in particular, provide clues to understanding the Syrian American relationship to whiteness and to Asianness in the American West.

A case in point, Antoine Vitar (probably Bitar in Arabic) came into the United States at Laredo, Texas, having lived first in Monterrey, Mexico. He declared his intention to become an American citizen in 1938 at the age of twenty-five. The form lists his occupation as "furniture springer," his color as "white," his complexion as "dark," his race as "Syrian," and his nationality as "Syrian." But the declaration of intention form for his brother, Helias, who entered the United States at the same time in 1920, lists his race as "Syrian," his color as "white," his complexion as "light," and his nationality as "Mexico" (sic).[45] Helias (Leo) and Antoine (Tony) were the children of Mary and Salah Vitar. Their household on Hollenback Avenue consisted of five children, of whom three were born in Mexico and two in Syria.[46]

Antoine Vitar's declaration of intention reflects the dominant pattern in the documents, that is, for clerks in California to assign to Syrian applicants for citizenship the color "white," complexion "dark," and race "Syrian." Based on this data, Syrians would seem to fit into historian Thomas Guglielmo's argument of a variation, but ultimate security within whiteness, an argument he develops in great detail for Italians in Chicago for the pre–World War II period. While Italians were subject to harassment and reviled for their foreignness, Guglielmo writes, they were "consistently and unambiguously" placed on the white side of the color line by a variety of peoples and institutions (including naturalization courts).[47] On the surface, then, there are obvious parallels with the Syrian experience that would make them just another immigrant group whose whiteness was slightly suspect but never really denied.

There are, however, important reasons to argue for the specificity of Syrian processes of racialization, reasons that make them different from the Irish, Italians, Jews, or Slavs who were able to consolidate their whiteness through various institutional, psychological, and material measures.[48] First, while the canonical works on whiteness focus on the above-named European immigrants, the Syrians were from Asia. Here again the naturalization records are instructive. When, for example, George Shishim filed his declaration of intention to become an American citizen in Los Angeles in 1907, he listed his last foreign residence as "Beirut, Syria," and renounced forever his allegiance to "Abdul Hamid II, Sultan of Turkey." It was very much his link to Asia that was an issue for the naturalization examiner.[49] Asians were not considered to fall within the provisions of the naturalization statute, which limited naturalization to "aliens being free white persons, and to aliens of African nativity and to persons of African descent or of African nativity or descent."[50]

Second, the backstory to the Shishim naturalization case involved the accusation that, even though he was a policeman, he could not give testimony in a court of law because he was not a "white man." The legal precedent used to support this claim was *People v. Hall*, a mid-nineteenth–century California ruling that barred the Chinese from testifying against whites in court.[51] Complicating the matter was the fact that the Asianness of Syrians was undergoing redefinition because the relationship of their place of origin to Asia and to their nationality was not entirely clear. When Syrians first started arriving in the United States, immigration officials classified them not as Syrians but as immigrants from "Turkey in Asia," as the western Asian territories of the Ottoman Empire were called in official English publications (as opposed to "Turkey in Europe"). By the early twentieth century they were designated as "Syrians" in federal immigration statistics, and by 1917 Syria was excluded from the Asiatic Barred Zone (the regions of Asia from which persons could not immigrate to the United States).[52]

The story of the Syrian claim to whiteness is a tangled one, connected to the construction of a new Asian space in the American imaginary, a space from which Syria, and southwest Asia more generally,
was disassociated and a new category of belonging was created: the
Middle East. For Syrians in Southern California, we see repeatedly in
the US documents of racial classification these Asian palimpsests—the
layers lying underneath the official classification of "white." The 1910
manuscript census entries (that is, the original schedules on which the
enumerators wrote in the data for a household) for Seba Esmaloof and
Sails (sic) George show this process at work. Both were residents east
of downtown Los Angeles, near what was at that time the Pilgrim Iron
Works. They were also naturalized merchants with large families as well
as lodgers. Their race is listed as "W," for white, their language spoken
as "Syrian," and their birthplace as "Syria." But above the word *Syria*
the enumerator has written "Ty Asia," for Turkey in Asia, in order to
signal their distance from whiteness.[53]

While the perception that Syrians were Asian pulls their story
away from much of the whiteness literature, yet another factor was
that many Syrians who came to Los Angeles were *Latin* American
before they were *US* American, and thus the Latinness of a significant portion of the community shaped interethnic solidarities that
developed between Syrians and communities of color in places like
Boyle Heights and downtown Los Angeles. If we approach the racialization of the Vitar brothers solely as a question of "How did they
become white?" we miss the processes by which they had already become Mexican. We also miss the fact that racial variation ran along
several axes. Of the forty-five Syrian entries from Mexico held in the
Los Angeles Southern District Court's naturalization repository, four
different kinds of race are listed (Syrian, Arabian, French, and Hebrew), and twenty-one different occupations, including seamstress,
mechanic, and meat peddler. And while all but one of the forty-five
lists the individual's nationality as Syrian, twenty-six different places
of birth within Syria are registered.

The indeterminate racial status of Syrians, including their purported Mexicanness, had already generated concern among immigration officials, and had fed into the discourse of racial inassimilability. In 1906 the Bureau of Immigration dispatched an employee named S. A. Seraphic to investigate improper border crossings by Syrians and reports of corruption along the US-Mexico border. Central to the bureau's concern was the possibility that carriers of trachoma, a contagious infection of the eye, could slip across borders undetected.

Like other immigrant groups whose fitness for US citizenship was called into question by government officials, Syrians were linked to contagion and disease and to social indicators, such as transience and poverty, that eugenicists argued defiled the nation.[54] But Seraphic's report revealed more than this exploitative scheme in El Paso. Traveling to several locations within Mexico, including Tampico, Veracruz, Mexico City, Monterrey, Nuevo Laredo, Matamoros, Porfirio Díaz, Torreón, and Juárez to assess the living conditions of Syrian populations and to gather information on methods of travel to the United States, he unwittingly described extensive Syrian networks consisting of men and women who had no intention of coming to the United States.[55]

While Syrians were on the radar of US immigration officials, they were also on that of the Mexican government, which amplified its own nativist campaign in the postrevolutionary decades.[56] In July of 1927 the Mexican Department of Migration suspended the immigration of laborers (possessing capital of less than ten thousand pesos) of "Syrian, Lebanese, Palestinian, Arabic, and Turkish origin."[57] These restrictions made Syrians the targets of antiforeign rhetoric reminiscent of other American campaigns to identify outsiders to the nation.[58] In 1932 the Mexican government went further and established the National Registry of Foreigners, obliging all foreigners over fifteen years of age "to appear before the proper authorities and show their personal identification papers." The municipal president of Mazatlán, in the state of Sinaloa, made clear the kinds of foreigners within the law's reach: "only Chinese, Russians, Syrians, Czechoslovaks, Hungarian[s],

Bulgarian[s], and Turks."[59] At the same time Syrian landowners became in many places the focal point in the rising demand for tenants' rights, which had been central to the revolutionary program of land reform. The interplay of postrevolutionary dynamics and the language of nationalism could produce quite complicated results in the lives of Syrians in Mexico. Ramón Duarte documents the case of Julián Assem, a merchant in Torreón who was expelled from Mexico, only to make his way back into the country via the southern state of Chiapas to join his Mexican wife. In appealing his case to President Calles, Assem wrote: "My only intention is to be Mexican, because I have lived in this country for over eighteen years and I identify completely with its nationals, and working with them I have managed to form what small capital I have."[60]

As in other parts of the Americas, Syrians in Southern California, including those who had come to the state during periods of heightened Mexican nativism, were caught in an ambiguous racial position. They could be celebrated as model citizens, as demonstrated in the governors' tribute to them in the 1937 *Pacific Syrian-American Guide,* but they could easily fall into suspect categories: they were at times too Asian, at others too Mexican, and sometimes not Mexican enough. The public patriotic language of Syrian elites suggested their eager incorporation into whiteness, but private correspondence reveals their concerns over the potential repercussions their liminal racial status would provoke. After an extensive five-year study of the Maronite communities in the United States, including the one in Los Angeles, the apostolic emissary Father Youssef Eid produced a lengthy report for the patriarch in Lebanon. He wrote matter-of-factly about the activity of the Ku Klux Klan, arguing that it posed a major impediment to the security and well-being of Syrians and other foreigners.[61]

Syrian proximity to other racialized ethnic groups further distanced them from whiteness. The Vitar, Esmaloof, and George families lived in neighborhoods that were decidedly mixed, consisting of Anglos, Russians, Syrians, Mexicans, and others.[62] The census records suggest the ambiguity at play in the assignation of these categories. The Garcia and Alvidiez families, neighbors of the Vitars, were first listed as white, but the enumerator put a second marking over the "W" and wrote "MEX," perhaps remembering that for the 1930 census, enumerators were to classify persons born in Mexico or with Mexican parents as Mexican, not white. This racial designation of "Mexican" disappeared from subsequent censuses.[63] Although the Vitars did not undergo this racial reassigning, other Syrian families did. Michael Tanasha, an immigrant from Palestine and a neighbor of George Shishim in Venice, confused the census enumerator. Tanasha's mother tongue is listed as "Arabic," while Shishim's a few lines above is listed as "Syrian." Tanasha's race is listed as "Ot" for other, but it is crossed out and a small notation beside it reads "W" for white. On the side of the schedule, the enumerator has written "Arabian" as if to clarify and qualify this whiteness. Even Emilia Vitar's naturalization was not straightforward; notations are crossed out and asterisks are added (see Figure 5).[64]

The different categorizations of immigrants from Syria and Mexico suggest again that racial categories could often be palimpsests. On the surface we see one designation, a dominant one, written in bold or asserted by an interlocutor unequivocally, but a closer reading reveals the traces of another. Rather than view these traces as mistakes, as assignations to be corrected and effaced, we can productively view them as racial markings that point to prior histories, to other possibilities, and to unexamined solidarities.

In the above instances, the practices of enumeration and naturalization attempt to pull Syrians out of whiteness. In others, the designation of *Syrian* allowed those with power to aggregate them with other racialized and vilified communities. Such was the case of the men with Arab names held in San Quentin prison, who had run afoul of the law during the economic difficulties of the 1930s. In page after page of intake ledgers, the booking photos reveal the range of incarcerated men, yet Syrians are among the groups whose ethnic marking merited a large notation in red pen. Others included "Coons," Filipinos, Mexicans, Armenians, and Indians.[65]

This marking was an example of how encounters with law enforcement criminalized entire groups of people. Mexican Americans were particularly prone to being scapegoated in this way, and one of the clearest examples of this was the *People v. Zammora* case, which would dominate Los Angeles headlines in October of 1942. The lead

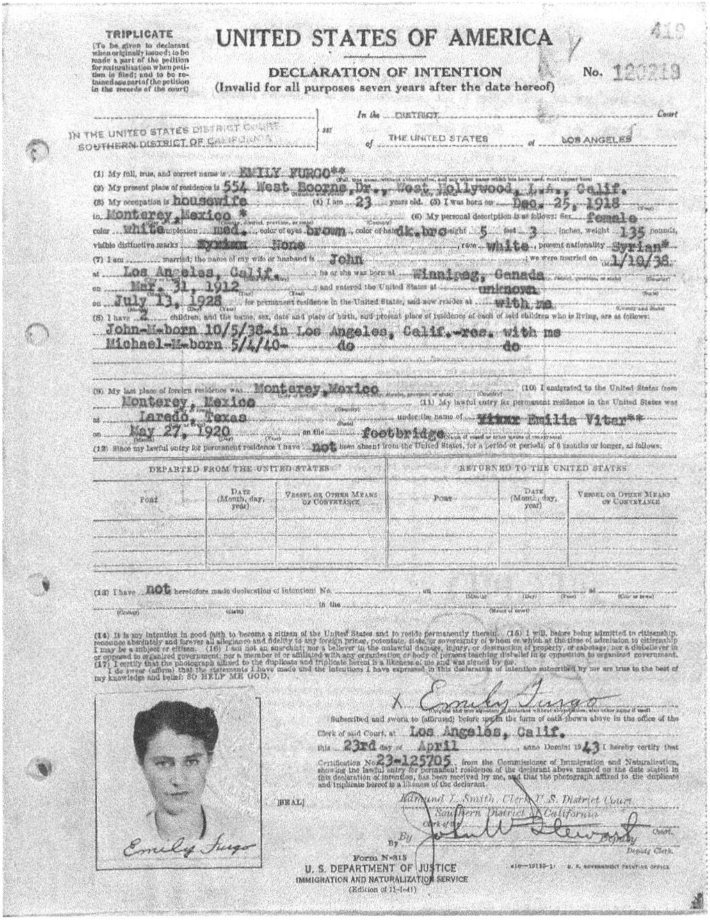

FIGURE 5. Declaration of Intention of Emilia Vitar (Furgo), 1943. Source: National Archives at Riverside, CA. Ancestry.com.

defense attorney in the case was George Shibley, the son of Syrian immigrants to Long Beach, and a staunch critic of the race-baiting and
rush to judgment of the young Mexican American men at the center
of the trial. The next chapter explores George Shibley's role in the case
as a way to examine a set of theoretical questions about Syrian social
and political life in Southern California and in interethnic coalitions.

CHAPTER 2

MURDER AT
THE SLEEPY LAGOON

OCTOBER CAN STILL BE VERY HOT in Los Angeles. Add
to the heat the nicotine habit of many of those present at the trial of
People v. Zammora in the fall of 1942, and one begins to sense the
insalubrious state of Judge Charles W. Fricke's courtroom.[1] The trial
that quickly came to be known as the Sleepy Lagoon murder trial,
in which twenty-one young Mexican American men and one Anglo
man were tried en masse for the murder of twenty-two-year-old José
Díaz,[2] has been written about from various angles and dramatized in
both the 1978 play by Chicano playwright Luis Valdez and the 1981
film starring Edward James Olmos, Tyne Daly, and others.

The rich and layered historiography and archive of the case have
yielded impressive accounts of the Sleepy Lagoon Defense Committee (SLDC), which worked tirelessly to secure the acquittal of the
twenty-two young men, seventeen of whom were convicted. Perceptive scholarship around the case has argued that the position of
Judge Fricke, the prosecution, and the mainstream press typified the

pervasive racialization of Mexican Americans as not quite American, as predisposed toward criminal activity, and as biologically inferior to whites. "From the beginning the proceedings savored more of a ceremonial lynching than a trial in a court of justice," wrote SLDC member Carey McWilliams in his magisterial *North from Mexico*.[3]

Throughout the trial the defendants were not allowed to sit with counsel, nor were they allowed to change their clothes or trim their hair until several weeks into the proceedings. The prosecution insisted on referring to the young men as members of a "gang" and repeatedly referred to them as Mexican, as if to underscore their foreignness. Exacerbating the prejudicial bias in the case were the fraught social tensions in wartime Los Angeles that had roots in rapid demographic shifts, patterns of segregation, and youth rebellion.[4] All of these factors heightened Anglo supposition that Mexican Americans constituted a fifth column, a supposition that "put them in the direct path of the storm" following the internment and vilification of the Japanese American community.[5] The organization and activism that undergirded the movement to free the "38th Street Boys," as the male defendants came to be called, which culminated in a successful appeal and release from prison, has thus been described as "a remarkable triumph in collective action and coalition politics."[6]

The purpose of this chapter is not to retread on familiar historiographical ground but to pull at unexplored strands of the case that lead to different paths of interpretation of the significance of the Sleepy Lagoon trial for American ethnic studies. Specifically, I focus on George Shibley, the thirty-two-year-old Syrian American defense attorney in the case, in order to ask a set of questions about interethnic solidarity and Arab American activism in Southern California. I explore how Shibley's defense of four of the Mexican American defendants and his repeated objections to the court on issues related to their right to counsel arose from his understanding of ethnic stereotyping facing the Mexican-descended population in the US, as well as from his grasp of the lines of solidarity across the Latino/a and Syro-Lebanese communities in Southern California and throughout the Americas.

In a write-up Shibley penned for *New West* magazine in 1979, after viewing the Luis Valdez play *Zoot Suit,* he revealed himself as the "real George Shearer" (as Valdez names the character based on Shibley). He asserted that his character "was and is an Arab whose ethnicity motivated his role in the Sleepy Lagoon case and other legal battles over the years." Tracing his ancestors to Moorish Spain, he added that he was "a blood brother of every Hispanic, including the Chicanos of North America."[7]

What made Shibley think of himself in 1979 as a "blood brother," as someone closely allied with "the Chicanos of North America?" Did this stem from the points of contact between the Syrian and Latino/a communities in Los Angeles in the 1940s? Do they help explain why Shibley spent $10,000 of his own money on the case and was willing to endure the reprimand, abuse, and ire of Judge Fricke in order to lay the groundwork for the appeal that led to the acquittal of the defendants and by extension the end of mass trials in California?[8]

When we place Shibley at the center of an analysis of the Sleepy Lagoon murder case, a number of arguments can be made. First, while many scholars have noted the multiethnic alliances mobilized by the case, the presence of a Syrian American at the heart of the defense has gone largely unexamined and undertheorized. This is part of a second, wider practice within California studies, including the new western history, of overlooking the history of Arab-descended communities in the state and of ethnic studies having a highly presentist frame of analysis for exploring Middle Eastern Americans.[9] In other words, while multiple fields are increasingly and appropriately concerned with systems of marginalization and exclusion that mark Arab and Muslim bodies as other, they have generated a scholarship disproportionately weighted toward late twentieth-century and post-9/11 histories. By tracing earlier connections, this chapter contributes to the

history of solidarity politics that accounts for the synergies and tensions between Syrian American and Latino/a activist projects, and it
argues for a continuum of engagement that stretches back from 1967,
a period often marked as one of political awakening among Arab
Americans.

By focusing intently on one individual, I do not claim that he speaks
for the whole Arab American community in Southern California. Rather,
his story reveals the traces of Arab American involvement in several
emerging social movements: World War II antiracism, gay rights, and
Palestinian liberation. By finding Shibley in the archives of these movements, and by bringing the archives of Arab Americans to bear upon
them, I advocate for an archival practice that opens up spaces for further
exploration in which the activities of a single individual offer a lens to
probing broader social relationships and political positions.[10]

"MAD DOG AT THE BAR": SHIBLEY'S ROAD TO AND REFLECTIONS ON SLEEPY LAGOON

In a 1979 interview with Paul Fitzgerald, former president of California Attorneys for Criminal Justice, George Shibley was asked about
his Arab background. Fitzgerald was trying to flesh out for the reader
what he described as Shibley being "a very improbable character generally, but a most improbable character to be representing these Mexican
American defendants."[11] The choice of Shibley for the Sleepy Lagoon
defense team has often been credited to his involvement in labor-
related cases. When the *People v. Zammora* case started, he was known
as a seasoned Congress of Industrial Organizations lawyer and had
recently won a settlement for striking workers at Ford Motor Company in Long Beach.[12] He was also a friend of Alice Greenfield (later
McGrath) and of labor activist LaRue McCormick, who asked him
to replace the court-appointed lawyer, Richard Bird, on the case soon
after the trial began in October of 1942.[13]

But Fitzgerald's question allowed Shibley to point to additional
reasons for his involvement in the case. He responded, "I am of Arab

descent. And my ancestry includes Christians, Moslems, and Jews, some of whom lived in Spain . . . I have always had an empathy for people who were members of minority groups because in my life in New York, in New Jersey, and later in California, I have always been identified with whatever minority was being picked on at the time."[14]

From an Arab American studies perspective, the interview touches on some standard themes in the historiography. There is the trajectory from New York to New Jersey, signaling the Shibley family's membership in an Ellis Island–oriented wave of early Arabic-speaking migrants from Syria to the United States. George Shibley was born in New York City in 1910 to Samuel A. and Sarah S. Shibley, who had immigrated to New York in 1899 from what is now the Republic of Lebanon. George's uncle, Samuel Barbari, had come to the United States in 1887 and found work as an interpreter (from Arabic and French) at Ellis Island.[15] The Shibleys lived for a while in New Jersey but then moved back to New York. According to the 1920 census, George's father operated a drugstore, and the family lived among Jewish, Greek, and Italian migrants near Broadway and West 160th Street.[16]

Other parts of the interview with Fitzgerald point to less developed strands in the Arab American narrative, notably the reasons for the move out west and to Long Beach in particular. Valdez's play has a reference to the family having lost its money in the stock market crash of 1929, but the Shibleys had already relocated in the mid-1920s and appear to have attained a semblance of middle-class life on Elm Street.[17] George and his brother, Wadieh, attended Long Beach Polytechnic High School. The boys made the Long Beach headlines in 1927 when they "evidenced oratorical aspirations and declamatory ability" in the "Fourth National Oratorical Contest on the Constitution" at the high school.[18] A few years later George went to college at Stanford University and graduated from Stanford Law School in 1934. That year he set up his law practice in Long Beach.

When the Shibleys moved to Long Beach, they became part of an expanding Syrian American community there. *The Pacific*

Syrian-American Guide of 1937 captures the expanse of the community, with particularly large concentrations in Los Angeles and Venice,
and smaller groupings in Santa Monica and Long Beach. There was
hardly a community in Southern California without a Syrian presence. They were in Calexico, Compton, Corona, El Centro, Glendale,
Hawthorne, Huntington Park, and Inglewood, to name a few.[19]

The examples in the previous chapter pointed to ways in which
Latin American migrations to California were Arabized in unexpected
ways, while it also encouraged thinking through Arab connections to
Latinidad. The latter was at play in Shibley's explanation of his involvement in the Sleepy Lagoon case and in his insistence that it be understood as being a product of Syrian Mexican affiliations. In particular,
his assertion that "I have always been identified with whatever minority
is being picked on at the time," and his reference to a long-standing
personal interest in Spanish-speaking populations, emerges not as a
nostalgic claim of leftist credentials or of an extracurricular activity,
but as a choice made intelligible by his familiarity with the deep Latin
American connections of the Syrian Californian population.

He tells Fitzgerald that he started taking Spanish classes in seventh
grade, although he later admitted that he never achieved fluency. In
a self-effacing and humorous reflection on an interaction with one of
the Spanish-speaking mothers of the Sleepy Lagoon defendants, he
recounted how he had translated "I am slightly embarrassed" with
"Estoy embarazado," or "I am pregnant," at which the Chicana mothers convulsed with laughter.[20]

Shibley's remarks to Fitzgerald also demonstrate a keen analysis
of systemic racism in California, including the practices of de jure
and de facto segregation, and the insidious ways in which prejudice
manifested in the legal system and was reinforced in the mainstream
press. Asked by Fitzgerald about "the climate of racial opinion against
Mexicans in the 1940s in LA," Shibley responds: "There was great
prejudice against Mexican Americans among all facets of the population." He recalls the historical prejudice "which had been nurtured at

least since the Treaty of Guadalupe-Hidalgo when the United States
stole most of the Southwest from Mexico," and reminds the reader
of the practice at public swimming pools in Los Angeles of exclud-
ing blacks and Mexicans. The particular example that came to his
mind was the Bimini Baths on Vermont and Third Street, which had
a sign reading "No Dogs or Mexicans Allowed." He then describes
"an intentional newspaper campaign" against Mexican Americans
in wartime Los Angeles, noting the practice of headlining divorce
cases involving Mexican American men with words emphasizing
their brutality and criminality. "You could look through the daily
newspaper and be led to believe that most crimes were committed
by them," he observes.[21]

While the historiography on the Sleepy Lagoon case pays scant
attention to Shibley (a point to which I return below), Fitzgerald
presciently notes: "It's quite obvious that the appellate court reluc-
tantly overturned this case, but only because you [Shibley] had made
such a detailed and lengthy record." Later in the interview he calls
Shibley "a model of advocacy" for his "tireless, tenacious work in the
face of a hostile judge, press, and prosecution team."[22] That same
tenacity and in particular his practice of using preliminary hearings
as an instrument of discovery earned Shibley a derisive nickname,
coined by a deputy district attorney who disliked him: "The Mad
Dog of the Bar."[23]

Shibley remarks in the interview with Fitzgerald that he "was always receiving veiled and sometimes not veiled threats from the trial
judge concerning what was going to happen to [him]." The court
transcript reveals Judge Fricke's contempt for the Mexican American
defendants and the ways in which this contempt appears to have infused his interactions with Shibley. Four days into the trial, on October 26, 1942, Shibley politely drew attention to the appearance of the
defendants and made the point to Fricke that "for the past two weeks
we have been trying to get money to them so they can get haircuts
and have clothes."[24] Fricke interrupts and tells him he "will take the

matter up outside of the presence of the jury." Shibley tries again, and again Fricke cuts him off: "I will take it up outside of the presence of the jury at recess. *I hope counsel understands the English language*" (italics added).[25]

It is not entirely clear whether Fricke was motivated in this instance by anti-Syrian animus, but given that he did not cast aspersions on the other lawyers in this way,[26] and reserved this insult about not understanding English for the Stanford-educated, olive-complected lawyer of Syrian parentage, the likelihood is high. Orientalist theories of race inferiority had fueled the case from the start. Edward Duran Ayres of the Los Angeles sheriff's department's Foreign Relations Bureau had presented a report to the grand jury on "the extent, nature, and causes of Mexican American juvenile delinquency."[27]

After a seemingly sympathetic introduction noting the restrictions on access to public spaces, entry into certain kinds of labor, low wages, and discrimination faced particularly in unionized trades, Ayres ventured into more familiar racist terrain: "But to get a true perspective of this condition we must look for a basic cause that is even more fundamental than the factors already mentioned . . . Let us view it from the biological basis."[28] Drawing on Rudyard Kipling's writings on the "Oriental," Ayres argued that "the Indian [from which he claimed the majority of Mexicans descend] is evidently Oriental in background— at least he shows many of the Oriental characteristics, especially so is his utter disregard for the value of life."[29]

Anti-Arab and anti-Mexican sentiment drew upon similar tropes. Elisions between Arabness and violence were standard in Hollywood representations of Middle Easterners.[30] Indeed, the derisive nickname the deputy district attorney had given to Shibley ("Mad Dog at the Bar") was most probably drawn from a popular 1940s Looney Tunes cartoon that featured a hook-nosed, lecherous desert Arab named Ali Baba, the "mad dog of the desert."

Fricke's insulting comment should also be considered in the context of Shibley's very careful and persistent argument against the prosecution's reference to the defendants as members of a "gang" and as "Mexicans" (instead of Mexican Americans, or Americans of Mexican origin), descriptors that put them at a disadvantage in the eyes of the jury. Shibley instead used language that humanized the young men and added nuance to their lives. He noted that they had been arrested in the kind of clothing in which they went to parties and "*not the clothing in which they go to school or their places of employment.*" By not allowing them to change their clothes, and by referring to them as a gang, Shibley argued that counsel "is purposely trying to have these boys look like mobsters, like disreputable persons, and is trying to exploit the fact they are foreign in appearance."[31]

In this exchange and in subsequent ones throughout the lengthy trial, Shibley builds the case to re-Americanize the defendants and to force the court to recognize their rights as citizens entitled to due process. He reminds jury members that they attend school, that they have other clothes that are worn to "their places of employment," and that they are quintessentially Californian. For example, on December 9 and 10, he called upon the defendants to testify as to their age and birthplace, an exercise that reveals that most were seventeen years old at the time of arrest and that, with one exception, all were born in Los Angeles County.[32] To underscore his point, Shibley entered into evidence the birth certificates of defendants Manuel Reyes and Robert Telles and the certificate of baptism of Eugene Carpio.

Despite his careful legal defense of the 38th Street Boys, the jury returned convictions on Friday, January 15, 1943. Three of the twenty-two defendants were found guilty of first-degree murder; nine were found guilty of second-degree murder and two counts of assault; five were convicted of assault; and five were acquitted.[33] The eight young women who had been arrested in relation to the murder of José Díaz (and who refused to cooperate with the prosecution) had been defamed in the press, declared wards of the state, and sent to the notorious Ventura School for Girls—an institution that, according to scholar Elizabeth Escobedo, "completely rivaled the state prisons at the time."[34]

On the day that the convictions were handed down, Shibley immediately made a motion for a new trial. He and the other lawyers were given ten days to prepare their request. On February 1 Shibley subpoenaed the jury in an attempt to demonstrate that "the public hysteria, public opinion, and the publicity was such that a fair trial could not have been had with these jurors or any other jurors within the County."[35] He attempted to introduce his fifty-page presentation consisting of newspaper and magazine clippings, which "inflamed public opinion on the subject of zoot suits and Mexicans" during the trial. Fricke shot the request down on the basis that there was no proof that jurors actually read the newspapers. In short, in his motion for a new trial, Shibley laid the groundwork for the appeal based on the argument that the defendants' right to counsel had not been protected and that the prosecution repeatedly engaged in misconduct.

Unsurprisingly, Fricke denied the motion for a new trial and proceeded with the sentencing of the defendants, twelve of whom were sent to San Quentin prison for terms ranging from five years to life.[36] As the team of lawyers began working on the appellate brief, Shibley was drafted into the army. Ben Margolis, also a seasoned labor lawyer, continued to work on the case and would serve as principal counsel upon appeal. In an oral history interview conducted in 1984, Margolis remarked: "George was the only one who tried to get in evidence what should have been gotten in and wasn't allowed to be put in. George was the only one who objected to the race-baiting and so forth that was going on . . . Except for [him] there wouldn't have been a record made. The boys would have gone to jail, and nothing further would have been heard of them."[37]

Following the convictions, the SLDC mobilized into action, overseeing a campaign to "free the San Quentin boys." Among the committee's public outreach efforts was the distribution of screenwriter Guy Endore's gripping pamphlet, *The Sleepy Lagoon Mystery*, which was particularly scathing of the *Los Angeles Times* coverage of the case. Following a sardonic four-paragraph introduction in which Endore plays with the reader's sense of complacency with the line: "Go ahead: you sleep [in peace]. As for me, I can't;" he exclaims, "beatings, forced confessions, newspaper terrorism, official racist policies openly enunciated: Is this America? Is this California? I say the Sleepy Lagoon case is no sleeping matter."[38] "It is the story," wrote Alice Greenfield in the letter accompanying the pamphlet, "of the 17 Mexican American boys who were convicted of murder and assault last year. Convicted not because they were guilty of murder—but because they are of Mexican descent."[39]

High-profile actors Rita Hayworth, Orson Welles, and Anthony Quinn, energized by the efforts of Josefina Fierro de Bright—wife of screenwriter John Bright and an activist with the SLDC precursor, Citizens' Committee for the Defense of Mexican American Youth—raised money for the appeal. Alice Greenfield, in her capacity as executive secretary of the SLDC, worked to advocate on behalf of the imprisoned young men and to challenge the racism that had sent them to prison in the first place. She visited them at San Quentin, wrote them letters, liaised with groups on the left, and served as the main archivist for the SLDC. These coordinated efforts helped lead to a historic result: in October 1944 the appeals court reversed the verdict, and the twelve imprisoned 38th Street Boys were released.[40]

The appellate court had taken up several elements of the brief, including the claim of misconduct by Fricke, who had made veiled threats and false accusations against Shibley. The appeal judges drew at length from the trial transcript, inserting large portions verbatim in their decision. They assessed, for example, a key moment in the trial when Shibley objected to a witness (a deputy sheriff) holding a document in his hand that Shibley could not see. Fricke admonished Shibley and told him "before you make any accusations . . . you should be a little careful." In one of the many instances in which Shibley refused to be silenced, or cowed by the threats, he responded to Fricke: "If Your Honor please, I assign this manner of speaking to me as misconduct, and ask that the jury be instructed to disregard it." Fricke instead accused Shibley of "serious misconduct" and claimed again that the witness was not using the document. After considering this incident and others, the appellate judges wrote in their October 1944 decision:

> The record herein discloses that throughout the protracted trial because of the number of defense counsel and the seating arrangements in the courtroom, counsel, and at times the court, experienced difficulty both in hearing and seeing what was transpiring. Instead of being 'guilty of serious misconduct' as charged the court, counsel [Shibley] was, in apparent good faith, attempting to protect the rights of the defendants. This was not only his privilege, but his sworn duty. The reprimand and severe castigation administered by the court was as undeserved as it was unwarranted.[41]

In what was the clearest area of agreement, the appellate judges concurred that Fricke's constant admonitions of Shibley during the trial could have affected the jury's decision. In the judges' words: "Imputations upon the good faith of counsel made in the presence of the jury can unjustly inure the cause of a defendant and thereby deprive him of that fair and impartial trial to which everyone is entitled."[42]

Thus, while Shibley was not physically present at the appeal, his participation in *People v. Zammora* and his legal strategies are repeatedly referenced. It is not an exaggeration to say, as Ben Margolis did, that without Shibley's original record made during the first trial, the appeal would have failed, and the 38th Street Boys would have languished in San Quentin prison.

These arguments of the appellate judges emphasizing impartiality should also be placed in the wider context of the international reverberations of the case, what Shana Bernstein has called a "public relations fiasco [that] jeopardized US alliances."[43] After twenty months of coverage of the trial, and the eruption of the Zoot Suit Riots in June of 1943, the court was no doubt aware that this case of local discrimination had become a hemispheric issue. The Mexican press ran article after article on the racism experienced by Mexican American youth in

Los Angeles, coverage that had the potential to hand the Axis alliance
a propaganda coup as well as damage Latin American contributions to
the war effort.[44]

AFTERMATH: MOBILIZATION, MEMORIALIZATION, AND A CASE FOR ALTERNATE NOTATIONS

Given Shibley's central role in the Sleepy Lagoon case and the praise
that other lawyers accorded him, including Fitzgerald and Margolis,
it is not entirely clear why he, with a few exceptions, did not receive
the kind of scholarly attention that other members of the defense
team and SLDC received.[45] Nor is it clear why, in repeated references
to the fact that the movement to free the 38th Street Boys consisted
of an interethnic coalition, the presence of an Arab at the center of
the coalition is systematically overlooked. The recollections of Carey
McWilliams are typical of this kind of omission. The case, he writes,
"was a joint effort. Mexican Americans took part in the defense committee's work. Anglos took part. Jews took part, Blacks took part. It
was an extremely successful joint effort."[46]

   Part of the answer to these questions around omission resides in
the way the historical record has been archived and organized. There
is an odd silence around Shibley in the voluminous SLDC archives,
and in the papers of Alice McGrath, housed at UCLA Special Collections. To be sure, Shibley's drafting into the army in March of 1943
and subsequent military service meant that his work on the appeal
trial was curtailed.[47] He nonetheless tells us that he worked on the
motion for the appeal and prepared the format for what became the
appellants' opening brief.[48] While the standard narrative of the case
has Shibley disappearing from the appeal process with his induction
into the army, his own recollection reinserts him.

   Shibley is "there" in the archive even if his name so often is not.
In a stunning photo showing the release of the convicted young men
on October 2, 1944, his jubilant expression is clearly obvious in the
crowd (see Figure 6). He stands to the side of Hank Leyvas, a cigarette

dangling from his mouth, his dark, fiery eyes focused on something or someone outside the frame. His face reveals the excitement of the moment. His elation is combined with fatigue and the physical markings of hard work. He makes us want to celebrate the victory with him. Yet there is something damaging and soul crushing about the notation on the back of this photo that speaks to a larger process of erasure of Arab Americans from the case and from Southern California history more generally. In neat penciled handwriting, the notation reads: "Coll. 1490, Box 5, F. 6, Copy Print, Sleepy Lagoon defendant Leyas [sic] shaking hands w/ Ben Margolis."

What difference would it make if this caption read: "Defense lawyer Shibley stands with Hank Leyvas as he shakes Margolis's hand?" This kind of notation would not only recognize Shibley as a central figure in the case but also encourage positioning Arab Americans and other Middle Easterners in the ethnic coalition that challenged white supremacy in California at the time.

FIGURE 6. George Shibley, far left with cigarette, with Hank Leyvas, and Ben Margolis after the release of the Sleepy Lagoon convicted young men from prison, 1944, UCLA Special Collections.

Alternate notations would also reinscribe Shibley into the drama of the 38th Street Boys' release from prison, and they would position and point the researcher in different directions. She might pause on the name of one of the "38th Street Girls," Ann Kalustian, and ask why an Armenian American girl was so recalcitrant in her testimony in court, refusing to bend to the prosecution's attempt to have her say that those who had been arrested in the dragnet constituted a "gang." There is not much in the archive about Ann Kalustian, but one record, the 1940 census, reveals considerable overlap with working-class Syrian American families.

Ann's parents were immigrants from Armenia, having made their way to Los Angeles after many years on the East Coast, living in small towns in New Hampshire, Massachusetts, and Pennsylvania. They rented a downtown flat near what became Little Tokyo alongside other immigrant families. Ann's father was a shoemaker, her older sister a finisher in a men's clothing factory, and her brother a delivery boy for a florist. By 1942 Ann had made friends with several of the young women who ended up at the Delgadillo home the night José Díaz was killed. If her defiant face in the police lineup photo and her terse testimony is any indication, she wanted to express her solidarity with an Eastside youth culture into which she had immersed herself.[49]

Like Ann, many Syrians were familiar with Mexican American realities in Southern California. They lived beside Mexican immigrants and their children, went to school with them, worked with them, and formed families with them. A significant number of Syrians in Los Angeles were, in fact, Latino/as. They were Arabic- and Spanish-speaking migrants who had come to Southern California from Mexico or other parts of Latin America. They understood, as did Shibley, what it was like to be "identified with whatever minority was being picked on at the time." They did not endure the degradation of the repatriation campaign that targeted Mexican Americans, but they faced quotidian reminders of their in-between status in the Californian racial landscape: ethnic slurs at school, nominal whiteness in the courts and on the census, Orientalist tropes that cast them as mysterious and other, and an uneasy relationship to Anglo-dominated spaces.[50]

Shibley's legal acumen and willingness to take on the cases of marginalized communities soon appealed to other disenfranchised groups. In 1952 members of the Mattachine Foundation, one of the earliest gay rights groups in the United States, contacted him regarding the arrest of Dale Jennings. Jennings had been arrested in an all-too-routine case of police entrapment, in which an undercover police officer followed him and requested sex acts. According to Jennings, he did not comply, but the presence of the officer in his apartment was enough to generate an arrest for "lewdness and vagrancy," a category of offense that allowed for the indiscriminate targeting of homosexuals. Under the organizational name of Citizen's Committee to Outlaw Entrapment, the foundation retained Shibley to defend Jennings and to pursue a novel defense strategy. The defendant admitted he was a homosexual in court but denied the lewd and dissolute conduct. After ten days of testimony, the charges were dismissed when one juror's intransigence—allegedly proclaiming that he would acquit a homosexual when "hell freezes over"—produced a hung jury. According to Mattachine Society notes, Shibley was disappointed by this outcome, as he was sure that he could win on a retrial, a decision that would have produced an important legal precedent in favor of homosexual rights. The district attorney, however, perhaps sensing a court defeat, declined to try the case a second time. In an open letter to the Friends of the Citizens' Committee to Outlaw Entrapment soliciting funds for the legal defense, the foundation wrote: "This is a GREAT VICTORY for the homosexual minority and for all citizens interested in equal justice under the law." The letter also stated that "George E. Shibley, brought to the jury and spectators an understanding of the discrimination to which homosexuals are subjected, particularly at the hands of the Los Angeles City and County Police."[51]

According to the minutes of a 1953 meeting, a motion was passed to invite Shibley to a Mattachine Foundation event. However, 1953 was the beginning of a profound and bizarre disruption in the life of George Shibley and his family. Brought up on charges of government-records theft, he was found guilty and sentenced to three years in prison in January 1954. The charges ensued after Shibley represented a man stationed at El Toro military base in a court-martial case. The soldier had been charged with asking for money from other military personnel for driving them to Los Angeles, which was apparently quite a common request. Indeed, Shibley argued that the practice was so common that the commanding general of the base was doing it himself, an assertion that stoked the case against him.[52]

Although entitled to a transcript of the proceedings, Shibley allegedly received a copy in the mail from an unknown source and was subsequently charged and convicted with theft of government records. "A really silly kind of prosecution," Margolis noted, "and one that wouldn't have happened but for the nature of the times and for the kind of defense he [Shibley] put up." The "nature of the times" included a rising anti–civil rights tide, virulent anticommunism, militarism, loyalty oaths, and conservative legislation in California.[53] One supporter of Shibley wrote a letter to the editor of a local paper, stating: "If the military can reply to criticism by strongarming those who find fault with any specific military procedure, all of us sleep in fear of rifle butts smashing against our doors."[54]

Despite an appeal on which Margolis worked and a probe by the Senate Judiciary Committee, Shibley surrendered to begin his three-year prison term in January 1957. He was accompanied to the police station by more than one hundred of his friends and by members of the Shibley Defense Committee.[55] Although he was released on parole in June 1958 and cleared by the State Bar Association to resume the practice of law, the case took a toll on Shibley's health, financial wellbeing, and reputation. The *Long Beach Independent* dubbed him "the stormy petrel of Southern California legal circles."[56]

Thus, some of the silences in the story of Shibley and the Sleepy Lagoon case may have to do with what Kevin Hillstrom called his

"Controversial Later Career." "Practicing with his sons William and
Jonathan," writes Hillstrom, "he displayed a continued willingness to
represent unpopular clients who he felt were not receiving their full
constitutional protections."[57] One of these clients was Sirhan Bishara
Sirhan, a young man from a Palestinian family that had been displaced
by the Israeli army in the war of 1948 and eventually moved to Pasadena.[58] On the fifth of June 1968, Sirhan was arrested and later convicted for assassinating Senator Robert Kennedy during a presidential
primary appearance in Los Angeles. Approached by Sirhan's mother,
who hoped to get her son's death sentence reduced to life in prison,
Shibley and two other lawyers, including rising Arab American civil
rights attorney Abdeen Jabara, from Detroit, filed an appeal to the
California Supreme Court.[59] Although they did not overturn the first-
degree murder charge, the appellate judges changed Sirhan's sentence
to life in prison, consistent with an earlier ruling that the death pen-
alty constituted cruel and unusual punishment.[60]

Shibley had not served as Sirhan's original lawyer, but the case
interested him from the start for some of the same reasons that had
drawn him to the Sleepy Lagoon trial. Three days after the assassination, he stepped into unconventional territory. Penning an open letter to Ethel Kennedy, widow of Senator Kennedy, from the "United
American Arab Congress of Hollywood," he wrote: "On behalf of
the American Arab community in Southern California we wish to
express . . . our heartfelt sorrow at the tragic assault upon Sen. Robert
Kennedy." He continued, "As Americans of Arab origin we deplore
violence in any form, whether committed upon individuals or upon
nations." He then went on to place the assassination in a wider context. Predicting the press attempts to portray Sirhan as a madman plain
and simple, Shibley expanded the conversation to include American
foreign policy in the Middle East. "The accused assailant, although a
Palestinian by birth, is a product of American society. American foreign policy dictated by pressure politics caused the destruction and
rape of his homeland, and made him a refugee. From the time he was

a boy of 12 he has been nurtured in a society of violence, a witness to a foreign policy that progressively despoiled him and his kinsmen of their homes, their lives and their dignity."[61]

Shibley's knowledge of the Palestinian-Israeli conflict deepened through his involvement in the Sirhan case. Jabara, who served of counsel in the trial and co-counsel on appeal,[62] and who stayed in contact with Shibley throughout the trial, believed that Sirhan's childhood trauma of expulsion from Jerusalem and his sense of betrayal by US foreign policy could bolster the defense strategy of establishing "diminished capacity." The original trial transcript contains pages of testimony by Sirhan on the "Palestine problem." One news report noted that Sirhan "astonished spectators at his murder trial with an impassioned—and accurate—discourse on the growth of Zionism, Palestinian history, and England's behind-the-scenes agreement on Palestine's future."[63]

In letters to Sirhan in prison (in Tamal, California), Shibley connected to his own Arabness with salutations in Arabic and by acknowledging Palestinian dispossession. In one letter, Shibley wrote: "The pot in the Middle East is boiling, as you know, but things look very hopeful. Inshallah, you and I will celebrate Christmas some day soon in Jerusalem in a free and independent Palestine."[64]

In much the same way that Shibley had humanized the Sleepy Lagoon defendants, he worked with Sirhan's defense team to present him as an articulate, complex individual with a history of tragic personal loss. Once the appeal process was over, however, and conspiracy theories regarding a second shooter began to circulate, Shibley cautiously extricated himself from public advocacy for Sirhan.[65] He did remain attuned to the Palestinian cause, however. In November 1977 Shibley was among a small group of Arab Americans requesting a meeting with Governor Jerry Brown in order to challenge his support for Israeli policies of land expropriation in the Occupied Territories.[66]

All of these factors—Shibley's defense of a man charged with murdering a popular presidential candidate, his advocacy for Palestinian rights, and his aversion to grandstanding and self-promotion—may help explain his marginalization in the historiography of Sleepy Lagoon. These same factors also provide clues for understanding his insistence on reinscribing an Arab dimension to the popular narrative around the case in the 1970s.

THE VALDEZ PLAY: THE DISAPPEARANCE OF AN "ARAB RADICAL"

The slow erasure of Shibley from the public discussion and memorialization of Sleepy Lagoon was evident in the production of Luis Valdez's play, *Zoot Suit*, in 1978. The massively popular play, performed at the height of the Chicano movement, captured the miscarriage of justice and abuse of the defendants throughout the trial.

Valdez worked on the play for more than two years before its premiere at the Mark Taper Forum in downtown Los Angeles. In four drafts of the play, he developed the narrative; introduced new plot devices, including his alter ego, Pachuco; and substantially incorporated trial proceedings in the script, almost verbatim. The character based on George Shibley undergoes interesting changes throughout the drafts. In the first draft George Shearer is introduced very early in the play as a "Big hearted Arab American . . . a courageous committed radical lawyer, who was the scourge of Judge Fricke at the Sleepy Lagoon Trial." He speaks Spanish and reminds Henry (the character based on Hank Leyvas) of "those other little things [mainly words like *ojala* and Guadalajara] we Arabs gave to the Spaniards. Seven hundred years we were in Spain. Then the Conquistadores brought all that culture to Old Mexico. It's all part of your heritage."[67]

The second draft of the play adds some detail about Shearer's family, noting that George's father was "one of the shrewdest merchants that ever hit these shores from Lebanon."[68] George's dialogue includes the lines

[my father] traded grains and made millions in the twenties. As a kid I knew I was different than the little Protestant children I played with, but I was rich, so it didn't matter. Then came the Stock

Market Crash in '29. My father lost everything, and we came out West to Long Beach—the nouveau poor. Makes a lot of difference to be poor and different at the same time.[69]

By the penultimate draft (marked as "final" in the archive), George enters as George Shearer; references to his radicalism are gone, as are the earlier references to his father. "He is a lawyer, strong and athletic, but with the slightly frazzled look of a People's Lawyer," reads the stage direction in the script.[70] In the draft marked as "final revised," he remains Arab American with a nostalgic recollection of the Moorish past but is now rendered as "playful." In an exchange with the defendant referred to as Joey, the character of George opines: "as an Arab I take great pride in Arabic contributions to the beautiful Spanish language, but what you boys have done to Español is a mystery to me."[71]

Alice McGrath was one of Valdez's principal interlocutors in the development of the play. The character of Alice, wrote Valdez in a letter to her, "symbolizes a real progressive social consciousness taking root in America during World War II; a deep awareness of racial equality that preceded the Civil Rights movement by a decade. In the dramatized history," he continues, "Alice's relationship to Henry Reyna, the so-called pachuco ring leader of the 38th Street 'gang,' provides the meaning of the entire play. As her character puts it, they are: 'Two symbols of everybody's love and trust and belief in the cause. A Mexican and a Jew. Only Hitler and the Second World War could have brought about that combination.'"[72]

There is an extensive and at times quite convoluted correspondence in Alice McGrath's papers about her advisory role on the play, and whether and to what extent she would be compensated for the film adaptation of *Zoot Suit*. Much of the correspondence was routed through her lawyers. A case in point, in a letter dated April 14, 1978, to the Center Theatre Group/Mark Taper Forum, on a Post-it that McGrath placed on the first page, she affirms: "This is the release I did *not* sign. I insisted 'to [grant the right to use her name and likeness] . . . to Luis Valdez."[73] In another letter of explanation penned three days later to her lawyer, Ken Brecher, McGrath writes: "Geez, I barely have got to the point where I would allow anyone to take my picture! And you expect me to arrive at a point where I would sign a release to an abstraction . . . The Mark Taper Forum is fully protected by the release which I gave to Luis. But it is not protection which I gave to Luis—it was a gift of a piece of my life. One doesn't give away a thing like that lightly."[74]

Shibley was not involved in the development of the play, but he nonetheless attended the opening at the Mark Taper Forum. Soon thereafter he penned a critique combining praise of Valdez for having written a "great musical drama [that has] pricked the conscience of California and the nation," but that also perpetuates "some seriously damaging distortions of the realities of the Sleepy Lagoon murder case." "Chief among these distortions," Shibley continued:

> are the myths that the Mexican Americans themselves had little or no part in the organization of the Sleepy Lagoon Defense Commit-tee; that no ethnic group other than the Jews came to the aid of the 22 defendants; that the case was won almost singlehandedly by the unmarried heroine, Alice, whose Jewish identity impelled her to set up a defense committee, hire a lawyer, and then fall in love with the chief defendant, Henry Reyna; and that the defense lawyer, who was called George Shearer in the play, acted alone in his legal battle on behalf of the Mexican American defendants.[75]

Shibley's published comments on the play in *New West* magazine and in *Newsweek* irked *New West* editor René G. Rodriguez and caused McGrath considerable distress. She was so upset that she wrote a let-ter to Shibley explaining: "I am at a loss to understand your public sneer at me and at the play which, in my view, ennobles and digni-fies the characters who symbolize a countervailing force against social injustice." In the note to her lawyer in which she asked for advice on whether to send the letter, she adds, "He has done me harm. He has assaulted my credibility and demeaned my role in the event. When the film rights for Zoot Suit are being negotiated this may not be important since it is the dramatic ALICE who counts."

It is not clear from the correspondence in the archive whether the letter was ever sent. McGrath sent it to Carey McWilliams for review, and he replied that the *Newsweek* piece was "very sad . . . but of course the media would like to heat up a big hassle." "I think the best bet," he counseled, "would be 'a more in sorrow than in anger' tone."[76]

What does seem clear is that the theatrical and filmic adaptation of the events of Sleepy Lagoon, the extent to which they would depict the lives of those involved, and whether or not they would be compensated for releasing the rights to be depicted, generated intense debate and apparently some acrimony.[77] René Rodriguez's letter to Shibley was cutting:

> The next time you see a play, Mr. Shibley, understand that playwrights write plays not history . . . George Shearer is not a historical character, but a creative composite of qualities chosen by Valdez for dramatic effect . . . You'll find that in general facts matter little in imaginative works, and that sometimes completely fictional characters such as my favorite, Don Quijote de la Mancha [sic], can become more 'real' in our lives than real people in the way we remember them.

In a private explanatory note to McGrath, Rodriguez writes that, "I guess Shibley 'got my dandy up' . . . My first inclination was to forget the whole thing, but Shibley isn't just some crackpot venting his spleen, however much he's coming to resemble one."[78]

Without wading too far into the possibility that these letters reveal a clash among strong personalities and some indelicacies of phrasing, it is worth considering that this criticism of Shibley never gets at his central point, which was to restore the Arab dimension to the story of Sleepy Lagoon and to emphasize the multiethnic makeup of the coalition to support the defendants. A close read of his letter to *New West* reveals that he was more concerned with reminding readers that persons of Arab origin and descent were part of the coalition than he was with any sort of self-aggrandizement. "The real-life George Shearer," he writes, "was and is an Arab whose ethnicity motivated his role in the Sleepy Lagoon case and other legal battles over the years." And it is telling that in the myriad ways in which the trial has been analyzed, and the play performed and critiqued, that Shibley's Arabness has not been a point of exploration. Rodriguez may have been right that "George Shearer is not a historical character, but a creative composite of qualities chosen by Valdez for dramatic effect," but the repeated casting of white actors in the role has virtually ensured that viewers do not retain the fact that Shearer was based on Syrian American lawyer George E. Shibley.

Like all archives, the SLDC folders from which much of the material for this chapter is drawn contain silences and omissions. They are also a product of Alice McGrath's collecting and accretions, and an overreliance upon them can skew narratives of the Sleepy Lagoon case in directions that lend primacy to her role. As Carlos Larralde has argued, the popular and scholarly focus on Alice McGrath has overlooked the role of other members of the SLDC, most especially of Josefina Fierro de Bright, whose influential contacts and fundraising were critical to the survival of the committee.[79] Yolanda Broyles-González, in her book *El Teatro Campesino,* laments the prominent place given to the "white saviors" in *Zoot Suit.* Alice Bloomfield, she writes, "has the first and last words in the play including a highly patronizing, trivial, and lengthy closing monologue directed at an absent Henry Reyna [Leyvas]."[80] The filmic adaption of the play, she continues, attributes to the white heroine work that was actually done by Latina activists Luisa Moreno and Josefina Fierro de Bright.

SLEEPY LAGOON TODAY

At a 2005 UCLA commemorative symposium entitled "The Sleepy Lagoon Case, Constitutional Rights, and the Struggle for Democracy," Professor Carlos M. Haro introduced the sessions by referencing the

connections between the Sleepy Lagoon case and the patterns of racial profiling against Middle Eastern immigrants for "national security
interests." He observed: "Now with the War on Terrorism currently
unfolding, one can see clear parallels between what happened in World
War II and what is happening today. Middle Easterners, Sikhs, Muslim
immigrants, immigrants from Mexico and Central America are being
treated as suspect groups, and they have been targeted and harassed."[81]
Haro's attention to the resonance between the racist discourse directed
at the Sleepy Lagoon defendants and the rhetoric of the war on terror
was important and apt. But it positioned the parallels as being ones
between Mexican Americans in the 1940s and Middle Eastern immigrants post-9/11, shifting the synergies to a contemporary moment
and occluding those of the past. Conference participant Luis Alvarez's
eloquent emphasis on interethnic solidarity and on the multiple origins of zoot suit culture also missed the opportunity to recognize the
Arab at the center of the story of the Sleepy Lagoon case.

My insistence on recognizing Shibley, and on the importance of
drawing upon earlier histories of interethnic alliance, does not stem
from a clichéd call for inclusion, but from a concern that engagement
with Arab realities within US ethnic studies reinforces the idea that
Arabs are new immigrants to America. While this engagement has
produced a vibrant debate within the academy and English-language–
dominant associations, such as the American Studies Association,
around support for Palestinian rights, this debate has not adequately
attended to the thick layers of Arab American activism in the United
States, Canada, and Mexico.[82] Nor has it sufficiently accounted for
the decades-long marginalization of issues related to anti-Arab racism,
Islamophobia, and imperial meddling in the Middle East *within* the
US academy and in liberal activist circles.

This chapter has focused on one case in which an Arab American
aligned himself with a multiethnic movement working to dismantle
systems of exclusion and race privilege, yet there are many more. In August of 1973, twenty-four-year-old Yemeni farm worker Nagi Daifullah

was celebrating a union victory outside a bar in Lamont, California, when a policeman ordered that the small gathering disperse. In the ensuing scuffle, the policeman clubbed Daifullah over the head with a flashlight. He died the next day. More than seven thousand people marched in his funeral procession, carrying his coffin from Delano to the United Farm Workers (UFW) headquarters. Photos of the procession are dominated by the black eagle–emblazoned flag of the UFW, but visible too are placards bearing the image of Egyptian President Gamal Abd Al-Nasser.[83] The struggle for farmworkers' rights in California was thus inflected with Arab anti-imperial coordinates.[84]

In an effort to build on these earlier collaborations and to learn from their strategies, tensions, and even their failures, we might listen again to the words of Shibley attesting to the resonance of the Sleepy Lagoon case for him *because* of his Arab background and *because* of his understanding of marginalization. Doing so will help to further historicize the connections between and within Arab American and other ethnoracial groups. It will also contribute to a more collaborative, historically minded American studies that finds emancipatory possibilities in the stories of radical Arab Americans, past and present.

This kind of work can also serve to counter a contemporary tendency to redress exclusion and invisibility only with assertions of patriotism and hypervisibility. In the second act of Valdez's 2017 revival of *Zoot Suit,* after the audience learns that Shearer has been drafted into the army, Valdez adds to his dialogue "I am a proud Arab American." The audience is thus given a more concrete ethnic category for Shearer and a resolution to his ambiguous musings in the first part of the play ("What If I'm an Arab? What if I'm a Jew? What difference does it make?").[85] Unlike in the original 1978 production, Shearer appears in his US military uniform throughout the second act, as if to underscore his patriotism. While the character of Shearer, now played by a bearded and olive-complected actor, appears sharp and adroit in his military garb, it reaffirms the limited options available to Arab Americans for inclusion into American popular culture.[86] Other than this one reference, we learn nothing about the content of Shearer's Arabness from the 2017 production of the play.

And while critics have remarked on the timeliness of the play in this current historical moment of a Trump presidency (Charles McNulty of the *Los Angeles Times* writes that the 2017 production is "an exhilarating revival that couldn't have come at a more opportune time"), not a single review in the mainstream press makes the connection between the Syrian at the heart of the Sleepy Lagoon defense team and the executive order to ban Syrian refugees from entering the country.[87]

That there would not be an interest on the part of critics in making this connection, and in reckoning with the presence of Arab Americans in US social movements, has much to do with the way that representations of Arabs have circulated in various areas of cultural production. Shearer can appear as a "proud Arab American," whose presence on the stage comes at an "opportune time," because there is such a stubborn persistence in theater, film, and television of the common archetypes of Arab as terrorist, Arab as un-American, Arab woman as escapee from patriarchy, and Arab as Muslim reactionary. Shearer's military-uniform–clad lawyer comes as a relief in an otherwise dehumanizing repertoire of bomb-toting sadists. And yet, had there been some attention to the real George Shearer, that is, George Shibley, there might have been an interest in the complex forms of self-representation by Syrians who lived in Los Angeles through the Zoot Suit era. The next chapter turns to an overlooked arena of cultural production, the outdoor festival, or mahrajan, as a site for the development of Arab American aesthetics and world-making during the 1940s and 1950s.[88] The musicians, actors, and participants at these festivals make clear that a wide-ranging set of representations were available, yet only a few were broadly circulated.

CHAPTER 3

MEETING AT
THE MAHRAJAN

IN SEPTEMBER 1953, the same year George Shibley faced a
prison term, Danny Thomas's situation comedy *Make Room for Daddy*
debuted on the American Broadcasting Company (ABC) television
network. Loosely based on Thomas's own career as an entertainer who
traveled so frequently that upon his return his children "had to make
room" for him, the show told the story of Danny Williams and his
daily travails with work and family life.[1] Up-tempo and interspersed
with musical numbers, *Make Room for Daddy*, along with *I Love Lucy*
and the *Dick Van Dyke Show*, produced quintessential representations
of middle-class American family mores in the era of McCarthyism.[2] In
scholar Lynn Spiegel's compelling reading, the show supported a set
of new domestic technologies that offered "a panacea for the broken
homes and hearts of wartime life."[3] Thomas assumed the role of Danny
Williams shortly after his successful turn playing a Jewish-American
veteran of the Korean War in the 1952 remake of *The Jazz Singer*.

Although *Make Room for Daddy* won an Emmy for best new show in its first year, and Thomas won an Emmy for best actor in the second season, the initial run had poor ratings.[4] Thomas attributed the low ratings to "odd-ball" scheduling times in some cities, and to having to compete with "powerhouses" like comedians George Burns and Bob Hope in others. The show was reintroduced on the Columbia Broadcasting System (CBS) TV network in 1957 as *The Danny Thomas Show*, with a reworked cast that included a new wife, a stepdaughter, and a Lebanese uncle named Tanoose, whose character was based on the brother of Thomas's mother.[5] It ran on Monday nights in the slot vacated by comic actress Lucille Ball when she went on hiatus. Not surprisingly, this Thomas series fared much better in the ratings than his first.

A fixture in the US television viewing public for more than forty years, Danny Thomas was a prominent member of the Syrian American community and remained attached to his Syrianness throughout his life. The son of immigrants from Bsharri, Lebanon, he was born in Deerfield, Michigan, given the name of Muzyad Yakhoob, and raised in Toledo, Ohio. He catapulted to stardom after a fitful set of years as an actor and singer in and around Detroit. According to his autobiography, he was so grateful for his good fortune that he spearheaded a campaign to found a children's research hospital in honor of one of the twelve apostles, St. Jude Thaddeus, the "patron saint of impossible, hopeless and difficult causes."[6] The organization that took on the task of raising money to operate the hospital, which was dedicated to no-cost treatment of children's catastrophic diseases, consisted primarily of other second- and third-generation Syrian Americans. Founded in 1957, it was appropriately called the American Lebanese Syrian Associated Charities but became better known by its acronym, ALSAC. Housed initially in a six-by-six-foot space in a tobacco and candy business, using recycled stationery for correspondence, ALSAC would go on to become one of the largest philanthropic organizations in the United States.[7]

In his remarks at the opening ceremony of the hospital in Memphis, Tennessee, in 1962, Thomas proclaimed: "It took a rabble-rousing, hook-nosed comedian to get your attention, but it took your hearts and your loving minds and your generous souls to make this fabulous dream come true."[8]

Thomas's self-deprecating, some might say self-Orientalizing, reference to his "hook nose" was telling, since he had navigated the pressures of assimilation in an entertainment industry that valued whiteness and Anglo middle-class ideals. The practice of name changes to de-ethnicize actors was an old and storied one in Hollywood, and Danny Thomas was certainly not the first actor to adopt a new stage moniker. Rita Hayworth, who had lent her support to the Sleepy Lagoon Defense Committee, started her dancing and acting career using her birth name, Margarita Carmen Cansino. At the urging of Columbia Pictures studio head Harry Cohn, who thought her look to be "too Mediterranean," she changed her hair color to red and underwent electrolysis to raise her hairline. She also started using her mother's maiden name, Hayworth. Danny Thomas recounted that when he was also pressured to change his look and "fix" his nose by Cohn, he refused.[9]

The only other identifiably Syrian American actor in Hollywood to achieve a modicum of success before Thomas was Frank Lackteen, whose birth name was Mohammed Hassan Yaqtin. Lackteen was very much a working actor and had parts in more than 135 films, but they fell relentlessly into the same category, the dark villain. In the silent-era films *The Fortieth Door* (1924) and *The Last Frontier* (1926), for example, he played Hamid Bey and Pawnee Killer, respectively. In the sound era he was cast as Mustapha the Beggar in *I Cover the War* (1937), with John Wayne, and as Shamba in *The Jungle Girl* (1941), but he often played minor character and bit parts for which he was uncredited. His biography on IMDb describes him as a "swarthy, pock-marked, cadaverous-looking character actor, born in Lebanon . . . [who] portrayed exotic villains in US films for five decades from 1916."[10] Lackteen's Syrianness was harnessed by Hollywood (he worked for Paramount,

Universal, Vitagraph, and Columbia) to play foreign and domestic others interchangeably. He was typecast as an Indian, half-breed, native, witch doctor, servant, Oriental, Arab, and Mexican.[11]

Thomas chose to both defy these stereotypes and redirect them. His de-Arabization in the mainstream entertainment industry was never complete. One of his most successful early routines was called "Ode to a Wailing Syrian." It was a long skit that began in Levantine Arabic with the welcoming words: "Peace be upon you, welcome, American people." The routine builds with suspense, relating the story of a Syrian man executed for opposing the Ottoman government. Condemned to the gallows, his last gesture is to sing a song that is heard by a beautiful woman who goes on to capture the hearts of her people. This skit, along with other parts of Thomas's repertoire, were popular with many audiences, so much so that *Life* magazine, in a write-up entitled "Top Comedians, They Make a Nation at War Forget Its Troubles," dubbed Thomas "a Syrian" and "1943's most promising new cabaret comic."[12] Thomas's use of a white tablecloth over his head to mimic traditional female head covering has elicited rebuke by some contemporary critics. Yet his deft handling of the themes of hardship and adversity, conveyed in an Arabized register, resonate today with the comedic acts of a young generation of Arab American comics.[13]

Thomas continued to draw on his Syrianness to craft his characters and to shape his comedic material throughout his career. Key moments in *The Danny Thomas Show* provide relief from the arsenal of negative images of Arabs in film and television, and supplement the biblical epic as the main interpretive lens for understanding US connections to the Middle East and to Middle Easterners.[14] In one episode Danny introduces his new wife, Kathy, to Uncle Tanoose, referring to him as "the old sturdy cedar of Lebanon." He addresses Tanoose as "'*ami*" (uncle in Arabic) and they talk about another cousin, Salim. A post-dinner scene shows the family in repose in the living room, with Danny playing the piano and singing "Day by Day." Uncle Tanoose, smoking a pipe and with his young grandniece on his knee says: "that

was lovely . . . now play a Lebanese song." Danny begins to play a
song on the piano, while his older daughter asks what the song means.
Uncle Tanoose responds that the song is as "old as our people." It is
about a man who, when separated from the woman he loves, climbs
to the top of a hill to profess his love for her in song. Again, prodded
by Danny's daughter, "What does he sing?" Tanoose asks Danny to
translate into English from the unuttered Arabic. We begin to hear an
'ud accompany the piano, which has now switched into Arabic musical scales. Danny complies: "Through the night, beloved . . . through
the long endless night, your silhouette hovers over my mind. I fear the
time and distance between us but, my beloved, I shall be content with
the time and patient with the distance, so long as that which troubles
my mind troubles yours."[15]

The scene is one of the few cases in which Arab American aesthetics and cultural expression find an outlet in primetime television in
the 1950s. The question is, What did these expressions mean? How
is it that, instead of the widely available and grotesque fantasy-driven
images of the Orientalist imagination, *The Danny Thomas Show* was a
place where Arab American musical culture seeped in and was allowed
to signal intergenerational curiosity and care? In the discussion below,
I focus on three interrelated factors that help answer this question.
First, *Make Room for Daddy* and *The Danny Thomas Show* incorporated Arab American expressive culture because Danny Thomas was
immersed in it.[16] References to it in his television show were extensions
of his connection to Arab American performance, much of which was
anchored in the Southern California Syrian festival culture. His appearances at Syrian outdoor festivals (mahrajans), what Sally Howell
might call "intensely parochial sites of cultural production," served
as incubators of his material and as venues for connecting to a wide
network of individuals involved in early Arab American associational
life.[17] Second, the festivals helped cultivate an audience—Syrian and
non-Syrian alike—for whom these expressions were recognizable and
resonant. Although a wide range of scholarship on the patterns of

otherizing of Arabic-speaking groups in media and television exists, I am interested in how Arab American expressive culture, produced in large urban environments like Los Angeles, allowed for mainstreaming of certain forms of Arabness. Third, and relatedly, the show coincided with a postwar period of consolidation of Syrian and Lebanese whiteness, and to appeals to ethnicity within whiteness. We see pieces of this process unfolding on *The Danny Thomas Show,* where Danny's whiteness is signaled as difference from his heavily accented, mustache-wearing, old-world uncle, Tanoose, a whiteness already made resonant in a household staffed by an African American housekeeper.[18] But the show also suggested that this racialization process was not linear. In short, while aspects of Thomas's film and television career supported Hollywood's whitewashing project (notably the remake of *The Jazz Singer*), the productions in which he was most creatively involved pushed against it. In several episodes Thomas veers away from overwrought representations of Arabs, in some cases flipping the script in unexpected ways. In the same episode where Uncle Tanoose meets Thomas's new wife, Kathy, for the first time, a dinner scene appears to fall into the trope of male dominance and female subservience as Danny asks his wife to prepare and serve food to his uncle. Danny acts out the role of an Arab patriarch, only to be challenged and reprimanded by his uncle for doing so.

Another episode has Danny capitulating to his agent's request to surgically reduce the size of his nose, but then backing down at the last minute. It is his Anglo American wife who challenges Danny's agent against the procedure and who is the most relieved by the decision not to operate. She reminds her husband that "beauty is in the eye of the beholder."[19] And in the postdinner scene described above, it is a "Lebanese song" that fills the space of the American living room, cohering a mixed-ethnicity family. These examples do not mitigate the aspects of the show that followed rote sexist and racial stereotyping that was typical of the era—the limited roles for African American actors being the most obvious. They do, however, encourage asking

questions about the source of Arab content and the role of Syrian artists like Thomas in attempts to shape an anti-Orientalist, Arab American repertoire. Thomas credited his interest in comedic storytelling,
as opposed to one-liners, to storytellers he had heard in his youth.
"When I was a kid, the entertainment was somebody from the old
country or a big city who came and visited and told tales of where
they came from," he noted.[20]

The same year that Thomas launched his career as the affable Danny
Williams, endearing himself to millions of American television viewers, he recorded a set of Arabic folk songs, the proceeds of which ben-
efited St. Jude Hospital Foundation. Thomas was no stranger to Arabic
music, having grown up in a household where his father, a peddler of
dry goods, played the *mijwiz*, a single-reed woodwind instrument, and
was sought after to perform at weddings and christenings in the Arabic-
speaking community.[21] The 1953 recordings of Thomas, accompanied
by the renowned 'ud player Toufic Barham, reveal the actor-singer's ca-
pable handling of the difficult and popular Lebanese genres of *mijana*
and *'ataba*. They also capture sonically his connection to the Syro-
Lebanese communities in the Americas, a connection that he fostered
in multiple ways, including by singing Arabic songs in revered guest
performances until a few months before his death in 1991.[22]

Thomas was a mainstay of the Syrian mahrajan festival circuit, and
through it he deepened his friendship with members of the community
who would take the lead in forming ALSAC. *Hollywood Magazine*,
published in Los Angeles by Nazih Massaad in Arabic, English, and
Spanish to build "deeper understanding and mutual respect between
the peoples of America and the Arab and Moslem World," featured
Thomas on the cover of the October 1951 issue and succinctly shows
Thomas's multiple affiliations. Relaxed and on the Warner Bros. movie
set of *I'll See You in My Dreams*, starring Doris Day, he is photographed
reading the magazine with a photo of King Faysal of Iraq on the cover
(see Figure 7). The heading below reads: "Danny Thomas: The Pride
of Lebanon."[23]

Rather than view these spheres of Thomas's life as separate or as reflecting his divided public and private persona, this chapter explores Syrian festival culture in Southern California as a site of community formation, image fashioning, and marketing that rendered Syrian and Lebanese culture familiar to multiple viewing publics. The discussion herein contributes to studies of Arab American representation, which

FIGURE 7. Danny Thomas on the Warner Bros. set, reading *Hollywood Monthly Magazine*, 1951. Source: St. Nicholas Antiochian Orthodox Cathedral Library.

have ably tracked the proliferation of negative Orientalist tropes—"rich oil sheiks, sultry belly dancers, harem girls, veiled oppressed women, and, most notably, terrorists"—that continue to feed the practice of stereotyping in film and television and in the mainstream media.[24] I focus on an overlooked post–World War II moment in which Syrian Americans produced affirming images of their communities that sat within a broad repertoire of Arab American cultural production and that resonated in Syrian homes, halls, churches, picnic grounds, and playhouses. Drawing on Evelyn Alsultany's theorization that seemingly positive images do not in and of themselves solve the problem of racial stereotyping, and on Melani McAlister's post-Orientalist reading of American culture as "obsessed with domestic diversity," I explore the meanings of these cultural productions in the context of Syrian ethnicization.[25] In this regard the mahrajans did some of the early work taken up by church-sponsored food festivals and Arab American owned restaurants that promoted their food and a "safe and friendly ethnicity to an American public hungry for (de-politicized) diversity."[26] But mahrajans also did more. They were spaces where participants renewed their Syrianness and its particularized iterations, and they served as a framework for organizing Arabic-, Spanish-, and English-speaking Syrians into a Pacific place. The mahrajans provided venues for Arab American musicians and performers to meet and to hone their craft. Because of their proximity to Hollywood and the entertainment industry, many of these artists hoped to influence representations of Middle Eastern culture, but a shifting tide of anti-Arab sentiment made this a difficult task.

CELEBRATIONS "THAT KNEW NO TIME"

"Syrian Fiesta Draws Carnival Throng to Barbeque." So began the *Los Angeles Times* article on the Syrian festival of 1940. "Tambourine twirling . . . Lahamishwee—barbequed lamb—spitting fat into a bed of cherry-red coals . . . Fezzes bobbing like a churning sea . . . This was the gala carnival scene yesterday at Riverside Drive Breakfast Club as more than 3500 persons assembled for the Mahrajan—Syrian fiesta."

It was "the biggest event of the year for the more than 15,000 members of the Southland's Syrian colony."[27] Perhaps unsure how to best translate the Arabic word *mahrajan*, the newspaper used the easily recognizable Spanish word *fiesta* to signal the large-scale and decidedly non-Anglo character of the event.

Mahrajans were massive undertakings for Syrians in California and throughout the Southwest. Participants remember family members coming from neighboring states and Mexico for days at a time to take part in the festivals, which combined live music, dance, and barbeques. It is hard to imagine that the gatherings did not generate interest beyond the Syrian community. The 1937 mahrajan attracted seven thousand visitors to the Riverside Drive Breakfast Club, a popular gathering site on the edge of Griffith Park in Los Angeles. The Syrian-American Mahrajan of 1940 was just one of five major Labor Day events announced by the *Los Angeles Times*. Twenty thousand marchers were expected at the San Pedro Congress of Industrial Organizations (C.I.O.) parade, and "8,000 participants from 25 states at the Mahrajan."[28]

Mahrajans were part of Syrian homeland culture that were adapted to the Californian environment in ways that met the needs of a scattered diaspora. Participants used the occasions as focal points for community formation. The events took months to plan, enlisted the service of old and young, and became sites for the display and adaptation of Arab culture. The conviviality extended beyond the festival grounds into the living rooms of local Syrian community members housing relatives from out of town. The mahrajans were, to use Robert Orsi's formulation for the Italian *festas* of East Harlem, celebrations that "knew no time."[29] As historian Adele Younis remarked, "children could meet one another, family ties would be reestablished, and friendships reaffirmed and honored."[30] There is some anecdotal evidence that the festivals were popular places for Syrians to meet future spouses, with one writer familiar with the Arab American music business calling them a "marriage market."[31]

In Los Angeles two brothers, Samuel and Norman Mamey, spearheaded the organization of the earliest mahrajans. Very often connected to religious organizations, the events were not, however, religious festivals like Semana Santa but large-scale gatherings over two or three days that incorporated various dimensions of Syrian diasporic life: food, music, performance, speechmaking, storytelling, prayer, and family networking.

There is surprisingly little work in the sociology literature on the Syrian mahrajans, an omission that is akin to ignoring the central place that quinceañeras have for Mexican American ethnicity.[32] Arab American studies scholars have focused their attention primarily on charting activist voices in the community, and on capturing political mobilization and alliance building. In this framework, mahrajans have been downplayed as "social affairs," as large parties that prioritized food and fun. They fit within a broader narrative that characterizes the pre-1967 generation as politically quiescent, overly focused on assimilation, and clueless on the question of Palestine. Edward Said wrote dismissively of this generation: "Compared to other ethnic groups here, Arabs (mainly Syrians and Lebanese) have always been politically conservative, interested in seeing themselves in a sort of harmless folkloric light (of the kind used, say, by Danny Thomas in his career), tirelessly assimilating and accommodating."[33]

Unfortunately, Said's rendering misses the important way that mahrajans brought community members together to converse, to network, and to re-create expressive culture. Ethnomusicologist Anne Rasmussen has underscored the importance of the mahrajans for the development of a new Arab American musical culture that fostered intergenerational participation. "The music played and the practices articulated by musicians, audiences, and patrons of the middle period [mid-1930s to early 1970s] comprised significant and solidifying aspects of community life."[34]

In addition to their role in the construction of Arab American cultural expression, as preceding chapters have argued, mahrajans were ways to fashion a collective space situated close to the Pacific. The 1938 mahrajan, organized by Samuel and Norman Mamey and announced as a "Two-Day Fete" by the *Los Angeles Times*, was cast as the sixth annual California Pacific convention, attracting Syrian Americans from eleven western states. When the Syrian-Lebanon-American Society organized its mahrajan in 1951, it was called "The Great Pacific Mahrajan." Attracting more than three thousand attendees, the event was held at the Croatian Recreation Center at 116th Street and Budlong Avenue.[35]

DRAWING IN THE YOUTH

By the early 1950s the mahrajans had become complex affairs intended to appeal to an intergenerational Syrian American community. They had to at once draw in Arabic-speaking first-generation immigrants while also catering to the youthful interests of American-born children and to an emerging professional class of Arab American entertainers who were making Los Angeles their home. Often the results could blend seemingly incongruent streams of Syrian American community life. The midsummer mahrajan held at Griffith Park in August of 1951, for example, was sponsored by Our Lady of Mount Lebanon Church. Father Boutros Daou, who was in charge of the event, seemed unphased by the appearance of the bare-midriffed dancers, Kanza Omar and Julia Hanna. Daou declared that the mahrajan, held in honor of Antonio Bishallany, celebrated by the organizers as the "first Lebanese pioneer to pioneer in the US," was a great success. Danny Thomas also performed, endearing himself to the "Lebano-Syrian Colony by remarks on the unity of the Arabic community."[36] It was not uncommon for the mahrajans to serve as major fundraisers for the different Syrian churches in Los Angeles. Joe Farrage, who was active in putting together several mahrajans, described it as a "50/50" arrangement: 50 percent of the proceeds to the church, and 50 percent to the clubs that organized the event.[37]

Syrian American youth, like other youth in postwar Los Angeles, participated in a multiethnic expressive culture, yet the mahrajans were places that were marked as authentically Syrian and Lebanese even

as they underwent adaptation. They were sites where the practice of
in-group marriage could be cultivated, as older generations sought to
keep their children connected to each other. Rasmussen draws attention to the postwar importance of mahrajans as places where young
people could dance, not just listen. The solemn attention that once
characterized audience reactions to Toufic Barham's 'ud playing, gave
way to a kind of impatient expectation to get on the floor and *dabkah*,
to hold hands and participate in the communal line dance. Musicians,
including those with classical training in Arabic music, found ways to
comply. Muhammad al-Bakkar, for example, "saturated the mahrajan
with dabkah and belly dancing, and subsequently, along with his con-
temporaries, infused the urban cabaret with Arab music."[38]

The Great Pacific Mahrajan in 1951 brought together several trends
that began to characterize the Syrian Southern California festival culture: opening remarks by a "homeland" politician, in this case George
Fuleihan, consul of Lebanon, serving in Los Angeles; appearances
by Arab celebrities, including Egyptian actress Amira Amir; performances by Arab American actors, notably Danny Thomas, and a group
of lesser-known singers drawn from the local community; and feature performances by entertainers, typically on tour from the Middle
East, such as singer Emily Ghannaji from Damascus. Younger participants were given the opportunity to dress and perform in "folkloric"
costume. However, as the reporter for *Hollywood Monthly Magazine*
noted, it was the communal dance that won the day: "The two days
were enjoyed by both old and young, dancing Lebano-Syrian folklore
dances, the 'DABKEH' [sic] being the favorite."[39]

Soon the venues began to change as well, and festival culture
moved into Westside hotels and places associated with middle-class
respectability. Even the names of the festivals began to change. By
1951 Syrian Americans associated with St. Ann's Melkite Church in
Los Angeles held a *Sahrajan* (from the Arabic word, *sahra*, or evening).
According to Al Asermely, who wrote and directed two Arabic skits
for the evening, "St. Ann's Melkites have coined a new word that now

signifies Arabic and American entertainment at its best." Conceived
as a fundraiser to assist in the building of a new church, the event was
held at the Los Angeles Breakfast Club and drew a crowd of close to
a thousand persons. While it showcased the musical talent of Syrian
American performers, notably Toufic Barham, Odette Stambouly,
and violinist Lou Shelby, it was an interethnic affair featuring a
ballet interpretation by Dan Takeuchi and a dance number by the
Ernest Hidalgo troupe. Ed Miller and his orchestra provided music
for "moonlight dancing" on the patio.[40]

Other forms of community engagement also began to draw on the
energy of the community. "Sweetheart Balls" became popular among
well-established Syro-Lebanese families, such as the one held at the
Beverly Wilshire Hotel in February 1952.[41] The yearly national conventions convened by major Syrian organizations increasingly took
time to plan and required financing from Southern California community members. The Western Federation of Syrian Lebanese American Clubs, for example, began holding yearly conventions in 1945.
In 1957 it affiliated with the national organization and held its yearly
convention in Las Vegas. It included twenty-one affiliated clubs from
Arizona, California, Colorado, Montana, Nevada, Oregon, and Washington. Besides working on a scholarship fund, a home for the aged,
and an adoption program for orphaned children, the 1957 meeting relayed the cable sent from the Western Federation to President Camille
Chamoun of Lebanon, commending Chamoun for his "pro-Western,
anti-Communist Lebanese Government policy."[42]

This last sentence lends credence to Edward Said's assessment
of the pre-1967 generation as "politically conservative." Yet the records of federation meetings and other sources suggest that this assessment needs nuance. It is not an accident that some of the early
activist voices in the community attended the mahrajans and that the
hard-and-fast demarcation that Said makes between "political" and
"cultural" groups does not capture the slippage between them. In
Southern California, community members participated in different

dimensions in Syro-Lebanese organizational life—*haflats* (social gatherings often involving dance), mahrajans, conventions, unions, civic associations—and they were not seen as contradictory or mutually exclusive. A full-page photo and article in Nazih Massaad's *Hollywood Monthly Magazine,* a publication that frequently carried coverage of weddings and engagements and that was the main organ for delivering news and reports on the mahrajans, also carried appeals for support for Palestinian refugees.[43]

The magazine also carried striking coverage of the National Association of Syrian and Lebanese American Federations meeting with President Harry S. Truman in October of 1951. The meeting was intended to urge Truman—who had personally recognized the establishment of the new Jewish state of Israel in May of 1948—to reorient US foreign policy on the Palestine question. Specifically, the delegation encouraged Truman to "implement a seven-point program designed to restore the lost friendship and confidence in American democracy of the fifty million Arab inhabitants of the strategically important Arab Near East."[44] Frank Maria, who attended the meeting in his capacity as president of the Syrian and Lebanese American Federation of the Eastern States, remembered that it had been at a 1947 convention of the federation that he had been inspired to act, as an American citizen, against Truman's philo-Zionism.[45]

There was in fact a high degree of organizational overlap between the mahrajans and the conventions, and they often served as incubators for later activist activity. The National Association of Syrian and Lebanese American Federations brought together four regional federations: those of the eastern, southern, midwestern, and western states. The Eastern Federation was especially active, combining advocacy for the Syrian and Lebanese communities of the East Coast with "news and events" and support for literary production—poems, short stories, and essays. Its official organ was the *Federation Herald,* a monthly magazine that was a polished example of an engaged ethnic press. Editor James M. Ansara, known in Arab American studies as the author of one of the first books on Syrian and Lebanese immigration to the United States, published the first iteration of this work in the *Federation Herald*. Contrary to Said's quip that the Syrians and Lebanese were "tirelessly accommodating," the editorials of the *Federation Herald* frequently reference the urgency of the Palestine question. The February 1953 issue carried an editorial by Charles Malik (then the Lebanese ambassador to the United States) calling for restitution, the right of return, and an internationalization of Jerusalem. In his words, "it is naïve to suppose . . . that this problem can be divested of its political overtones and can be treated on a purely humanitarian or economic basis. . . . the only reasonable and in the end practicable solution of this problem is to make it possible for the greater part of the refugees to be resettled on Palestinian soil."[46]

To be sure, the federation did contain hallmarks of a certain kind of political conservatism (a saccharine politeness when interfacing with US State Department officials and a skepticism of communist organizations), but it was not quiescent.[47] In fact, the same February issue of the *Federation Herald* contained letters to the editor alerting the readership to swelling "anti-Arab Propaganda" in the United States.[48]

What kept the federations going and what energized them were the yearly conventions. The *Federation Herald* is peppered with advertisements for these meetings. The August 1953 issue contains a full-page ad for the Seventeenth Annual Convention of the Syrian and Lebanese American Federation of the Eastern States in New York City. The image accompanying the ad engages in some cringeworthy self-Orientalizing: a smiling couple on a camel's back heading to the Hotel New Yorker. But the text got to the heart of the convention's purpose: "to renew old friendships and form new ones, to vote for your favorite candidates, to promote your favorite measures."[49]

Danny Thomas tapped into this web of connection created by the federation structure to pursue his "favorite measure" of raising funds for St. Jude's Research Hospital. The driving force behind ALSAC in the early years was Mike Tamer, who was president of the Midwest

Federation of Syrian Lebanese American Clubs, as well as a wholesale tobacco and candy business owner in Indianapolis.[50] LaVonne Rashid, also of Indianapolis, and former typist for the District Works Progress Administration Office, served as recording secretary and a member of the board of directors.[51]

It is not entirely clear why the Western Federation was not as active as the Eastern. The answer may lie in part in the older structure of the Eastern Federation and a membership base that was concentrated in a smaller geographic expanse. Relevant too was the decision of the national association to sponsor what it called an "Overseas Convention" to Lebanon and Syria, which attracted participants from across the nation and channeled resources, financial and otherwise, into that endeavor.[52]

When asked about the reasons for the decline in mahrajans after World War II, the interviewees who remembered often referred to the "spreading out" of the community, the process through which the concentration in and around downtown Los Angeles and in Santa Monica thinned as families moved into the San Fernando Valley and Orange County. A representative sampling of families in the 1937 and 1955 directories captures this movement quite strikingly, and it is a through line in the oral histories of those who were young adults in postwar Los Angeles.[53]

A shift was also emerging within Los Angeles Arab American musicianship. The advent of the nightclub scene allowed performers with knowledge of Arabic music and instrumentation to have regular employment and a space for innovation. But it was a scene rife with paradoxes. Consisting of polyethnic audiences, often with "limited aural capabilities," they clamored for sounds and images that drew on the Orientalist repertoire. Arab American musicians gave audiences what they asked for, not only in the space of the nightclub but in music packaging—scantily clad and gossamer-veiled women, as well as camels, pyramids, and references to Mecca can all be found on record jackets of the postwar period. As Rasmussen notes, "Western European

puritanical characterizations of Oriental culture were reproduced with
enthusiasm and naivete for public consumption . . . it was a brilliant
advertising strategy . . . "[54] Whereas the mahrajans had been complex
intergenerational Syrian spaces, the nightclubs, even those owned by
Syrian Americans, could not escape the risks of commodification. Lou
Shelby's nightclub The Fez, which opened in 1957 on Sunset Boulevard and Vermont Avenue, was the first of these to garner success.
Frequented by Hollywood celebrities including Jayne Mansfield, Lee
Marvin, and, of course, Danny Thomas, The Fez featured Middle Eastern–inspired acts with musicians, many of whom, like Shelby (Shalaby
in Arabic), had been mainstays at the mahrajans. Former Fez dancer
Feiruz Aram recalled that the establishment "was decorated to capital-
ize on Americans' fascination with Orientalism—influenced by Hollywood's version."[55] Even so, there was also a sense that their artistry
was an improvement on the misappropriations of the mainstream entertainment industry. Another Fez dancer, Jamila Salimpour (of Iranian descent), remembers how excited she was when Syrian American
Antoinette Awayshak began dancing at The Fez, because it allowed
viewers to see another kind of belly dancing. Before this, she asserted,
"Ruth St. Denis, who disastrously interpreted the Danse du Ventre,
was considered the expert dance consultant for the biblical biographi-
cal blockbusters of D. W. Griffith and Cecil B. DeMille."[56] She argued
that those who learned to dance by training with Middle Eastern artists
could help alter the prevailing "disastrous interpretations." Acknowledging the role that outdoor festivals played in cultivating Arab American
artists, Salimpour remembered meeting Awayshak at the Los Angeles
Supper Club's Arab American reunion in Griffith Park, attended "by
Arabs from across America, Canada and Mexico."[57]

     In many ways, the pattern of postwar Syro-Lebanese community
formation resembled that of white ethnics, who also moved into the
suburbs and out of racially mixed neighborhoods like Boyle Heights.
As George Sánchez has argued for the Jews of Boyle Heights, this movement—often facilitated by access to the benefits of the G.I. Bill—served

to consolidate whiteness.[58] In the case of Syrians and Lebanese in Los
Angeles, this proximity was very often a literal and real proximity to
Jewishness. It is worth returning to where this chapter began, with actor
Danny Thomas, in order to elaborate on this point.

PLAYING IT AGAIN

The decision by Paramount to remake *The Jazz Singer* in 1952 confirmed that major studio executives were still committed to a set of
representations that denigrated African Americans, including through
mechanisms that allowed Jews to shore up their whiteness. While the
original 1927 production of *The Jazz Singer,* starring Al Jolson, had
pioneered the use of sound in film, it had also perpetuated the use of
blackface and the appropriation and distortion of African American
musical aesthetics.[59] It likewise allowed for the jazz singer to escape
his immigrant identity through blackface.

The 1952 remake dispensed with blackface, but it kept key themes of
the story intact. Danny Thomas, playing the character of Jerry Golding,
embodies the drive of a highly assimilated Jewish American man, seemingly detached from the piety of his cantor father. The detachment does
not sever entirely the connection between Jewishness and Americanness,
however, as Jerry resolves his identity crisis in the penultimate scene,
where he appears in the synagogue to sing the Kol Nidre on Yom Kip-
pur. It is a story that resonates with other immigrant groups who, as
Matthew Frye Jacobson argues, became part of a consolidated post–
World War II white race.[60] Following this logic, Thomas's Syrianness
doesn't matter because he represents the story of white ethnic incorporation into the American mainstream and into a cozy collaboration with
white privilege. *The Danny Thomas Show* (and other shows, such as *I
Love Lucy,* featuring Cuban actor Desi Arnaz) churned out a domestic
narrative that placed ethnic men into "safely middle-class settings where
their ethnicity was just one or more running gags."[61]

In many ways, this was also a continental story, resonant with
popular Mexican incorporations of immigrant narratives into film

and television. A year before *Life* magazine heralded Danny Thomas as "1943's most promising new cabaret comic," Mexican actor Joaquín Pardavé starred in and directed the film *El Baisano Jalil*. It was released during the golden age of Mexican cinema and featured not only the highly revered Pardavé but also Sara Garcia, known as "the grandmother of Mexican film."

The film revolves around the story of two Mexican families, the Farads and the Veradadas. Jamil Farad and his wife are immigrants from Lebanon, their Lebaneseness made obvious in their heavily accented Spanish and in their pronouncing of *p* as *b*, as in "*baisano*." In an opening flashback we learn of Jalil's rise from humble origins, as a kind and good-hearted itinerant merchant, to the owner of several department stores managed by his suave and sophisticated son, Selim. The Veradadas are presented as old-stock, landowning Mexicans recently ruined by debt. Unable to truly come to terms with their economic descent, they cling to bourgeois sensibilities and patronizing judgment of the Farads. In one particularly drawn-out scene at the Veradada hacienda, Jalil and his wife, Suan, are repeatedly made the butt of jokes: Suan can't ride a horse properly and is laughed at for overgesticulating while describing how kibbe is made, and Jalil overdresses in tails at dinner. The film veers perilously close to grotesque stereotype when Jalil sings in unintelligible, fake Arabic a song from his homeland, his sissified dancing causing the dinner guests to convulse in laughter.

There is some relief from the relentless parody.[62] Selim is smitten by the Veradadas' daughter, Marta, and the film eventually follows a familiar filmic trope of love conquering social and class divides. It is a story of harmonious exogamy that propels national integration, but one in which the poles of difference are carefully chosen. Produced by two Jewish Mexicans, Gregorio Wallerstein and Alfredo Ripstein, the film uses immigrant fiction to support Mexican cinematic values that stress the importance of family, hard work, and marriage.[63] But as coproducer Wallerstein maintained, he did not think the Mexican viewing public would readily accept an on-screen marriage between a Jew and a Catholic.[64] The signifier of difference is the Arab, but the Arabic pronounced in the film is a pastiche of pseudo Arabized words. Some have suggested that the script was informed by the real-life friendship between the screenwriter Adolfo Fernández Bustamante and José Helú, the son of a Lebanese immigrant, a friendship that may have helped save the Farads from complete Orientalizing.[65]

Both *El Baisano Jalil* and *The Danny Thomas Show* play with the themes of assimilation that mark Arabized bodies as congruent with middle-class masculinity. Coded as hard work and love of family, Selim's Arabness delivers him into a space unmarked by accents and nostalgia for a foreign place of origin. Whereas Pardavé uses faux Arabic to signify difference and relies on the peddler trope, Thomas uses real Arabic to develop the character of Uncle Tanoose and allow for a more sustained engagement with Arabness.

In other aspects of Thomas's career, we see the fissures in this process of accommodation and an unwillingness to let his Syrianness slip away into political irrelevance. His ALSAC work on behalf of "Leukemia Stricken American Children" involved pushing for the first integrated hospital in Memphis; the mahrajans in which he sang laid the groundwork for activist projects; and proximities to Jewishness began, in the post-1948 period, to push against profoundly different views of the founding of Israel.[66]

Thomas appears to have read the pulse of many of the controversies provoked by these issues in the Syro-Lebanese community, and he navigated them in ways that are not consistent with a reading of him as "tirelessly accommodating." In an interview with writer Greg Orfalea, he recalled being harangued publicly by a Maronite priest for including "Syrian" in the name of ALSAC, as if this were an offense to Lebanese nationalists. He reminded the priest: "Don't forget. We were all Syrians when we came here. There was no Lebanon."[67]

In 1982 Thomas's decision to narrate the film *To Lebanon with Love*, produced by pro-Israeli American evangelist George Otis, was panned in the Arab American activist community. Arab American

Anti-Discrimination Committee (ADC) director James Zogby wrote him to criticize the decision to work with Otis. Rather than run away from the issue, Thomas appeared in the next year's ADC event to support the victims of the Lebanon war.[68]

In short, proximities to Jewishness were not stable, and advocacy for Middle Eastern populations displaced and dispossessed by the Palestinian-Israeli conflict was one of the principal ways that Arab Americans fell out of whiteness.[69] Once Lily and Sol Ajalat, longtime members of the Syro-Lebanese community in Los Angeles, began speaking out against human rights violations against Palestinians in the Occupied Territories, they felt a distance emerge with their Jewish neighbors in Toluca Lake.[70] In his autobiography *Just Farr Fun*, Jamie Farr (born Jamil Farah) who first came to California in 1952 to enroll in the Pasadena Playhouse, waxed nostalgic about his close working relationships with Jewish writers, directors, and producers (notably Pedro Berman, Gene Reynolds, and Larry Gelbart).[71] He had landed the role playing Thaddeus in the 1955 biblical epic *The Greatest Story Ever Told* and had invited most of the cast to his wedding at St. Nicholas Antiochian Orthodox Cathedral. But he could not escape a particular reading of his Arabness when a Coke commercial he was making in 1968 in the Yuma valley was pulled. Citing "renewed hostilities between the Jews and the Arabs in the Middle East," Farr lends his characteristic wry humor to the decision, noting that the commercial "tried to show that even Arabs know things go better with Coke."[72] The results of the cancellation were not so funny. Then a struggling actor with a newborn son, Farr lost $10,000. Undeterred, he kept the words of his friend and the patriarch of a large Syro-Lebanese family in Los Angeles, George Sadd, in mind: "Remember, Jamie, a newborn baby always brings a loaf of bread."[73] Farr went on to achieve commercial success by playing the Lebanese American dress-wearing Corporal Klinger (who longs to get out of wartime Korea and back to Farr's own hometown of Toledo) in the smash television hit *MASH*. The Coke commercial incident did, however, underscore his probationary whiteness and provided an example of how, in the aftermath of the 1967 war, in which Arabs were vilified in the mainstream press, corporations were loath to allow an Arab, even one clad in Orientalizing garb, to embody the thirst-quenching desires of the American consumer public.[74]

The decline in mahrajans, the move to the suburbs, the disaffection of many youth with traditional religious organizations, and the advent of virulent anti-Arab bias in the post-1967 period produced a feeling of distance from community among third-generation Syrian Americans. However, consistent with the oscillations of the past, many soon found ways to reconnect to their Arabness by seeing the lives of first-generation relatives in new light. This was not just a "roots craze" or "the principles of third-generation interest" analyzed by other scholars of ethnicity, it was a process of retrieval that spoke back to the erasures of Arab American voices in the post-1967 period of liberal multiculturalism.[75] The next chapter explores this dynamic in the context of several family stories. It charts the importance of archival activism and the place of Southern California in the route to ethnic consciousness.

CHAPTER 4

FRAGMENTS OF
THE PAST, IDENTITIES
OF THE PRESENT

LIKE MANY THIRD-GENERATION Syrian Americans com-
ing of age in the 1960s, Lisa Halaby was not especially attached to, or
cognizant of, her Arabness. Her father, Najeeb, embodied the ethos
of a highly assimilated ethnic American. The grandson of Syrian immigrants who had come to the United States from Damascus, Syria,
in the late nineteenth century, Najeeb spent his childhood in Dallas,
Texas, in a solidly middle-class family connected to the high-end furniture business. At age twelve he moved with his mother, Laura, to Los
Angeles, having lost his father suddenly to an illness. Najeeb went on
to graduate from Stanford University, where he was captain of the golf
team, then from Yale Law School. He served as a pilot during World
War II, became fascinated with flying, and began a career in aviation
at the war's end. In 1961 President Kennedy appointed him director
of the Federal Aviation Administration and by 1965 he was senior
vice president of Pan American World Airways, better known as Pan
Am.[1] His wife was American-born of Swedish descent; he attended a

mainline Protestant church and lived in a predominantly white en-
clave of Santa Monica, California. There didn't seem much that was
overtly Arab in the Halaby household.

Yet, according to her memoir, Lisa began ever so slowly to connect
to the Arab part of her identity after a conversation with her mother.
She described the shift in this way:

> I first learned the history of my family when I was six years old in
> Santa Monica. . . . One day, in my parents' bedroom overlooking
> the ocean, my mother told me about my Swedish and European
> ancestry on her side of the family and my Arab roots on my father's.
> I remember sitting there alone after our conversation, staring out
> the window at the limitless horizon of the ocean. It was as if my
> world had suddenly expanded. Not only did I have a new sense of
> identity; I felt connected for the first time to a larger family and a
> wider world.[2]

Lisa Najeeb Halaby, better known to the American public as
Queen Noor of Jordan, opens the chapter "Roots" in her memoir *Leap
of Faith: Memoirs of an Unexpected Life* with this starting point of her
journey toward Arabness. We learn of her grandfather and great uncle,
the "dashing brothers Halaby" (originally from Aleppo, Syria), and of
the family's "entrepreneurial instinct." Much in this opening section
of the memoir draws on the tropes of the assimilatory Arab American
narrative: a pioneering Syrian patriarch laying the groundwork for the
incorporation of his family into the American mainstream, a celebratory up-by-the-bootstraps story of thrift and capital accumulation and
of cross-generational success. There is, however, as the subtitle of her
memoir suggests, something "unexpected" in Lisa Halaby's story. Her
father takes a job working for the Jordanian airlines company and in
this capacity meets King Hussein of Jordan. He introduces the king
to Lisa, his eldest daughter, and after a brief and storied romance, the
two are married in 1978. Raised Christian, Lisa converts to Islam and
takes the name Noor al-Hussein ("the light of Hussein"), becoming

"the first American member ever of an Arab royal family."[3] The marriage of the young, Princeton-educated Halaby to the thrice-married monarch, sixteen years her senior, caught the media by surprise.

The register of surprise did not pervade the mainstream media only, but also persisted long after the marriage and eventual death of King Hussein in 1999. In an interview with Queen Noor as part of his 2010 *Faces of America* television series, Harvard University scholar Henry Louis Gates Jr. notes that Lisa Halaby was "the ultimate all-American girl." "Few people realized," he continued, "that [when she married King Hussein of Jordan], she was reversing the journey of her grandfather Najeeb."[4]

Gates's commentary suggests that he viewed the union as something incongruous, an unlikely development that an "all-American girl" would marry an Arab Jordanian. His casting of her journey to the Middle East as a "reversal" of an earlier one that had been embarked upon by her Syrian grandfather was also curiously ahistorical, a truncation of the transnational ties that characterized the Syrian diaspora, and of the Halaby family in particular. While Gates's made-for-primetime series has helped fuel the genealogy craze in the United States and for-profit websites such as Ancestry.com and 23andMe, in this particular episode on Queen Noor, he reinforces the perception that she cannot be "all-American" and Arab at the same time.

This chapter seeks to pull at the unexplored threads woven into Gates's narrative of incongruity about Queen Noor, for they extend far beyond this one case. Implicit in his reading of Queen Noor's Arabness is that it is brought into being by her marriage to a "real" Arab (King Hussein) who lives where real Arabs are supposed to live: the Middle East. And yet Queen Noor tells us that she confronted her Arabness long before her marriage but did not have the language to let it sculpt her "wider world." She writes of her first year of college that she was "confronted by a couple of upperclassmen who taunted me about my Arab background, one more reason I spent so many Saturday nights of my freshman year alone, reading in my room."[5]

Queen Noor's comments suggest how Arab Americans are subject to the "hyphen that never ends." They have been repeatedly represented as "not quite free, not quite citizens, not quite American."[6]
This mode of representation is most obvious in the repeated use of
negative images to portray Arabs in film, television, and the news
media, but it is also more subtly suggested in the Gates documentary
on Queen Noor. It lays bare a fundamental problem facing second-
and third-generation Americans of Arab origin and descent: how to
inflect their Americanness with Arabness in ways that do not merely
negate damaging stereotypes or reinforce imperative patriotism, but
that underscore a deep engagement with family history and the craft-
ing of activist Arab American identities.

Nadine Naber has written about the process by which middle-class
children of Arab immigrants in the San Francisco Bay Area fashioned
a sense of self and community in the presence of "bifurcated concepts of culture."[7] They struggled against Orientalism's dehumanizing
tropes, but they also faced the pressures from their parents of "reverse
Orientalism" and its binary categories ("good Arab girls versus bad
American girls," for example). "Dominant articulations of Arabness,"
Naber argues, "were structured by a strict division between an inner
Arab domain and an outer American domain, a division that is built
upon the figure of the woman as the upholder of values, and an ideal
of family and heterosexual marriage."[8]

Elements of this process reverberate in this chapter, but I also take
the analysis in different directions, following the leads of my interviewees. Since all are the grandchildren of Syrian migrants, the connection to Arabness is intensely mediated through the relationship to,
and memory of, a grandparent—a dynamic I develop below.

While Queen Noor of Jordan has navigated this "bifurcated culture" with the benefit of a skilled media relations team, and within
the comforts of the Arab ruling class, it is nonetheless striking that
she begins her memoir by emphasizing how connecting to her Arab
roots gave her a "new sense of identity." Important parts of her family's

story resonate with the history of the Syrians that this book develops: a grandfather ensconced in business in the Southwest; a great uncle who went to Colombia, South America, thrived in the textile trade, and married there; a father who moved to Los Angeles with his mother after her husband's untimely death and who became connected to the Syrian community there.

This process of coming to understand oneself anew by revisiting the past is a recurring one in the lives of the children and grandchildren of Syro-Lebanese migrants. I explore the complexity of this process and in particular the way that it intersects with California coalition politics, and involves an active and ongoing curation of family history; that is, the assembling of archival material that has the potential to speak back to the erasure that has characterized official narratives and to the silences in established archives. Just as Chapter 1 asked how we can productively view processes of becoming as ones of renouncement, this chapter asks how the concept of "return" might better be understood as a process of "rearrival" through which short-term returns to original Arab homelands ultimately lead to the reassessment and reclaiming of the *US* terrain. Analyzing a set of Arab American texts in which the protagonists travel to their families' places of origin, literary scholar Carol Fadda-Conrey argues that they return with new self-understandings that "enable them to ultimately rethink the ways in which they interact with, belong to, and claim the US as a permanent home. It is the self-reflection gained during their time in the Arab homeland that enables many of these characters to reassess the version of Arab identity they grew up with or developed in the US."[9] This reclaiming involves a recalibration of a sense of alienation from Arab identity and a bridging of worlds often thought of as distinct.[10]

I explore this reassessment and rearrival in the life stories of several Southern-California Arab American women, all of whom are the granddaughters of Syrians introduced earlier in this book. While other scholars have written productively on the trope of the grandmother in Arab American literary studies, sometimes cautioning against its use as

an emblem of culture, I extend it here for reasons specific to my historical analysis.[11] First, it is often in the context of mourning, of having lost
a grandmother or other family member, that the women here begin to
reflect on their Arabness in new ways. The loss has a catalytic effect on
the process of writing and on reflecting upon Arab womanhood. Ad-
ditionally, this reflection propels deep engagement with the documentary past—with passports, interviews, letters, photos, and other kinds of
sources—to such an extent that I call this engagement "archival activism,"
and a form of history-making outside of the academy.[12] In short, I am
interested in how these women use the tools of history to assemble and
narrate their relationship to female elders and how, in that assemblage,
they discover longer trajectories to their own radical politics. I therefore
use the concept of rearrival not so much as a literary trope but as a component of a wider, longer process of retrieval, reclamation, and refusal.

In addition, I chart the complex work lives that this encounter
(my own and that of each of the women at the center of this chapter)
with these sources reveals. The grandmothers here are supervisors,
seamstresses, grocery store workers, door-to-door salespersons, and
members of charitable organizations. They do not so much represent
the ancestral homeland as "culture-bearers," but a model of being Arab
in America that grounds the renarrativization of their granddaughters'
own stories. Finally, their reflections unfold in a transnational frame
and are interspersed with travel to the Middle East, most especially
to Palestine, which serves to organize new understanding of Arabness
and of being Arab in America. I explore these threads, this archival
nourishment *from* grandmothers, in the lives of Kathy Saade Kenny,
Vicki Tamoush, Diane Shammas, and Therese Saliba.[13]

"THE FIRST PEG"

In 2003, as her elderly mother's health deteriorated, Kathy Saade
Kenny began that all-too-often difficult task of sorting through her
belongings. Tucked away in a closet of her mother's home was a See's
Candies box. The contents of the box would soon mitigate some of

the sadness surrounding her mother's final days, for in it were stacks of letters, more than 130 in total, written not by Kathy's mother but by her grandmother, Katrina. Kathy had never seen them before, and she could not read them because they were in Arabic; thus "she could only guess what secrets these letters contained."[14] For Kathy Saade Kenny, the closing of one door opened a new window to her history as she began the journey to understand the contents of the letters. It was a journey that would augment her connection to her extended family in Bethlehem, Palestine, and in Saltillo, Mexico, while it also forged new ties to California and honed a new form of activism. Kathy would come to understand her Arabness anew through a reconsideration of her grandmother's multisited journey as a migrant.

The window that opened for her was also one that allowed her to contribute to an Arab feminist tradition in which one woman passes her story—and her voice—to another who makes that voice the basis of her own writing and creation. Pauline Homsi Vinson, writing on the novels of Etel Adnan and Nawal El Saadawi, calls this "a reciprocal act of support and empowerment as well as a hope for meaningful change in the future."[15] Kathy finds previously unknown parts of her grandmother's story, told in her own voice, in the letters in her mother's closet. The un-silencing of these letters is made possible by Kathy's decision to route her activism in different directions, to retrieve and find meaning in her family's continent-spanning story, and to create and disseminate her own archive.

Kathy described growing up in a family that "was not at all political," where "the subject of Palestine didn't come up as a political question."[16] As a young girl, she remembers participating in cultural events of the Syrian community in Southern California, including the mahrajans in Bixby Park in Long Beach. The more specific identifications were to family members in Bethlehem and in Saltillo, where, as Chapter 1 detailed, her grandmother Katrina married her first husband. Kathy experienced this connection for the most part as "a cultural and food thing." It had nothing to do with politics.[17]

When she was in her early thirties, Kathy told me in an interview in April 2017, she decided to take a year off from work to travel. She started her journey in Palestine, arriving on Orthodox Easter Sunday in 1979. Because of a mail strike, the letter she had sent to her family in Bethlehem, alerting them to her upcoming visit, had not been received. She arrived unannounced, greeting them with "Hi, I am Kathy. I am your cousin from California." "They embraced me completely," she recalled, "it was wonderful."

Kathy spent approximately six weeks in Palestine, living in Jerusalem but making her way to Bethlehem frequently to visit with her family. The Israeli military occupation of the West Bank and Gaza Strip was in full tilt, but her family was not eager to talk about the political situation. It was a Jewish American woman she met in Jerusalem who "started the process of [Kathy's] political education." "She sat me down and explained to me the settler movement. . . . That was the first peg."[18]

Kathy returned to the San Francisco Bay Area, settling into her career in gerontology. It was close to ten years after this initial trip that a decisive shift occurred in her thinking on Palestine and on her Arab identity. Watching a CBS news report on the intifada, the Palestinian uprising that broke out in December of 1987 against the Israeli occupation, she witnessed Israeli soldiers using batons to suppress stone-throwing children. "All of a sudden this light went on, and it was like . . . that could have been my cousin," she remarked. "It became really personal for me. . . . That was the awakening."

As part of this awakening, she began to gather information on the Palestinian-Israeli conflict. She remembers calling the Washington, DC, office of the Arab American Institute after hearing its president, Jim Zogby, interviewed on National Public Radio. "It was the first time I had heard someone talk positively about the struggle of the Palestinians. I was so taken aback." Inquisitive and inspired, she called his office the next day and asked, "How do I plug in?"

Similar to other emerging activists, "plugging in" meant applying this newfound knowledge on the question of Palestine to the local political landscape. For Kathy, the opportunity soon presented itself in the controversy surrounding Proposition W on the San Francisco ballot of 1988. Proposition W represented the combined efforts of progressive Palestinians and Jews in San Francisco to inject discussion around Palestine into political discourse in the Bay Area. The proposition consisted of a resolution calling for the city government to support a two-state solution, an independent Palestinian state alongside Israel. When the ballot came out, Kathy noticed that the people who were against it, mainstays in the Democratic party, "were all the people I helped get elected." The list included Nancy Pelosi, on whose campaign for San Francisco supervisor Kathy and her husband, David, had worked tirelessly. "I got mad," recalls Kathy. She called Pelosi's office and demanded a meeting, which was granted. Accompanied by her husband and another couple, Kathy met with Pelosi for an hour and a half. "From then on, I took on Pelosi as my personal challenge. Anytime anything to do with Israel/Palestine came up, I would call her office. . . . I was on her like a cheap suit."[19]

Kathy returned to Palestine in 1989 as part of a delegation organized by Pax World Foundation. She met with a wide spectrum of activists and human rights advocates, and visited again with her family in Bethlehem. "It was like a college education," she recalled. After her return to the Bay Area, she connected with a group of women who held a weekly vigil outside city hall. The group was modeled on the anti-occupation organization Women in Black.

The pace of this involvement, however, was hard to sustain. Groups formed and levels of engagement intensified, but often dissipated. The devastation of the US-led Gulf War of 1990–1991, and the disillusionment over the Oslo Accords,[20] forced many activists to regroup and recalibrate their connection to movement politics—to the vigils and demonstrations that had characterized the activism of the 1980s. Nadine Naber calls this period the "dormant years" marked by generational shifts as younger, American-born Arab Americans began to chart different relationships to politics and activism.[21] In Kathy's case, she became involved in planning the Arab Film Festival in San Francisco. She asserted that her expertise in gerontology actually translated well to this endeavor. The patterns of representations of older people, particularly ones that characterized them as feeble and unproductive, reminded her of the tropes that the mainstream media relied on to represent Arabs. "I saw the same things with how Arabs were portrayed . . . no one represented themselves. [It was] full of stereotypes, patronizing."[22]

Kathy remained at the helm of the Arab Film Festival for several years, but with the discovery of her grandmother's letters, she found that her activism took on a new form—reconstructing and telling her grandmother's story. She had the letters translated from Arabic into English by Palestinian historian Salim Tamari, and she self-published a book about her grandmother's life entitled *Katrina in Five Worlds*. She gave multiple presentations on the book in the US and in Mexico, and she organized and curated her family's papers. As she explained: "My principal form of activism over the past nine years has been through my grandmother's story and my book. I have found it to be a great starting point for a deeper conversation about Palestine—one that personalizes and humanizes through a story that many people can relate to. . . . On a personal level, it's my way of honoring my roots and heritage, and ensuring that the next generation in my own family takes pride in our shared history."[23]

Kathy drew on the language of kinship to further explain her archival activism, noting that she did not have children of her own but made a contribution to her extended family in this way.[24] "Any immigrant story should be preserved," she remarked. "I felt it was important to tell the story, to make sure the family had the story too." Being a caretaker of the family history is also at work in a second interview to which we know turn.

"I CAN'T DENY WHAT I ALREADY SAW"

The Santuario de Nuestra Señora de Guadalupe sits atop a small hilltop in East Los Angeles, sandwiched between the 60 freeway and 3rd Street. The church, built in 1926, features a stunning painting of the Virgin of Guadalupe behind the altar as well as several delicate stained-glass windows. After more than ninety years, it continues to serve as a site of prayer and devotion for its mostly Latino/a congregants, and on the day I met Vicki Tamoush there, it was the rehearsal ground for more than forty teenagers preparing for their confirmation.

On the east side of the sanctuary grounds, a long, wide stone staircase runs up the hill from 3rd Street. It was these steps that Shafiqa Hallal (Vicki's grandmother) climbed on her knees, making her way up to the church entrance and all the way inside to the altar. There, she gave thanks and payed homage to the Virgin for returning her son, John, from World War II alive. This painful climb was an act of piety that, according to Vicki, Shafiqa had learned from the Latina women she lived among in their Boyle Heights neighborhood. It was also for Vicki a memory that captured the tenacity of her grandmother, her devotion to her children, and the layers of her years living and working among Mexican American women. As a new immigrant to Los Angles (having arrived first in New York in 1911, making her way quickly to Portland, Oregon, to be with her sister's family, then moving down to LA), Shafiqa had found work as a seamstress, eventually serving as "forelady" (supervisor) in the downtown Los Angeles factory where she worked. Her skills as a seamstress were captured on the front page of the *Los Angeles Evening Herald* on January 2, 1918 (see Figure 8). Flanked by two other members of the Garment Workers Union, she helps to sew five hundred stars to a banner to represent the men of organized labor "now en route to the trenches."[25]

When I asked Vicki why she was the most active person in her family around Arab American issues, she replied that she was the oldest of her siblings and had had the most contact with the immigrant generation. As she put it, "I was more a part of my grandparents' lives when their ethnicity was more a part of their lives."[26] Vicki connected to her family's history in multiple ways, including by collecting, preserving, and disseminating objects that captured the stories of her parents' and

grandparents' generations. This documentary and material archive included family photographs; her grandmother Shafiqa's workshop led-
ger, with the piecework of those she supervised listed in the margins;
a rosary; and a handmade piece of embroidery that is now housed in
the Arab American National Museum. A photo of her grandfather,
Mansur, also hangs in the museum, with a note explaining that his
journey to California exemplifies the story of Syrian migrants who lived
and worked first in Central America and Mexico.

FIGURE 8. Shafiqa (Sophie) Hallal, middle, sewing stars on a World War I
banner, 1918. Source: *Los Angeles Evening Herald*, Los Angeles Public Library.

In January 2016 Vicki traveled with her Uncle Phil and Aunt Artie to New York to attend the opening of an Ellis Island exhibit on Syrian immigrants where her grandmother's embroidery was exhibited. Interviewed about the exhibit and Shafiqa's handiwork in it, Vicki said: "She rolled that up and brought it because she said she wanted to be able to prove that she had skills. This to her was like showing a diploma."[27]

As was the case with Kathy, these objects provided a window into the retelling of Vicki's family history to multiple audiences, helped her to craft an archival sensibility, and to connect and sustain relations with family members within a diasporic space. There were other parallels as well. While Vicki identified strongly with her Lebanese and Syrian ancestry, it was her involvement in the Palestine question that propelled her into activism, recalibrated her sense of Arabness, and broadened her understanding of community.

In 1981 Vicki joined a small group of activists associated with the Chicago-based Palestinian Human Rights Campaign on a three-week fact-finding trip to Lebanon and the Occupied Territories. The trip allowed her to gain firsthand knowledge of the reality of Palestinian camp life, the workings of the Palestine Liberation Organization, and the inequities of the Israeli occupation in the West Bank and Gaza Strip. It also consolidated her pull toward Arabness that had been largely understood as a product of her closeness to her grandparents.

The journey to Palestine and back gave Vicki what she called "new knowledge," yet she quickly learned to adjust when, where, and to whom she conveyed this knowledge. Living and working for several years in Chicago, she served as the facilitator of a small discussion group consisting of Arabs and Jews. It was a model for engaging on the Palestine question that aimed to break through the perception of inherent hostility between the two groups. One member had grown up in a small Ohio town with an active Ku Klux Klan presence. She was reared on left-wing Labor Zionist principles, emphasizing collective agricultural work and trade unionism. These principles were demonstrated by her attachment to a blue box "that all Jewish families kept, which was money sent to plant trees and so on." She also recalled that when she became aware of the Israeli occupation over Palestinians, "This was not the Israel [she] thought she knew."²⁸ Another participant was a Palestinian man from the West Bank who spoke of the childhood trauma inflicted upon him after he witnessed a young neighbor, to whom he was deeply attached, being hanged, purportedly as an "Israeli spy."²⁹ He also recalled the longtime illness his mother suffered after she attempted to return to the family home in Tel Aviv, only to find a motel built on what had been the family's land.

Following Quaker practice, the early sessions of the dialogue group involved sharing of personal narratives. A lengthy *Chicago Reader* article on their meetings, however, couldn't help but reproduce, indeed fabricate, the trope of hostility, entitling its story "Enemies."³⁰

After Vicki returned to Los Angeles, she found herself in a different environment, less activist on Arab American issues. Advocating for Palestinian rights within Lebanese American circles was often fraught with tension. Steeped in the factionalism of the Lebanese civil war, Arab-origin communities experienced cleavages that were often refracted along confessional lines. Vicki remembered a particularly searing moment when these tensions erupted. While attending the funeral of a family member at the Maronite church on San Vincente Boulevard, she began to hear a ruckus in the parking lot. She looked out in time to see a group of men attempting to tip her car over. The priest ran outside to confront them and they dispersed, but he scolded Vicki and said that they had been attempting to upend her car because of her bumper sticker. It read: "Palestinians have human rights too." "You really have to be more careful," the priest told her. "If you are going to come to this church, you shouldn't have this in your window." "Well," Vicki responded, "I guess the answer is I shouldn't come to this church." A few weeks later, at the Orthodox church that her father had attended, the priest told Vicki: "You can park in our lot anytime."³¹

Vicki decided that going forward she would not "talk politics with family," and that her activism as it related to Palestine would focus on the importance of people gaining experiential knowledge. "The most important political move a person can make is to go there," she asserted. Witnessing the on-the-ground reality, American travelers would not be able to "deny" what they had seen. Even those motivated solely by their faith to visit Jerusalem could be altered by the journey because "even the act of prayer is interrupted by the occupation." Vicki recalled interfacing with Christian evangelical groups, supporting their pilgrimage to Jerusalem, but adding: "by the way, go through Nablus, and then come back and tell me what you think." "Nothing will change them like that," she continued, "no book will affect them that much; no movie is going to hit them that hard." For Vicki, the act of refusal was a refusal to ignore what she had witnessed. As she put it, "I can't deny what I already saw."[32]

"MY DAD BELIEVED IN BUILDING COALITIONS"

The journey to Palestine was also transformative for Diane Shammas. Growing up in a household with a Swedish American mother and with a Lebanese American father, who had an "understated" sense of Arabness, Diane's pull toward Arab American identity unfolded gradually. Like Kathy and Vicki, her Syrian grandmother, Adeby, had been a strong presence in her childhood. Strong-willed and industrious, Adeby had moved from the East Coast to Los Angeles with her children after her husband had left the family. Adept at embroidery and familiar with the textile trade, she spent years cultivating a client base to whom she sold linens. Her labor required long hours away from home, and the frequent boarding out of her son and daughter with other families.[33]

Diane did not connect to her Arabness primarily through her grandmother, however, but through her involvement in coalition politics. Her father, Nickolas (Nick) Shammas, had set a precedent of active civic engagement. The owner of several car dealerships that

employed a mostly Latino staff, Nick Shammas helped launch the
Mexican American Political Association, which galvanized around the
election of Edward Roybal to the US Congress in 1962. Roybal had in
1949 become the first Latino to serve on the Los Angeles city council
since 1881.[34] Diane remembered being drawn to Chicano activism in
her youth, through the example of her father. When she was in tenth
grade, her class had traveled to the agricultural community of Delano
to meet with farmworkers and to distribute toys to their children. Her
father had loaded up the car to accompany her. "It was the first time
I really got political," she asserted.

For Diane, the road to Gaza, to which she would travel in 2009 as
a participant in the Code Pink delegation, was routed through Delano
and through her involvement in protests against the Vietnam War.[35]
Coming into an Arab American identity was an extension of her work
on other issues. The question of Palestine was initially a muted one in
her household, expressed largely as a broad-based sympathy for the
refugees. It also competed with the contradictions of the Lebanese civil
war and a sense of Lebanese pride. Her Arabness became more central
to her sense of self once she started going to Gaza. These journeys allowed her "to figure it out," as she put it, to rearrive in the US with
new capacities for critique of domestic and foreign politics.

Kathy, Vicki, and Diane were articulating here what women-of-
color feminists have called a "theory in the flesh," or "knowledge derived from narrating lived experiences and producing critical lenses
through which we see and analyze the social and political world."[36]
In telling her own life story, Vicki cast her grandmother not so much
as an emblem of culture, of someone who represented authenticity
and home, but as a catalyst for her own reassessments of Arab womanhood. The subtle and at times quite overt upending of patriarchal
authority in her grandmother's life, and certainly in that of Kathy's
grandmother Katrina, and of Diane's grandmother Adeby, gave them
each points of departure to challenge representations of culture and
propriety within their own communities. The broad perspective they

had gained from travels and activism also gave them the tools to
challenge the renderings of Arab women as passive and subdued that
were generated from without, most notably in the mainstream press.[37]
Moreover, their retelling of their grandmother's stories extended beyond a strategy of reinsertion that animated earlier oral history work
to ones that underscored the transnational dimensions of migrant experience and to cross-ethnic relations at the heart of those experiences.
Vicki understood her grandmother's piety, her bruised knees on the
steps of the Santuario, and her nimble fingers stitching the borders of
a union banner, as an extension of her relationships with other ethnic
women. Archival activism allowed these Arab American women, these
granddaughters of migrants, to see what Therese Saliba calls the "plural narratives of Arabness" and to frame their engagement with social
justice within longer, rediscovered, family histories.[38]

"WANTING TO NOT LOSE HER"

Therese Saliba describes her own route to a more engaged sense of
Arabness in ways that resonate with the themes of reconnection and
rebuilding in the face of loss explored thus far. Growing up in Southern California, she was extremely close to her grandmother, Victoria,
whose love and attention to her made her feel "very special." But the
content of her Arabness was contained within a "weekend and holiday connection," "a world of foreign foods, strange language, incense,
ritual, bazaar and bizarre."[39]

As an undergraduate student at the University of California, Berkeley, she began to absorb information on the Middle East in new ways,
within the prism of postcolonial studies. Then her grandmother passed
away. Deeply affected, Saliba describes "wanting to not lose her . . . to
use my writing to capture my memories of her." The fruits of this effort
to "not lose her" took shape in a short piece published in the *Berkeley
Fiction Review*.[40] It is, however, the second, more developed iteration
published in the ground-breaking book *Food for Our Grandmothers*
(1994) that is more widely read and cited.

This essay, "Sittee (Or Phantom Appearances of a Lebanese Grandmother)," begins with Saliba's musings on the racial incongruities
between her grandmother Victoria's passport and her naturalization
papers. The passport, issued by the French Mandate government
in Beirut in 1924, describes her forehead as "ordinary," her eyes as
"green," her hair as "chestnut," and her complexion as "white." Five
years later, her naturalization papers, issued in Los Angeles, reveal a
process of darkening, a trompe l'oeil affecting a naturalization clerk.
"Her complexion, hair, and eyes are now brown, dark brown even."
"Maybe," Saliba writes, "this is part of the process of naturalization,
the loss of years, the gaining of darkness, the irony of a procedure
that as it naturalizes an alien, making her 'as if a native,' defines her
as darker, as Other."[41]

Saliba deftly brings two documents issued by two different states,
each with an intent to classify and to regulate (regulate access to movement and classify those eligible for citizenship), into conversation with
each other. Her reflection on the categories of classification assigned to
her grandmother (*sittee*) serve as a departure point that allows the reader
to see that her grandmother was all of the things enumerated, but also
none of them. "As long as I knew my grandmother, her skin was fair
and her eyes were green," she writes. And while Victoria "spoke little
of her old way of life. . . . it bled through into everything she did."[42]

Victoria's death and Saliba's decision to "not lose her" leads her to
probe the documentary past and to come to know her sittee's history
that she heretofore knew "only in the confused and convoluted ways
of a child." As a teenager, "because I wanted to forget my Arabness and
to be like everyone else, I didn't have much time for Sittee."[43] The essay
in *Food for Our Grandmothers* is an attempt to find Victoria, to give
her more time, and to share with her a language of connection and of
self-identification. In fact, Saliba ends the essay by telling the reader
that she has come to know Arabic, the language of her grandmother.
She thus reconstructs a connection to a female elder that other Arab
American women lament not pursuing. Queen Noor, for example,
states in her interview with Henry Louis Gates Jr.: "I wish I had asked

her [grandmother] many more questions before she passed away." Joe Kadi also used this concept of a conversation never embarked upon to signal a desire for insights from his sittee. "I do wish I could talk to her, I have so many questions," Kadi writes in the introduction to *Food for Our Grandmothers.* But rather than remain in a place of am-biguity and unknowability, Kadi uses the oft-repeated refrain "there are things I once took for granted whose ugliness, endurance, and uselessness now astound me" to unmask the systems that invisibil-ize Arab Americans. Kadi offers in their place new stories, "beautiful, enduring and useful—to our grandmothers, to ourselves, and to the generations after us."[44]

Shortly after she published her piece in *Food for Our Grandmoth-ers,* Therese Saliba spoke with historian Alixa Naff about the inter-view Naff had done with her grandmother, Victoria, in 1962. The interview was one of a series that Naff conducted with elders in the Syrian and Lebanese communities of Los Angeles, Detroit, Montreal, and other cities. Naff focused on getting her interviewees to describe their places of origin and their journey to the United States. Victoria, for example, spends a good portion of the 1962 interview speaking about her hometown of Duma, and the ways in which migrants from there connected in the mahjar. She credits them with raising money that helped bring electricity to the town. In her words, "When Duma people get together for coffee, or at funerals . . . they request money for Duma instead of flowers."[45]

Therese Saliba's conversation with Naff was yet another way to tap into the archival legacy, yet it was also an encounter that produced a new sense of incongruity between the lived experience of Victoria, her own narration of her past, and the ways that Naff incorporated this past into *Becoming American.*[46] It is to some of these incongruities that the next, and last, chapter turns, exploring not only the disconnects between archives and history telling, but also the hidden palimpsest of California in Arab American historiography.

CHAPTER 5

PALIMPSESTS IN
ICONIC CALIFORNIA

IT IS A QUINTESSENTIALLY mid-century Southern Californian image, the kind that would fuel Americans' fascination with beach culture based on idealized representations of youth, beauty, and athleticism. Taken at the original Muscle Beach, just south of the Santa Monica Pier, the photo, like hundreds like it taken in the late 1940s, shows a group of tumblers displaying their acrobatic skill to an enthralled crowd. A young, lithe woman gracefully takes flight from the arms of two supremely muscled men as another, arms outreached, waits to catch her.[1] We can imagine in the ensuing seconds that the crowd erupts in applause and cheers. Then in the minutes between acts, they seek refreshments in the storefronts behind them, enticed by the huge Dr. Pepper, Pepsi, and Coca-Cola signs that hang above a strip of storefronts. A closer look at this photo and another taken in a similar spot (see Figures 9 and 10) reveals the name of one of the places in which so many of these beachgoers quenched their thirst: Khoury and Auad Café. Syrian-owned and operated, the café was run by business partners Leo Khoury and Abraham Auad and was one of a collection of Syrian establishments along the beach.

Leo Khoury was Elias Khoury Rayheb, originally from a place whose name was written on some documents as Cuba (probably Qobeh), Lebanon, the same village that Mansur Nahra came from. His declaration of intention to become a US citizen shows him arriving in the US in 1938 and lists his last foreign residence as Buenos Aires, Argentina.[2] It was in Buenos Aires that he most likely connected with Abraham Auad ('Awad in Arabic), who listed Khoury as his cousin on his World War II draft registration card.[3] The two men are enumerated as living together on Third Street in Santa Monica in the 1940 census. Both were unmarried at the time, with Khoury, at twenty-nine years of age, registered as "head of household" and Auad, at twenty-six years old, recorded as his "partner."[4] Auad had arrived in the US

FIGURE 9. Paula Unger (Boelsems) is thrown by two male gymnasts into the arms of Lyle Lytell, in front of Khoury's Café at Muscle Beach, south of Santa Monica Pier. Courtesy of Santa Monica History Museum, Santa Monica History Museum Collection.

from Buenos Aires in 1939. The ship's passenger manifest lists his nationality as Argentinian, the language spoken as Spanish, and his race
as Syrian.[5] In other words, both men were Latin American Syrians.

Rather than see the presence of the names Khoury and Auad as
incidental to the photo, a marginal notation in a much grander story
of the constitution of California beach culture, this chapter reinserts
them as central to the conditions that helped produce that culture. In

FIGURE 10. Four male gymnasts in acrobatic balancing stunt in front of
Khoury's Café at Muscle Beach, Santa Monica, CA. Courtesy of Santa Monica
History Museum, Santa Monica History Museum Collection.

much the same manner that I repositioned George Shibley into the narrative of Sleepy Lagoon and proposed alternate archival notations on the photo with Hank Leyvas, I Arabize this iconic representation of the original Muscle Beach by excavating a particular piece of the image title. Collected as part of a digital project of the Santa Monica Public Library, the image bears the notation: "Paula Boelsems flying toward Lyle Lytell on Muscle Beach in front of the Khoury and Avad [sic] Café, Santa Monica, Calif."

I pause on the last part of the description "in front of" (the misspelled place name) to suggest how considering the subjects of this photo relationally (the acrobats, the café owners, and the crowd) informs a reading practice that captures the Syrian American contribution to Southern California history. I tie together threads of earlier chapters in order to push against the narrative of arrival in Arab American studies that focuses on Ellis Island and Little Syria in New York as the iconic "mother colony," toward one that incorporates geographies of California, the Southwest, and Latin America into our understanding of the Syrian American diaspora. I do so by reading three final sets of texts through the lens of the Syrian Pacific: a set of photographs, including the beach images referenced above; Lebanese author Rabee Jaber's prize-winning novel *Amerika;* and the oral histories that historian and "mother of Arab American studies" Alixa Naff gathered in Los Angeles in 1962.

OUT TO THE PACIFIC: SYRIANS AND SANTA MONICA

The photographs taken of tumblers at the original Muscle Beach orient the Syrian presence in California to the shores of the Pacific Ocean. Khoury's Café was one of at least eight Syrian-owned cafés on Ocean Front that catered to the throngs of beachgoers there. Two doors down from Leo Khoury's café was Eddie and George Drake's store, advertised in the *Directory of California* Syrians as home of the "Famous Hamburger." Vera Tamoush's uncle, Ruffie, also had a café in the same strip of businesses, as did Bashara and Nicholas Haddad.[6]

Santa Monica, Ocean Park, Redondo Beach, and Venice were home to many Syrian families, a number of whom operated service-related businesses such as hotels, restaurants, and cafés. Mrs. Abdo (Mary) Hilaiel ran a liquor store on Pico Boulevard, which she took over after her husband's death. George Shishim, whose racial fitness for citizenship had been debated in the Los Angeles press in 1909, went on to own a detective agency after serving as the police chief of Venice. His granddaughter, Edie Nassief, remembered growing up between the Syrian worlds of Santa Monica and downtown Los Angeles, as if the two communities were separate yet connected. "We were more Santa Monicans than Arabs," she recalled in a 2016 interview.[7]

Edie's father, George, and his brother, her Uncle Francis, followed the example of their father and became police officers. They are pictured in the *Arab-American Almanac* escorting another California icon, Marilyn Monroe, to a gala in 1959, ostensibly to protect the diamonds she was wearing around her neck. All three of the photo's subjects are beaming and, for the discerning reader, there is an underlying irony: two men whose father's suitability to become an American citizen was challenged in a Los Angeles court because he was thought to be racially unfit to be one were now entrusted with protecting a white American icon. The photo represents yet another lost moment in California historiography, where the presence of Syrians in the flow of major cultural events goes unremarked upon, as if it does not exist. The eyes of scholars who have written about the rich complexity of Southern California's racial terrain and its dynamic popular culture have not been trained to see it. They do not "see" that Shishim is an identifiably Arab name worth exploring.[8]

Pausing on this name, exploring its origin and its continued presence in the landscape of Los Angeles—something a high school student with online access to a public library can now do—leads to an important racial palimpsest: George Shishim's petition for naturalization. In Chapter 1 I discussed Shishim's case in relation to his Asianness and to the reasons that his eligibility for citizenship was called into question: his place of origin, Syria, was considered to be part of "Turkey in Asia." I return to the case here to focus on issues related to the document itself and its revealing marginalia. The document is both a literal palimpsest, with "diverse layers or aspects apparent beneath the surface," and a figurative one. Now digitized, his petition for naturalization shows through, peeking from underneath the original declaration of intention (see Figure 11).[9] The declaration is filled out in the elegant cursive script of the deputy clerk for the Superior Court of Los Angeles and signed by George Sulayman Shishim in June 1907. A half-page of handwritten notes was added to the petition of 1909, in the section entitled Order of Court Admitting Petitioner (see Figure 12).[10] Written by Judge George Hutton, the notes are remarkable for their detail among the thousands of petitions with which it is collected. The marginalia underscore the fact that this was not a run-of-the-mill naturalization case but a bumpy road to citizenship for Shishim. Hutton's notes remind us of the interstices of doubt between 1907 and 1909 regarding Syrian racial fitness for US citizenship.

The notations begin on September 22, 1909, with the motion by Frederick Jones, identified as a US naturalization examiner, to "deny said petition" on grounds that the "petitioner does not come under the provisions of Sec. 2169 of Revised Statutes of U." The next day, twenty-two-year-old Missouri native Byron C. Hanna appeared as the attorney for Shishim. Hutton notes that the "witness's satisfactory" [sic] and "knowledge satisfactory," referencing the law's provisions that an applicant for citizenship must have two witnesses testifying to his or her good standing and that a set of questions on US civics had been answered appropriately. This is followed by several continuances until the final notation of November 4, 1909, Shishim's sixth appearance in court, admitting him to citizenship, or more accurately, overruling the motion to deny him admittance. The last notation is telling: "Exception to above decision taken by Frederick Jones representing the Government through the Division of Naturalization Dept. of Commerce and Labor." The "exception" taken by Jones presaged the legal

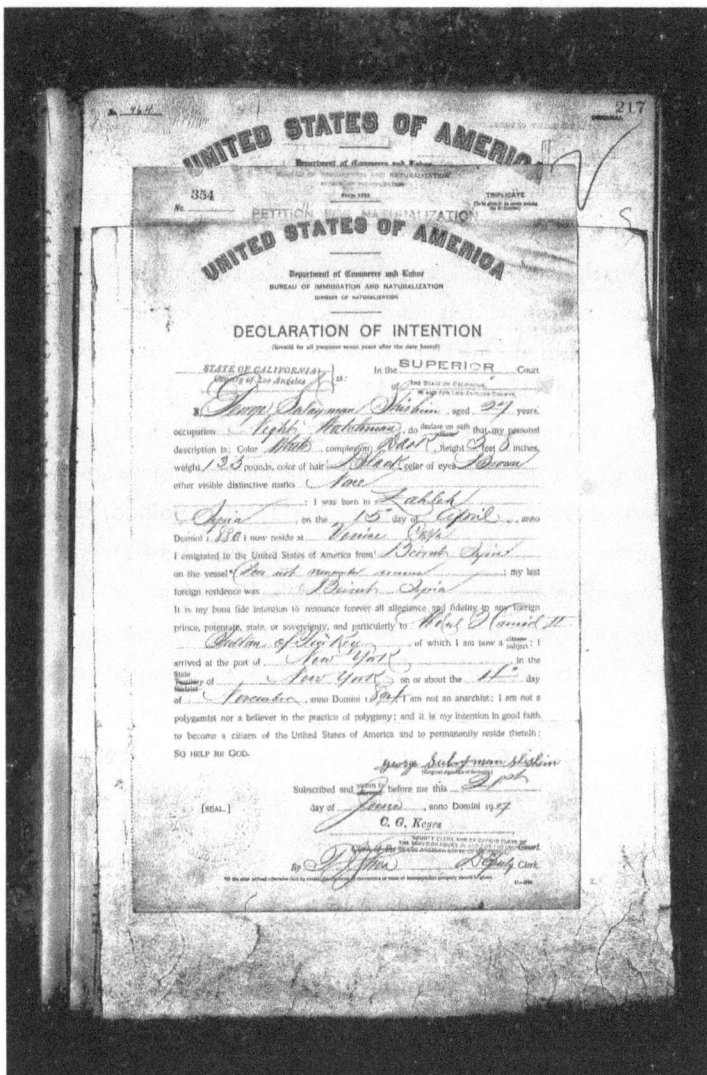

FIGURE 11. Declaration of Intention to Become an American Citizen of
George Sulayman Shishim, 1907. Source: National Archives and Records
Administration, Ancestry.com.

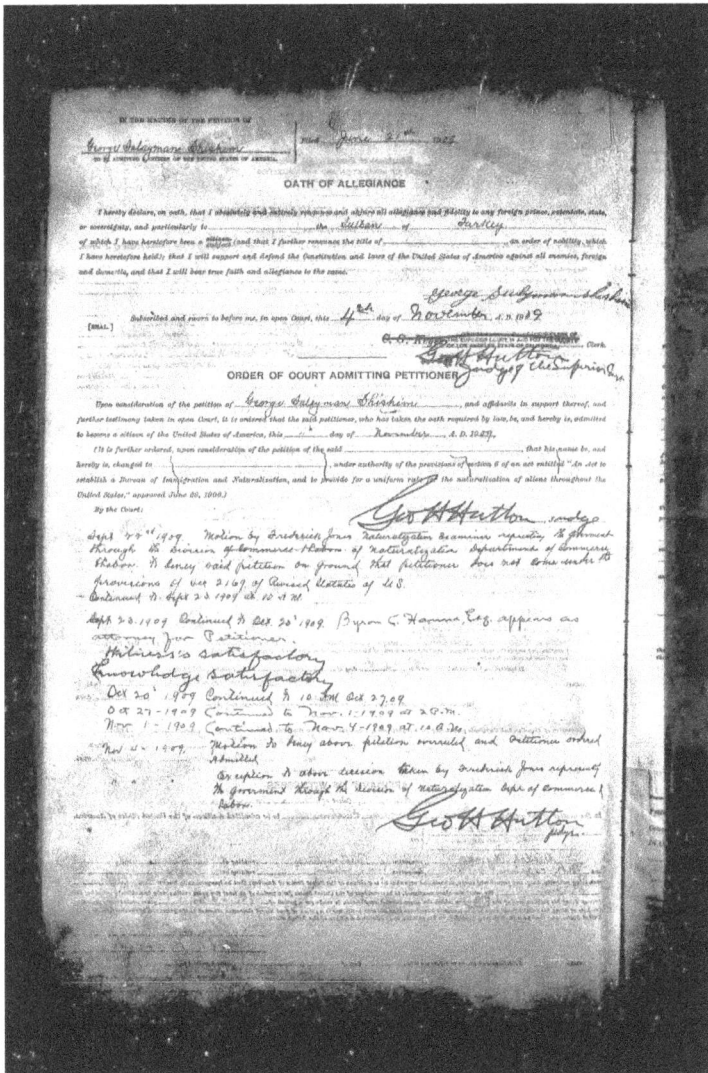

FIGURE 12. Order of Court Admitting Petitioner George Sulayman Shishim, 1909. Source: National Archives and Records Administration, Ancestry.com.

battles that were to come for Syrians around the question of their fitness for citizenship and that were not resolved from the standpoint
of naturalization law until 1914.[11]

The fifty years between the racial-prerequisite case of George Shishim
and the photo of his two sons arm in arm with Marilyn Monroe can be
read as a classic tale of assimilation, of the "exception" taken by Hutton
challenging Shishim's qualifications to be an American fading away into
irrelevance. But it is not so simple. If we look again at the *Arab American
Almanac*, we see on the same page as this photo another entry suggesting
the continued need for Arabs in California to advocate for their rights
and to push for an Americanness open to Arab concerns.[12] In 1960 the
Arab American Arab Society of Orange County was established, and
that same year a group of women in San Francisco founded NAJDA
(Women Concerned About the Middle East). NAJDA's main goal was
to raise money for United Nations Relief and Works Agency for Palestine Refugees in the Near East (UNRWA) scholarships for Palestinian
youth. In 1959 Arabs in America were on the precipice of a national
campaign that would vilify them, and it is worth noting that these stir-
rings in the late 1950s and 1960s are organized in the "New Directions"
section of the *Almanac*. They interrupt a chronology that posits 1967
as a watershed moment for Arab American activism by pulling back to
earlier ones, and they point to California as a place of "new directions"
where advocacy was always in play.

Taken together, the photo of Khoury and Auad Café at Muscle
Beach, that of the Shishim brothers escorting Marilyn Monroe to an
event, and the founding of new organizations in San Francisco and
in Orange County capture the interconnected layers of California's
Syrian American history. And while the 1950s are often considered
a decade of increased assimilation of Arab Americans, they are also
a period of new beginnings where Syrian identity was mobilized to
tighten connections to Arabness.

The symbol of starting anew is well established in California history, and it permeates narratives of migration into the state.[13] New

beginnings unfolded differently for different ethnoracial groups, however. African Americans sought refuge from de jure segregation in the Jim Crow South; poor whites from the Midwest were enticed by the boosterism of Southern California's Anglo elite; and Chinese men built railways, all the while enduring government policies and cultural backlash that pathologized them. Mexican bracero families labored in the agricultural economy, sustaining it, while being subjected to race-baiting and California's own brand of segregation.[14]

Syrians also saw California as offering possibilities for a new beginning, but it was not a tabula rasa for them. They tapped into pre-existing networks, relied on co-ethnics, and navigated the racial fault lines in ways that were predictable but also at times quite unexpected. Rabee Jaber's novel *Amerika* is a text that probes the meaning of new beginnings in the Syrian diaspora by pushing against linear models of movement and assimilation. The journey of the central character, Marta Haddad, ends in Pasadena. Her move is one that exemplifies a quest for security after the economic crash of 1929, yet it is also one that allows the reader to position California as a window onto the Syrian diaspora and its Latin American coordinates.

"UN NOUVEAU DÉPART": RABEE JABER'S *AMERIKA*

Amerika, first published in Arabic in 2009 and translated into French in 2013, is a text that both reproduces the tropes of arrival in the Arab American narrative yet also incorporates different destinations that are recast, in fact, as "new beginnings."[15] Marta's journey from Lebanon to "Amerika" is familiar for those with even a modest grasp of the history of Syrian migration. The first chapter, titled Ellis Island, evokes the themes of excitement, anxiety, and state regulation that are found in other novels on the early twentieth-century immigrant experience.[16] Marta disembarks and finds herself thrust into a sea of humanity that is directed to numerous halls and corridors like "ants burrowing underground." It is a depiction of arrival that conveys bewilderment, the inability to communicate to the prodding immigration inspectors, a search for friendly faces, initial fright, and even panic. "We are in the spring of 1913," the narrator declares, "and it is here that everything is decided, entry or return" (*amma al-dukhul aw al-'awda*).[17]

Jaber then begins to weave his intricate tale of Marta: "I want to tell you a little bit about the journey (*rihlatiha*) that brought her from Btater to the doors of America."[18] Barely a few chapters in, the reader grasps that she embodies the changes that the silk-producing region of Mount Lebanon underwent in the early twentieth century. Marta has learned to read and write at a village school opened by the Russians, and delights in the taste of fruit as she reads her book "underneath the mulberry tree" (the crop that feeds the silkworms).[19] Perhaps most significantly, like thousands of other Lebanese women, she is caught up in the dynamic of transatlantic migration. She marries Khalil Haddad, who "took her to his bed, then left for America." She embroiders handkerchiefs for him to sell, ones that an American supplier admires so much that he tells Khalil that "no one embroiders like the women of Syria."[20] Khalil writes to Marta at first, but then there is a silence of a year and a half. She decides to leave Lebanon to find him.

Jaber's opening to this migration story seems to be a synthesis of the canonical works in Arab American history. While he states at the outset that the novel is the "fruit of his imagination and that any resemblance to real events or people is entirely fortuitous," it seems he means this more in jest.[21] Entire story lines of the novel resonate with the peddling thesis, with the focus on Ellis Island and Little Syria, and with the social networks created between old and new immigrants. Khalil excels as a peddler, his "*kasha* on his back."[22] His supplier tells Marta that her husband was one of the fastest and most hardworking of peddlers: "We started to send him whole cases by train, as far as Lincoln, Nebraska, and Tulsa, Oklahoma, he picked up the merchandise and hit the road. He then bought a horse and buggy and sent money regularly. All this in less than two years."[23]

Marta channels the pioneering spirit of the women whose oral histories shape the text of Alixa Naff's, *Becoming American.* She first works in a textile factory, then decides to peddle wares and is helped along in this endeavor by a Syrian matriarch and boarding-house operator named Hajja Mary. Other hallmarks of the early Syrian immigrant experience are found in the novel, including Marta's primary contact and confidant, Joseph Estephan, himself a former peddler and now a manager in the factory of M. Herman. Estephan serves as the intermediary between the world she has left and the world she is now trying to navigate. Finding her without a proper winter coat, for example, he takes her to the basement of a Maronite church where there are piles of clothes, free of charge, for her to pick from, to protect herself from the biting New York cold.

The chapters in the Little Syria section of Jaber's *Amerika* are so reminiscent of Konrad Bercovici's 1924 "Around the World in New York—The Syrian Quarter" and the *New York Tribune*'s "A Picturesque Colony" that they seem inspired completely by these articles. Jaber even uses Bercovici's device of asking the reader, "cher lecteur," to imagine a journey to Rector Street in Lower Manhattan, complete with the tram route that takes her there.[24] "Orient yourself west, pass several houses and voilà you are in Syria." Here you will find the answer to his previously posed rhetorical question: "Did you know, dear reader, that a part of Damascus or of Constantinople has been transported across the ocean here to America?"[25] Jaber appears to draw heavily on Naff for the development of his peddler characters. One section, told in the voice of a Syrian man in Slidell, Louisiana, relates how his father, when he was tired, hungry, and cold, pretended not to speak English, only knowing the words "thank you," in order to gain entry and rest at a farmhouse. It is lifted almost verbatim from the On the Road chapter of Naff's *Becoming American,* an intertextual move that brings Naff's oral histories into the purview of Arabic fiction.[26]

While *Amerika* thus seems informed by Arab American historiography, and the novel becomes what Wrisley calls "historiographic

metafiction," Jaber does not replicate the rags-to-riches story.[27] The
hardships that are mentioned in other nonfiction texts as minor obstacles that immigrants ultimately surmount loom in *Amerika* and have
a visceral, haunting impact on the reader. Marta's husband, Khalil, for
example, sees his supplier at one point change his shirt. On his body
are "the deep scars that the straps of the kasha left on his shoulders
and on his back."[28] When Hajja Mary and Joseph Estephan find Marta
listless in her room, her body having given out under the crushing
news that the husband she has traveled thousands of miles to find is
living with a "an American whore" ("une catin américaine"), we read
that "even the light that emanated from the window appeared to
him [Joseph] sinister and assassin-like."[29] The tight network of Syrian
migrants in which Marta finds herself enmeshed is both a source of
comfort and a source of oppression, as others engage in its whispering
campaigns and judgment of her.

Much is familiar in the mahjar of Jaber's *Amerika,* but he also
takes the narrative to places outside the dominant paradigm in Arab
American studies in what becomes an intricate and decidedly non-
linear account of Marta's life. Notable among the places the reader is
rerouted to is Louisiana as a destination for Marta on her quest to find
her husband. The long train ride south from New York is a pensive
one for her. When she arrives in Slidell, to the north of New Orleans,
she spots a store with signage in Arabic and English. The store owner
sits outside, a *tarboush* on his head, smoking his *nargileh* (water pipe)
and, thankfully, conversant in Arabic. Marta's interactions with this
man, Jamil Tarazi, stretch the narrative down to another port city with
a Syrian presence, mitigating temporarily the sense of aloneness that
she feels. But it is followed by a crushing deception. Marta continues
on to a plantation outside of New Orleans, where a festive banquet
is under way. There is music, food, and cacophony. The young black
servant who meets her carriage sees her staring intently at the master
("maître"; *al-sayyid*) of the house. The servant sees her see the face of
her husband, Khalil (now known as Joe), his mouth wide open in

surprise as he also recognizes his wife. Khalil says nothing and does not move from the side of the mistress of the house. Marta retreats in the same carriage, without so much as descending, and makes her way back to New Orleans and up north. On the train ride back, she catches a glimpse of her face in the window. It is "yellow and shattered."[30]

The New Orleans encounter is one of many ruptures in the assimilative arc of much of the early Arab American scholarship and of the idealized imagery of emigration produced by the modern state of Lebanon. Considerable evidence points to the fact that married men engaged in bigamy in the mahjar. Indeed, we have already encountered it in the life of Katrina.[31] Jaber chooses to foreground this open secret and to develop a complex character who takes charge of her life despite this affront. Marta marries again (only after she finds out that Khalil has died while serving in World War I) to another Syrian migrant, Ali, who Jaber casts as a peripatetic roamer. Having evaded inspection at Ellis Island by jumping ship and swimming to shore, Ali continues on a journey that leads him to South America, to the Texas-Mexico border, to Illinois, and to various locations in between. Together, he and Marta raise four children and work through the devastating years of the Great Depression. In the last part of the book, Jaber introduces a place that is both a destination, an end, and a beginning: Pasadena, California.

The family moves west after the stock market crash of 1929, a move that is made possible by Marta's fortuitous decision to buy an orange grove there several years before. These final chapters of her life do not represent a telos toward success, but a vantage point from which she elongates some connections and severs others. Widowed again by the age of forty, after Ali's premature death, Marta receives condolence notes from far and wide. "Some had American stamps, some not. She received letters from states whose names she did not recognize. Others came from Canada and Mexico and Argentina. *Kashshashs* [peddlers]—whose names she strained to remember, then found them in her old workbooks—wrote her from Brazil, Venezuela, and Peru."[32]

We are reminded here again of the toll of the Great Depression on many of these peddlers. In what is a dramatic interruption in the peddler-to-proprietor paradigm, Jaber describes how many of those who had purchased stores found themselves crippled by debt and unable to move the merchandise off their shelves. So they closed their shops and put their merchandise on their backs and peddled from door to door.³³ "Peddling (*la kacha*) made its return during the Great Depression, but it was a feeble return, inconsistent and with poor returns. People were always on the brink of hunger," Jaber writes.³⁴

In the closing chapters on Pasadena, Jaber develops Marta's relationship to Latino/as. She receives the letters from peddlers in Latin America while living on her farm, which she entrusts (*awkalat*) to Joaquim, who is originally from Mexico, to run. Joaquim has a Latina wife named Castilla, whose sisters and brothers come from Hobbs, New Mexico, one at a time to work the farm. She also cooks and (Marta's) children enjoy the dishes that she prepares. "This family—Joaquim, his wife, and the sisters and brothers of his wife—gave the farm a new life."³⁵

Marta's son, Jamil, grows close to Castilla's youngest brother Juan, and prefers to work on the farm and in the gardens instead of as a merchant. He spends so much time with Juan's extended family that he learns Spanish. He speaks it so well, it is as if he "had been born in Mexico."³⁶

In a few short paragraphs, Jaber disrupts several of the tropes in the Arab American narrative by accounting for the multiracial makeup of Los Angeles and the central place of Mexican American labor in the post-Depression economy (this, despite the massive attempts to repatriate Mexicans). It is Mexican American hands that give the farm "new life" and that nourish the children with food that is not the emblematic kibbe and hummus of a Syrian grandmother. The closing chapters of *Amerika* are recurrent reminders of Syrian proximity to Latinness just as those that detail Marta's journey to New Orleans involve underexplored proximities to blackness—blackness understood not as one pole in a racial binary but as generative space for critique, space that, as Therí Pickens argues, "troubles the ease with which one can accept or endorse the American dream and all that accompanies it."[37] Jaber's text has the potential to not only "trouble the American dream," but to subvert the peddler-to-proprietor paradigm and complicate it. Marta is, at the end of the novel, an owner not of a store but of a farm, one that is worked by Mexican Americans, while she rents a boutique on Arroyo Street in Pasadena that sells men's and women's clothing.

That Jaber's Marta is reminiscent of the women that Alixa Naff brings to life in her book, calling them "the most valuable economic asset to the [peddling] trade," is both ironic and revealing.[38] Ironic because of Jaber's claim that the novel is the product of his imagination and revealing because it points to ways that the peddling thesis (and the Naff archive itself) might productively come to terms with its western origins. Marta in fact resembles the women that Naff interviewed not in New York or the Midwest, but in Los Angeles, because that it where her research began. However, the location of Naff's informants in a Pacific space goes largely unremarked upon and certainly undertheorized in her analysis. Instead, there is an insistence on an idealized East Coast origin in Naff's *Becoming American*, and her subjects' stories rarely extend beyond the Midwest. Oddly, then, while Jaber's *Amerika* is a work of fiction that claims to be divorced from the archive, his Marta reads as a composite of the life stories that are actually contained in a real archive but that became truncated in Naff's usage. How might we productively bring the Naff archive into conversation with the character of Marta Haddad?

CALIFORNIA DREAMING: ALIXA NAFF'S
BECOMING AMERICAN FROM THE VANTAGE
POINT OF THE PACIFIC

When historian Alixa Naff died in 2013, tributes poured in, recognizing her role in shaping the field of Arab American studies. Helen Hatab Samhan honored Naff by calling her the "grande dame of Arab American studies," and the Arab American Institute signaled the importance of her foundational work by calling her the "'mother' of

Arab American studies."[39] The Arab American Studies Association followed suit by holding its second conference in her honor, noting in its program that "her preeminent publication, *Becoming American: The Early Arab-American Experience*, remains a pioneering and influential history of Arab Americans."[40]

When thinking about Naff's life and work, two places readily come to mind: Detroit and Washington, DC. Naff came of age in Detroit, working in her father's grocery store after school and then for Western Union. In a highly personal essay she wrote for *Arab Detroit: from Margin to Mainstream*, she notes: "No other city in which I have lived since has so legitimate a claim on my reminiscences."[41] The essay provides a window into a "thoroughly Syrian-Lebanese household" shaped by her mother's attachment to the traditions of her village of origin, Rashayya, and her father's fitful journey from peddler to store owner. Throughout the essay, the "Dragon of the Depression" lurks, and an acute sadness pervades the piece. We learn of her mother's heartache at losing first her parents, then her two brothers. These three tragedies structure the narrative as if foreshadowing a final devastating blow: the sudden death of Alixa's mother at the age of forty-nine.

Naff is candid about the toll of these various hardships, which also included intense anxiety while her brothers fought during World War II, the departure of her sister from the family home, and Naff's reluctant assumption of the management of the family store. The latter involved "leaving what I had come to consider the most meaningful part of my life (working at Western Union)." She described the store as "a narrow prison whose formidable bars seemed permanent to me."[42] After the war, she entered into a protracted depression while she was still in her twenties.

She does, however, punctuate the essay with moments of grace and beauty. These include a fond reflection on the family's house in Highland Park, Michigan: "It is the image of that house that my memory flashes up to me when I think back, as if there was nothing else worth remembering from those years."[43] The potency of this remark helped solidify Naff's identity as a quintessentially Midwestern Arab American, a product of the pioneering wave of immigrants that she devoted many years to studying. Her book, *Becoming American,* offers a comprehensive history of Arab American assimilation. In it she champions the peddling thesis—an argument that the economic activities of peddling allowed for English-language acquisition, capital accumulation, store ownership, and eventual incorporation into the American middle class.[44]

The fruits of Naff's scholarship were made available to researchers through the establishment of the Faris and Yamna Naff Arab American Collection at the Smithsonian Institution in Washington, DC in 1984. Alixa Naff became identified with the collection, not only because her material and in particular the oral histories she had conducted with early Arab American immigrants formed the backbone of the collection, but because she herself became so involved in organizing and cataloging it. Fittingly, in its tribute to her after her death, the Arab American Institute featured a photo of Naff sitting with a group of volunteers engaged in this endeavor, further solidifying the connection between Alixa Naff, the Smithsonian, and Arab American studies.

But a period between Detroit and Washington in the life of Alixa Naff lasted approximately twenty years, the same amount of time she lived in Detroit. It is her sojourn in Los Angeles along with her brothers and her father while she attended UCLA, and then took up an academic post at the University of California, Chino, before moving to the East Coast in 1977. While cursorily mentioned in Arab American studies scholarship, this period was foundational to developing her project, which would become synonymous with the field. A deeper exploration of the oral histories in the Naff collection pivots the canon west. Los Angeles is in fact the starting point for what came to be the Faris and Yamna Naff Arab American Collection.

To be sure, Naff does mention California in her personal essay in *Arab Detroit*, but the account is saturated with so much pain that it is as if she wants us to forget it. California opened up on the horizon of the Naff family when her brother, Nick, was stationed in San Francisco during World War II. "Like hundreds of other servicemen who breathed the clean, fragrant air of California and were captivated by its way of life," Naff tells us, Nick began a campaign to move the family to the Golden State. By 1949 the plan's last plank was finally in place, and Alixa Naff sold the family home in Highland Park. "But fate had other plans for the Naff family," she writes. "It dealt us an untimely and tragic blow as we were almost ready to leave for California. Mother, in the prime of her life, died suddenly and purposelessly. Broken hearted, Dad and I traveled to Los Angeles alone."[45] It seemed impossible for her to be sanguine about a new beginning when she was in the depths of grief.

In 1957 Naff enrolled at University of California, Los Angeles (UCLA), and it was within the framework of a class on immigration history that she first began writing on the Arab immigrant community. She was disturbed by the paucity of material available to her on library shelves, so she began collecting stories from her family and parents' friends.[46] Encouraged by an instructor to pursue the project further (an instructor who admitted that "he had never before given Arabs a thought"), she applied for and received a folklore grant in her senior year. Armed with a tape recorder, she began to gather oral histories in the summer of 1962, traveling around in a Volkswagen Beetle to sixteen communities across the United States and into eastern Canada.[47] This part of her scholarly trajectory is well known. Less obvious is the fact that the majority of interviews she conducted in 1962—twenty-three in total—were done with members of the Los Angeles Syro-Lebanese community. Yet there is little information about why or how people came to Los Angles in *Becoming American*. It is as if Naff stops them in the Midwest, anchoring their stories in a place that was, for her, infused with nostalgia, verging at times on the idyllic.

Naff's 1962 interview with Victoria Saliba, Therese Saliba's grandmother, is typical in this regard (see the discussion in Chapter 4). Victoria tells Naff that she arrived in the US in 1921 and "came straight to Los Angeles." One brother, "the doctor," came to meet her in New York, and they then came on to Los Angeles, where he started a medical practice. We don't learn much more about this part of the story. But other sources reveal that by the early 1920s, Victoria's brother, Dr. Assad Abdun-Nur, was running a medical clinic in near downtown LA, at 12th St. and San Pedro.[48]

Victoria does provide information on her life in Los Angeles, including quite detailed references to her involvement in the Episcopal church and the Doumanian Mutual Aid Society, an organization that connected Syrians with origins in the town of Douma (Duma), Lebanon. She also discusses a pridefulness among members of the community and an unwillingness to ask for help so as not to appear needy. There is, in other words, quite a bit of information that points to a complex communal life in Los Angeles and to cross-ethnic interaction. But the questions Naff asks throughout the interview lead elsewhere. When she incorporates Victoria Saliba's oral history into *Becoming American*, it is to support the argument around the insularity of the Syrian community and of a "social life centered on identity of the group." She uses Victoria's story to buttress her observation that membership was based on "religion, sect, village or family . . . Victoria S. had to resign from the Douma (Mount Lebanon) Society when she married a non-Douma man."[49] As granddaughter Therese Saliba observes, however, Victoria rejoined the group after her husband's death and had a strong sense of her civic engagement:

> By my grandmother's account, what she took pride in was her activities in a number of clubs and organizations, including her charitable work in founding the Doumanian society, her activities with the Republican party, in her Orthodox church [where she became involved in the 1950s] community, and in the neighborhood Council, which included people from twenty-two countries. Her civic engagement in such diverse community organizations complicates the construction of immigrant women in a pre-feminist era, but also the meaning of *Becoming American* in the diverse landscape of Los Angeles from the 1920s to the early 1960s, where my grandmother perceives everyone as a foreigner, yet all belonging to America.[50]

Many of Naff's oral histories are truncated in this way. This does not lessen their value as historical sources, but it does encourage reflection on her positioning as an interviewer. She seems most excited by the material that speaks to her own nostalgia for the Midwest, "the place worthy of her reminiscences." And she is most interested in narrating the story of those who fall into the up-by-their-own-bootstraps narrative, those with modest origins who prevailed against great odds to "become American." Victoria Saliba, who was from a wealthier landowning family, whose brother was a doctor in East LA, and whose Syrian husband was, she tells Naff, "a Southerner from the heart of Dixie," didn't fit this mold. Tellingly, Naff added a side note to the top of the handwritten transcription of her interview with Victoria: "This informant was too conscious of her status and therefore her responses are too general and distorted by this quality. The interview was continued out of courtesy."[51] In another revealing moment, Victoria sizes up Naff's focus in this way: "You are interested in talking to poor people who came. When we came it was in luxury. We came with big money and beautiful clothes and we adjusted easily."[52]

This truncation is also found in one of the documents that is not part of the oral histories but was obviously deeply cherished by Naff. It is the memoir written by her father, Faris, entitled "The Story of My Life: From the Age of 12 Until the End of My Days." Written in 1951 and 1952 in Los Angeles, it chronicles his childhood in Rashayya, his marriage, and his decision to emigrate to America. He spends many pages detailing the peddling circuit and then takes a diversion to a kind of hagiography of Fares Ghantous, the brother of his recently deceased wife. He never gets to Los Angeles, although it was there that he spent "the end of his days." In the introductory remarks to the manuscript, Alixa Naff notes that, "When he wrote them in 1951–52 he was not less than eighty years old, bereaved, bored, uprooted from life-long friends and places and approaching the illness which was to end his life and interrupt his narrative."[53]

One wishes that Alixa Naff had written an essay on this middle portion of her life, but it was not to be. Curiosity about the Syrian community in Los Angeles hardly figures in the Naff oral histories, and even less so in *Becoming American*. But California is there in the unexplored margins of her notes and in the unacknowledged living rooms of her interviewees. It is the underexplored layer, a palimpsest, of an archive identified with the East Coast and Midwest.

Naff did, however, write an essay in which she described her process of collecting artifacts and oral histories, and the relevance this activity had on her sense of self. Like Therese Saliba, she drew on the language of mourning to relate the urgency of the need to document and narrate the lived experience of the early generation of Syrian immigrants. "I began to mourn their passing and reflected on the libraries and artifacts I has seen in some of their homes," she recalled, while also noting the many occasions on which she was told that descendants had thrown out "that old stuff" once their parents had died. Naff reveals that it was only after she had finished her book that she came to understand the feeling that had surfaced in her. "Sometimes, like the breath of a ghost, it chilled me; sometimes its familiarity comforted me; but its definition eluded me." In language similar to that of the stories encountered in Chapter 4, she speaks of a turning point: "Then one day—I realized what was happening. I had been coming to terms with myself, with my inner being, with what I am and why. I had come to terms with my parents' generation, with its collective life and interests." Clues are then given as to why California doesn't figure in *Becoming American*: "Intimacy with the cultural heritage of which I had been largely ignorant or had deliberately shunned as irrelevant had washed away lingering shadows in my identity, strengthening my ethnic pride, and confirmed me, more clear-eyed, in my Arab-Americanness and Arabness."[54]

In a sense, Naff tells the reader that she had engaged in her own excisions and capitulations to sociological paradigms of assimilation that may have made her ambivalent about pursuing the material in her own home, material such as the Syrian American guides used in this book.

Indeed, thumbing through the *Western Pacific Buyers Guide* of 1954–55, we find Naff's father and her brother Nick living at 1788 Griffith Park Boulevard in Los Feliz, most likely members of St. Nicholas Antiochian Orthodox Church, which published the guide. Leo

Khoury is also listed there. He had once again taken out a quarter-page ad in the directory, and both his café and his residence are listed in the Santa Monica section, as are the homes of George Shishim Sr. and those of his two sons, George and Francis. Because the guide did not list the female members of a family unless they were heads of households, we do not find the names of Alixa Naff or the wives of the Shishim men. We can imagine, though, that all of their lives intersected in some way in the various Southern California worlds that they helped forge.

The directory also reveals a sizable community in Pasadena, including several Haddads. It is tempting to consider them as an unrealized support for the fictional Marta Haddad in *Amerika*, who lamented that "no one spoke to her in Arabic there." If Jaber has made "art from the archives,"[55] then it is entirely appropriate to send the archive explored in this chapter back to him or, at the very least, to ponder anew the relationship between fiction and history in the mahjar. As the reader nears the end of the novel, Marta strolls "along the Pacific" with her daughter Jenny. She prays for her son, Jamil, and his friend Juan (the brother of Castilla) who serves in the Korean war. "The wind caressed her face and the smell of salt and the marine algae made her forget the real world."[56] Perhaps she would have wanted in those minutes to shut out the bustle and sound of the crowd in front of Khoury's café. Knowing that it was there and giving a name to the Syrian hands that served the customers puts us in a better position to understand the world that was "real" in the Syrian Pacific.

MESTIZAJE IN ARAB AMERICAN FAMILIES

AS ONE BEGINS TO WALK through the permanent collection of the Arab American National Museum, opened in 2005 in Dearborn, Michigan, the city with the largest proportion of Arabs in the United States, a placard soon appears, orienting the viewer to the early history of the Arab American experience.[1] It bears the title "Hadj Ali's Adventures Out West." The description of the image begins by noting that "Hadj Ali is another well-known Arab who came to America in the 19th century. He was brought from Syria by Major Henry Wayne, upon the recommendation of Secretary of War Jefferson Davis." The accompanying image is a grainy, black-and-white photo pairing two animals: a horse and a camel. To the right the horse stands with its trainer; to the left the camel points its head toward two men. Although their faces are obscured, both men appear to be wearing the marker of Ottoman masculinity, the peakless hat, or *tarboush*. One appears to wear a frock coat. The caption reads: "Loading a camel at the US Army headquarters warehouse in

Wilmington, California, for a trip to an Arizona fort, ca. 1860." The placard identifies Hadj Ali as a member of the Camel Corps, established by Jefferson Davis to assist in the effort to build a supply route from Texas to California, after the US acquired the territory in its war with Mexico between 1846 and 1848. The camels were brought from the interior of present-day Turkey, accompanied by several Ottoman handlers, including Hadj Ali, whose name was corrupted to Hi Jolly. They landed at Indianola, Texas, in 1857, and began their westward expedition.[2]

Scholars and archivists have interpreted the story of Hadj Ali in several ways. Although there is ambiguity about his origins, the Arab American National Museum positions him as a "well-known Arab" and situates his life in the United States within the arc of American expansion west. Other mentions of Hadj Ali identify him as one of the earliest documented Muslims in the United States (although certainly not earlier than those enslaved from Africa), noting that he converted to Islam from Orthodox Christianity before he came to the United States from the port town of Smyrna (Izmir) in the Ottoman Empire. There has not been a substantial study of his life within Arab American studies, and he has been positioned primarily as an intriguing, adventurous figure in the origins discourse.[3] His appearance in the historical record helps advance the argument for a long-standing presence of Arabs in America, and his service in the US military serves to boost claims to patriotism, or as one recent news article phrased it, that Muslims are "more American than apple pie."[4]

More recently, there has emerged a contentious claiming of Hadj Ali's story by various nationalist constituencies. He is at once the "first Turk," the "first Greek," and the "first Syrian" migrant in the United States.[5] The most rigorous treatments of Hadj Ali's life have come from historians working in US military history, intrigued by the Camel Corps and its relationship to the development of trade, transport, and expansion in the Southwest. Many of these accounts draw on extensive newspaper coverage of Hadj Ali's exploits and a six-part series published in the *Arizona Republic*, written by local Arizona historian Roscoe Willson in the 1960s.

I am interested in revisiting aspects of Hadj Ali's story because much has gone unstated in its usage in the Arab American narrative. Although he is often written about as a quaint and esoteric figure, by no means typical of the majority of nineteenth-century Arab migrants in the US, his story can be read through the key conceptual frames of this book. First, and perhaps most obviously, Hadj Ali's story pivots Arab American history west. It places an Ottoman subject with Syrian origins in a space made available to particular forms of settlement because of military conquest. It also encourages us to reckon with American imperial interests that harness expertise from the Ottoman Empire to facilitate a US project of colonization toward the Pacific.

Second, Hadj Ali's journey should prompt us to ask questions about why he died in Arizona, what his life was like there, and what bearing if any this might have on Arab American history. Two aspects of his story are of particular interest: he was married to a Mexican woman from Sonora, and he naturalized as a US citizen. In this concluding chapter, I propose a rereading of this originary moment, the arrival of Hadj Ali to, and movement within, the newly consolidated United States. Widely cited and sometimes celebrated, his story merits reconsideration because of its relational and gendered implications, and for the ways it repositions the early Arab American narrative geographically, away from its eastern locations, and conceptually, toward a focus on interethnic contact.

"FIRST" SYRIAN FAMILIES

While aspects of Hadj Ali's life are still hazy in the historiography, his marriage to Gertrudis Serna is well documented. The two appear in a wedding photo that has been reproduced repeatedly from the Arizona Historical Society archives and that has proliferated online in various stories about Hadj Ali (see Figure 13). The photo, taken in 1880 in

Tucson, Arizona, shows Hadj Ali, identified by his purported original name, Filippou Teodora, sitting, as his wife Gertrudis stands by his side, her hand resting on his shoulder. It is clear that she is much younger than he. Based on the available sources, she was approximately fifteen years of age at the time, and he was approximately fifty-two.[6] They would soon have two daughters, and one of them, Hermina (Minnie),

FIGURE 13. Filippou Teodora (Hadj Ali) and Gertrudis Serna, wedding portrait, Tucson, AZ, April 21, 1880. Source: Arizona Historical Society, AHS-SAD, #19482.

provided this photo to Roscoe Willson when he wrote a series of articles titled "The Camels of the Desert." In it, Willson noted that "Hi Jolly" had "a friendly disposition and spoke very broken English. His Spanish was much better."[7] Minnie also relayed information about her father's abandonment of the family, his later request that they be reunited during a period of illness, and her mother's refusal to do so.[8]

Far from being idiosyncratic, parts of Hadj Ali's story read as familiar when set alongside other examples detailed in this book. His aborted attempt at settled domestic life seems similar to the youthful years of Katrina Sa'ade's second husband, who she discovered had another partner when they married. Afraid that she would be abandoned without support when he petitioned for divorce from her, Katrina appealed to the Orthodox patriarch in the Jerusalem ecclesiastical court to intercede on her behalf. It was an appeal that fell on deaf ears.

There is also something glaringly familiar in the age disparity of the two subjects of the wedding photo. Gertrudis's young age, set beside that of her husband, old enough to be her grandfather, is reminiscent of scores of other photos taken of marriages in the early Syrian American diaspora.[9] Marriages between older men and young, often teenage, women were common in the first decades of transatlantic migration and while often presented in the historiography as a cultural norm, they were sometimes fiercely challenged. Mahjar writer 'Afifa Karam a Lebanese immigrant to Shreveport, Louisiana, railed against the practice in her articles and novels, calling it "*zawaj al-tufula*," or child marriage.[10] A pioneer of Arab women's writing on reform in the late nineteenth century, she participated in the debate on broad societal change that would expand women's access to education and to the public sphere.

Marriage patterns that stretched the boundaries of propriety (because of age difference or their plural nature) have often been attributed to the transient quality of labor in the early Syrian diaspora. Desert ecologist Gary Nabhan notes that "Philip [sic] was constitutionally unfit for living in a fixed abode. He, like his camels, could not stay very long in one place before being overtaken by the urge to roam once more."[11] This may have been true, but assessments of Hadj Ali's temperament should be placed within a broader discussion of intimate partner relationships among early Syrian migrants. The scholarship has been wedded to the chain migration thesis for several decades, an argument that places a male migrant as the first link in a chain, someone who returns to the homeland to marry or sends for a wife to join him. It is a thesis that buttresses the theory of endogamous (in-group) marriage not only in the first generation but in the second also. There has been some attention to how migration stretched heteropatriarchal norms and was debated in the early twentieth-century Arabic-language press. Syrian intellectuals expressed concerns that high rates of male migration effeminized villages; that women who peddled in the mahjar were engaging in improper conduct; and that relationships outside of marriage were contravening norms established by religious institutions. In fact, religious officials began demanding statements from Syrian men returning to marry in Syria stipulating that they had not already married in the Americas.[12]

The evidence marshaled throughout this book presents fruitful possibilities for theorizing relationships that fall outside these paradigms of transience and impropriety that are purportedly resolved by endogamous marriage. What if we center a discussion of Syrian American marriages around a different set of questions and a different set of intimacies? Who was the woman that Katrina Sa'ade referred to in her letter to the Orthodox patriarch, the one with whom her husband, Suleiman Farhat, had a daughter? What more can we know of the Mexican wife of Julián Assem, with whom, as described in Chapter 1, he reconnected after being thrown out of Mexico? What kind of relationship might we imagine Khalil (Joe) Haddad, from the novel *Amerika*, to have had with the "catin américaine" he lived with in New Orleans? What if we think of Hadj Ali's marriage to Gertrudis Serna not as an aberration, a departure from the norm, but as a different kind of origin story?

The photo of Hadj Ali and Gertrudis Serna can lead us to think through a "first" Syrian American family at the center of which is an Ottoman (often described as Arab) subject and a Mexican woman. It allows us to imagine an interethnic Syrian family that butts up against ideals of endogamy and patriarchal authority, a family made possible by contact in a borderland space. Their relationship was not an unofficial one but was sanctified by a church wedding in Tucson, memorialized, and the image associated with it repeatedly reproduced. It is not clear what kind of relationship Hadj Ali and Gertrudis had after he left the family. By her daughter's account, Gertrudis agreed to meet with him when he was ill, but she refused reconciliation. She continued to live in Tucson and was enumerated on the census as Gertrude Tedro (erroneously listed as being of Greek origin), while her daughter Minnie took part in commemorating her father's story. Minnie's own death in 1958 was reported in a half-page article in the *Arizona Republic* under the title "Daughter of Hi Jolly, Famed Frontier Camel Driver, Dies."[13]

This family story of Hadj Ali is a reminder that we need a generative scholarship that probes the ways that interethnic relationships produced new forms of Arab American identity. Their relationship suggests that the Spanish-language discourse of *mestizaje*,[14] of mixture and cultural hybridity, can productively open up the historiography of Arab *Amairka* and shift it away from some of its epistemological inequalities; that is, its practices of knowledge production that have focused on particular communities of people, and on select historical and cultural processes, to the exclusion of others.[15] The goal of such an endeavor, a turn toward mestizaje, would not be to reproduce what Alexandra Stern calls the "Mexican cult of the mestizo," a romanticized vision of race-mixing that regulates, incorporates, and assimilates the Indian past (not a real valorization of its present). Rather, it would be to use mestizaje as a lens through which to view the messiness of Syrian racial classification and to render clear the limits of the whiteness paradigm.[16]

Put simply, ignoring Gertrudis Serna in the commemoration of
Hadj Ali is to forget the range of reasons that he ended up in Arizona,
stayed, and had a family there. Toward this generative goal, there is
much to be gained by revisiting already assembled material and minor
archives.[17] We might pursue what seemed like a casual comment by
Vera Tamoush that her family lived beside a Syrian man "who was married to a Mexican woman" in Boyle Heights, Los Angeles. We could
try and unpack Victoria Saliba's description of her husband as a Syrian
man from the "heart of Dixie"—a description she offered to historian
Alixa Naff from her home in North Hollywood. We might ask more
about the encounter between Marta Haddad and the black servant
in New Orleans who, as author Jaber phrases it, is the first to "follow
her gaze" when she sees her husband with the plantation mistress.[18]

We could also revisit long-held assumptions about other Syrian
American families. Because immigration histories are very often interested in particular kinds of firsts, what historian Rudy Vecoli called
"Mayflowerism"—a mythology of immigrant origins and successful
integration into the American mainstream—Arab American histories
often point to another "first family," the Arbeelys, as exemplifying Syrian flow across the Atlantic at the end of the nineteenth century.[19] To
be sure, much is noteworthy in their story. Yusuf Awad al-Kaloush
(Arbeely) and his wife, Mary Durany, had moved to Beirut from
Damascus after their home was destroyed in the sectarian violence
of 1860. Yusuf established a school there and became connected to
the American missionary scene around the Syrian Protestant College
(SPC), where he taught Arabic and modern Greek. Three of his sons
attended SPC.[20] In 1878, after exploring the possibility of emigrating
to Russia, the family instead made its way to the United States, landing
in New Orleans and then moving on to the port of New York. There
the family caught the eye of a reporter from the *New York Times* who
described them as "The first family of Syrian immigrants to the United
States," a designation that the Arbeelys would also later use.[21] The reporter used the occasion to engage in some fairly standard anti-Muslim

rhetoric, noting that the Christian Arbeelys had escaped the "Turkish Government, administered locally by ignorant Mohammedans."[22] The family soon moved on to Tennessee, where Yusuf taught Arabic in a school for American missionaries. It was here that the oft-reproduced photograph of the family was taken (see Figure 14).

The photograph shows six Arbeely sons, one niece, and the father, Yusuf, posed in bourgeois attire in a photographer's studio. Yusuf holds a sign in Arabic that reads: "Here I am with my children, happy in our freedom." Taken in the early 1880s, in Knoxville, Tennessee, the sign shows the date of their arrival to New York, 1878. Matriarch Mary is missing from the photo, having died before it was taken, her absent presence indicated by an empty chair. We can assume that the young niece, Amelia, took up much of the labor of the household. She is enumerated on the 1880 census from Maryville, Tennessee, as "keeping house."[23]

This photo and that of Gertrudis Serna and Hadj Ali on the day of their marriage are taken only a year apart. And yet it is that of the Arbeelys one year after that of Gertrudis Serna and Hadj Ali that has acquired almost mythic status in the Arab American narrative.

FIGURE 14. Arbeely Family, Knoxville, TN, 1881. Courtesy of Habeeb and Dania Arbeely.

Admittedly, the Arbeelys did much to promote their story of arrival to the United States. Three of the sons toured and performed in shows portraying the "Oriental manners and Biblical customs" of the Holy Land.[24] They also gave interviews to the press, stories that resonated with an American predisposition to see these peoples from the East as fleeing their Muslim overlords. As the first Syrian family, they propel Syrian Mayflowerism: they were successful; they were Christian; they extolled the virtues of America; and they lead us back east to New York where Nageeb and Abraham Arbeely established the first Arabic-language newspaper, *Kawkab Amirka* (Star of America). Nageeb's work at Ellis Island as a federal registry inspector and interpreter from Arabic and French to English further solidified the East Coast placement of the family.

Positioning the Arbeelys in this way is an ironic move in the historiography, given that important chapters of the family story unfolded in and around Los Angeles. Abraham married Anna Marie La Fetra there before they moved to Washington, DC. Fadlallah married in Monrovia and died there in 1890 at the age of thirty-five. Nageeb had purchased property in California but died prematurely of a stroke while living in New York. Patriarch Yusuf died in Glendora in 1894. Writing about his death, the *Los Angeles Times* noted: "the history of the deceased's life reads almost like a romance, and illustrates what may be attained by the exercise of pluck and energy."[25]

While the Arbeely photo has been used to reaffirm well-trodden ground in the scholarship, the Serna/Teodora (Hadj Ali) wedding photo leads elsewhere: a ruptured marriage, a husband living far afield of the family home, and to children with Spanish first names. It points us to alternate origins and different pathways that tilt toward the borderlands, where the Teodora family was part of a heterogenous community that included Syrian men married to Mexican women, Syrian women and men identified as Mexican, and their children choosing partners across ethnic lines. This variation in identifications reminds us that the category of "Arab American" is an essentializing construct; it can strategically mobilize communities, but it can just as easily flatten complexities within them. While popular discourse props up Hadj Ali's Arabness and finds in him a Muslim who is "as American as apple pie," it has not attended to the fact that, as one who met him remarked, he "spoke very broken English. His Spanish was much better."[26]

PARTING GLANCES

By the early 1890s, when Hadj Ali left Tucson for Quartzsite, Arizona, other Syrians were coming in to the town. The Joseph family, for example, lived on North 6th Avenue, where the father, John, ran a grocery stand. Their enumeration on the census is a mess, with the entries crossed out and written over many times, suggesting the liminal space they occupied in the racial schema of the day. They were Turks, Syrians, and Mexicans. They spoke English, but their children had Spanish names. As I have argued throughout this book, these palimpsests can serve to generate scholarship that explores their meaning and aberrations from the perceived norm. They allow us to see racial categories as being in flux, highly dependent upon local contexts.

It was not uncommon for Syrians to be marked in different ways at different times as they interacted with the racial state. Khalil Tabet was classified on the 1910 New Mexico census as being from Turkey, living in a household with his Spanish-speaking wife, Severa Gonzales. Their children, Dolores, George, Adela, Elena, and Anita, were classified as "other" on the 1920 census, part of a household in which the father spoke "Arabian." Both notations were modified on the schedule—the "Ot" becoming "W," and the Arabian becoming "Arabic." By the 1930 census, Khalil was listed as being from "Syria."[27] The Tabet children recalled this connection to Syria as having a profound impact on the culture of their household, noting that their mother, Severa, became "Syrianized" and cooked Middle Eastern food.[28] When Samuel K. Tabet Sr. died in 2012, his grandson remembered his youth in Mountainair, New Mexico, where he was known as "*el Arabito*," the little Arab. All of these designations shaped the identity of the Tabet children in ways that were obvious but often unarticulated. By 1944 eldest daughter Lola had moved to Oxnard, Southern California, and worked as a nurse cadet during World War II. Like other migrants to the area, she brought with her recollections of an Arabized Southwest youth.[29]

Remaining in a place of unarticulated Arabness, however, allowed for other people to distort it. In 1935, thirty-three years after Hadj Ali's death, the town of Quartzsite built a monument honoring him that features a small pyramid with a camel on top. The plaque reads: "The Last Camp of Hi Jolly, born somewhere in Syria about 1828, Died at Quartzsite December 16, 1902, Came to this country February 10, 1856, Camel driver—Packer—Scout—Over thirty years a Faithful Aid to the US Government."[30]

The monument is an odd tribute and one that has the potential to reproduce tropes that scholars have for decades been keen to avoid. There is the camel, which has been such a staple in Orientalist renderings of Middle Easterners, a recurring representation that does not allow for nuance or historical context. At the very least, it is worth noting that the camel represented atop the plaque in Quartzsite is different from the kind of camel that was used in the Camel Corps, the Bactrian two-humped animal native to Central Asia. The early write-ups on the plaque and on the life of Hadj Ali engaged in a kind of pastiche very typical of the Orientalist notebook. The *Montana Standard*, for example, featured a sketch of a cloak-wearing camel driver with headdress, hooked nose, beard, and desert motifs that were all shorthand associations for Arabs and the Middle East. There is also the pyramid, another Orientalist trope. In fact, the whole installation seems strikingly similar to the packaging on a Camel cigarettes box.

The plaque also contributes to a tradition of recognizing Arab contributions to the United States only when they can fit within the discourse of patriotism. In this case, we see an ennobling of Hadj Ali as a "faithful aid" to the US government. This has allowed for his story to be incorporated into a festive tradition in Arizona that celebrates the Camel Corps as a special chapter in frontier life. There is even a bizarre popular song that memorializes his exploits. But those who anoint parts of Hadj Ali's story in this way should also reckon with the stakes involved in this "swarthy Arab's" journey out west. The *Montana Standard* was quite clear, mockingly telling its readers that had he not been successful with the camels, he would have been lynched "with gusto and glee."[31]

By reinvestigating the life of Hadj Ali, not only can we rescue him from buffoonery, but we can also use his story as an entry point into rethinking some of the most established paradigms in Arab American history. The foundations for the field could just as easily be found in a church in Tucson, with the marriage of the young Gertrudis Serna to "Filippou Teodora." They could take us to routes that extend from Mexico, to the Southwest, and into California and encourage a return to the archives of Arab American history to un-silence the stories of the Syrian Pacific.

These routes, sustained by *intra-American* migrations, encourage a reconsideration of the patterns of movement of the Syrian diaspora, and especially the focus on New York City's Little Syria and Ellis Island as the iconic gathering place of turn-of-the-century migrants. Shifting the lens of interpretation to the intra-American context opens up questions about causation, or what an earlier model of scholarship called "push-pull" factors in migration history. With so many thousands of Syrians becoming American through a process of step migration, a focus on the reasons for leaving the homeland, understood as Syria, cleaves off the factors that propelled migration *within* the Americas. If transnationalism is understood as a process "by which immigrants forge and sustain multi-stranded social relations that link together societies of origin and settlement," the Syrian case suggests that there are *multiple* points of origin within the migrant's landscape.[32]

This multiplicity calls for different metaphors to narrate the stories of Arabs in America. With some variation, historians, sociologists, literary critics, and anthropologists draw heavily on the wave metaphor, and write of three important "waves" of migration of Arabic-speaking peoples to the Americas.[33] Each wave is conceived as being shaped by major socioeconomic changes in lands of origin and shifting immigration regimes in receiving countries. The first wave began in the late-nineteenth century and ran until the US Immigration Act of 1924; the second wave emerged in the interwar period, and was marked by quotas and restrictions; while the third corresponded to the disruptions and dislocations of several Middle Eastern wars, and the loss of Palestine in particular.[34] Scholars of Latin American Arab migrations have been less attached to the wave metaphor, preferring to use language associated with broad sociopolitical policies—the *Porfiriato* in Mexico, for example, or the *Estado Novo* (New State) in Brazil.[35] They have also, more recently, focused on "networks," "webs," and "peaks in mobility."[36]

Conceiving of the migration of Arab peoples from the Syrian lands in terms of waves is both apt and problematic. It is apt because it conveys magnitude and movement, a sense of traversal across wide expanses, and it is a metaphor that fits in with other terms in the migration lexicon that draw upon aquatic symbols—shores, ships, oceans, and tides most especially. It is problematic because it prioritizes the part of the journey that ends at the edges of the Americas—a telos toward arrival, where the wave washes up on shore. The wave paradigm makes it difficult to capture the internal migrations that preceded cross-oceanic ones, and it cannot account for the intracontinental travels that have figured prominently in this book: Mansur Nahra's move from Mexico to California, for example, or Leo Khoury's relocation from Buenos Aires to Santa Monica. Waves lose their conceptual power when people like Katrina Sa'ade move within and across them. She was part of the "first wave" and the "second wave," a migrant and a return migrant, someone whose multiple departures and arrivals placed her in interaction with various immigration regimes.

And because the wave metaphor leads toward shores, where it supports botanical metaphors of roots and seeds, it has often been connected to Ellis Island imagery in the Arab American narrative. It has helped solidify as iconic the Syrian migrant disembarking there after a long, fetid journey across the Atlantic.[37] As multisited as Rabee Jaber's novel *Amerika* is, for example, the cover of the French translation features a photo of passengers walking happily off the small vessels that have ferried them to the shore. This kind of image has come to stand in for others that must be conjured anew if we are to grasp the full complexity of the Arab American story. The cover of the Arabic version does offer a different set of possibilities. It is a 1905 painting by George Benjamin Luks of a bustling market scene on Hester Street on Manhattan's Lower East Side—a heavily immigrant and mostly Jewish area of the city. The French edition's cover suggests arrival, landing, and processing by those who police entry, while that of the Arabic captures the vitality of the world created by those who have already made New York their home.

Attachment to the Ellis Island imagery has allowed for certain mythologies to endure, not only those relating to Arab migrants, but for other ethnicities as well. In the fall and early winter of 2018, as thousands of migrants made their way in caravan toward the US-Mexico border, many journalists used the Ellis Island analogy to convince readers that the United States is a nation of immigrants, that it has a history of welcoming strangers who are integral to building the American polity. One story recounted how two men had turned their home into a supply center for migrants, walking essentials to them each day over the border at Brownsville, Texas, offering hot meals prepared by volunteers in an apartment rented specifically for that purpose. "In a sense, it's the new Ellis Island, but run by local volunteers," the article proclaimed.[38] Another story described a nonprofit in El Paso, Texas, called Annunciation House, which provides food and shelter to migrants, as the "Ellis Island of the Southwest border."[39]

The stories convey compassion and a willingness of ordinary citizens to circumvent the strictures of border policing, and of "zero tolerance" policies implemented by an intensely nativist government. However, evoking Ellis Island in this way—as benevolent and caring, as the antithesis of confinement—elides the fact that Ellis Island was the gateway for the enforcement of restrictive immigration laws. Ellis Island adhered to policies that excluded Asians and refused entry, often based on spurious rationales, to those deemed likely to become a public charge. It quarantined and deported others, separating them from their families for months and sometimes years. To be sure, Ellis Island did admit the vast majority who arrived, and excluded a mere one percent of the 25 million who landed there.[40] But those who were processed through Ellis Island went on to face a rapidly industrialized and racialized order that harnessed their labor and willfully abused it with, to echo the chilling words of the *Montana Standard*, "gusto and glee."

Those who devised these restrictive policies had no problem with the inconsistencies of this immigration regime. They did not mind that strict restrictions for some meant access to easy privileges for others. These contradictions included the removal of US citizenship from women who married men "ineligible for citizenship," namely Chinese, Filipino, Japanese, and other "alien husbands."[41] Another contradiction involved the massive loophole established for Europeans who had no record of entry and were allowed to "get legal" by simply going over and reentering via the Canadian border.[42]

In short, Ellis Island houses not only the lists of names of all those who entered, but the silences of oft-forgotten stories of those excluded, denaturalized, or denied entry on the basis of race. It holds the sediment of policies that are now resurgent, twisted in intent, and that dehumanize and deflect the ravages of inequality onto the bodies of the disempowered.

We don't need the language of Ellis Island to recognize how individuals with no legal training come together to recognize the rights of asylum seekers. We need to name this organizing for what it is: a refusal to accept a definition of *American* that is premised on fear and the scapegoating of outsiders. This definition has harnessed well-worn stereotypes, including the specter of nameless, faceless "Middle Eastern terrorists" slipping undetected into the caravan moving up from Mexico toward the US border.[43]

This book has argued that to understand the presence of Syrians in Southern California in the first half of the twentieth century is to come to terms with the connection to Mexico that so many among them had, a connection that manifested in repeated border crossings, the use of Spanish in their everyday interactions, and in the forging of family networks and solidarities that spanned the Americas. Indeed, it was to her family in Mexico to whom Katrina Saʿade turned when she tried to reunite with her son, George, who she had had to leave behind in Palestine when she returned to the United States in 1934.[44] George was born in Mexico and was not a US citizen. He did not have papers to prove his Mexican nationality either. Katrina asked desperately for her cousins in Saltillo, Mexico, to find the midwife so she could testify to being present at his birth, but they could not locate her. George remained in Ramallah, and eventually enlisted in the British Army during World War II. He was captured in Greece and taken prisoner of war by German soldiers. He was finally allowed to enter the US in 1945. It had taken thirteen years for him to be reunited with his mother and siblings.[45]

George had in fact interfaced with the US border regime before, when he had crossed back over with Katrina from Mexico in 1923.[46] While he was born in Hermosillo, his border crossing card listed his race and nationality as "Syrian." When George declared his intention to become a US citizen in 1948, having sailed from "Haifa, Palestine," his color was listed as "white," his race as "white," and his nationality as "Mexican." He petitioned for and was granted US citizenship in 1953. His form did not have a designation for race, but his color was listed as "dark."[47] Like his mother, his trajectory to Long Beach was multistranded, his designation as a Syrian, Palestinian, Mexican, and American imprecise but not incommensurate.

The stories of Syrians at the heart of this book demonstrate the ability of migrants to adapt, to learn new languages, and to use their skills to craft complex lives of work and leisure. They also document how those who have moved across borders to build and connect with community will fight for those ensnared by them.

ACKNOWLEDGMENTS

I am very grateful to the many people who helped shape this book. I want to first acknowledge those who entrusted me with their stories and their documents, and who connected me to a network of Syrian and Lebanese American families in Southern California. Vicki Tamoush has been at the center of this constellation. I'm blessed to be in her orbit. Thank you also to Sol and Lily Ajalat, Edward and Louise Deeb, Linda Jacobs, Edie Nassief, Therese Saliba, Carole and Diane Shammas, and the incomparable Bob Andrews. The late Joseph Haiek inspired me with his steadfast commitment to preserving Arab American history. I remember with fondness his family's generosity and the many wonderful meals at their home. I thank Kathy Saade Kenny for her willingness to share her personal archive with me. Her grandmother Katrina's journey to and through California allowed me to think of new ways to write about the multisited history of Arab American migrants and the pivotal role that women played in these journeys.

A fellowship from the National Endowment for the Humanities came at a juncture when I was particularly stuck in the writing of this book. I'm thankful that it gave me time to move forward with the project. Deans Dani Byrd and Peter Mancall at the University of Southern California facilitated my leave from teaching. Bill Deverell, Karen Halttunen, Nayan Shah, and John C. Rowe, my chairs in the departments of History, and American Studies and Ethnicity (ASE), were supportive in significant ways. The staff in the department of American Studies and Ethnicity, Sonia Rodriguez Flores, Kitty Lai Gallegos, and Jujuana Preston, were helpful on a multitude of administrative fronts. I am fortunate to count Ramzi Rouighi and Laurie Brand among my colleagues in Middle East Studies. Former colleagues in ASE, Jack Halberstam, Macarena Gómez-Barris, Robin D.G. Kelley, Laura Pulido, and Sarah Banet-Weiser all provided sound advice.

There have been many turning points in the research and writing of this book, moments when I gained momentum from conversations and feedback from friends and fellow academics. Keri Kanetsky helped me organize the Syrian naturalization documents at an early stage of assemblage, and her partner Gil Hochberg encouraged me when I said I wanted to write in a more accessible way. Alex Stern, a cherished friend since graduate school, gave me insightful feedback on my book proposal. Barbara Shaw and Carmen Aguilar, also of Chicago, sustained me with their gift of friendship. Evelyn Alsultany, Nadine Naber, and Pauline Homsi Vinson read portions of the manuscript and helped refine aspects of the argument. Carol Fadda, Melani McAlister, Michelle Hartman, Sally Howell, Abdeen Jabara, Ali Jihad Racy, Rashid Khalidi, Eve Troutt Powell, Suad Joseph, and Natalia Molina have been engaging interlocutors. Dorinne Kondo and Shana Redmond have been present for me as friends and as models of committed scholarship. Thank you also to Jody Aguis Vallejo, Manuel Pastor, and George Sánchez for organizing a workshop at USC in which I could present this work. Sahar Bazzaz, Farika McCarron,

ACKNOWLEDGMENTS   153

Karim Mostafa, Johnny Burke, and David Sartorius have shown up
for me when it really matters.

I had several excellent research assistants who impressed me with
their initiative and analytical rigor. Thank you to Christina Pushaw,
Audrey Weber, Jason Collins, Cathleen McCaffery, and Ryan Nhu.
They embody the great promise of so many talented undergraduate
students at USC. I would also like to give a shout-out to the many
wonderful archivists and librarians who helped secure my access to material at UCLA Special Collections, the National Archives at Riverside,
and the Santa Monica History Museum, to name a few repositories.

I have never felt so exhilarated at a Middle East Studies Association
Conference as when I met Kate Wahl, Editor-in-Chief at Stanford
University Press. Her meticulous reading of my manuscript, keen sug-
gestions around its core arguments, and beautiful grasp of language have
made *Arab Routes* a better book. The entire team at SUP with whom I
have worked has been a model of professionalism and commitment to
the world of learning and scholarly publishing. In addition to Kate, I
thank Leah Pennywark, Jessica Ling, and Geneviève Duboscq.

My father Antonio Gualtieri has been an advocate of my scholarship from the start, and he has also been wise to remind me of the
benefits of taking distance from it at our cottage in Ontario, Canada.
My sister Joanna has opened her home in Ottawa to me on many occasions with generosity and warmth. The memory of my late brother
Mark and late mother Peggy gave me strength during challenging
times. In Los Angeles, Eliane Fersan was supportive, providing love
and encouragement throughout the writing process.

I dedicate this book, the fruit of many years of labor, to my son
Anees, who has made an otherwise difficult decade an enchanting
one. And I am profoundly thankful to three people who were there
at the beginning of his life, on "day one and day two." My sister Julia
read most of the manuscript and provided feedback that improved it
immeasurably. I'm grateful beyond words for her devotion and care.

María Elena Martínez and I talked through the challenges and joys of writing history that matters during long walks in Griffith Park. I will leave a copy of *Arab Routes* for her in the secret pine forest, where I still feel and miss her graceful presence. My dear friend David Román has stood by me, never asking me too many questions, but always the right ones.

NOTES

INTRODUCTION: ARAB AMAIRKA

1. Kathy Kenny, "The Power of Place: Katrina in Five Worlds," *Jerusalem Quarterly* 35, no. 5 (Autumn 2008): 14; and Kathy Saade Kenny, *Katrina in Five Worlds: A Palestinian Woman's Story*, 3rd ed. (n.p.: Five Worlds Press, 2010), 26–27. Katrina lost her second child, Elena, to the flu—six months after Emilio died. I am following the spelling of Emilio (not Emelio) that Kenny used in her 2010 publication, *Katrina in Five Worlds*.

2. Kenny, *Katrina in Five Worlds*.

3. I use the term *Syrian* to refer to persons originating in the late Ottoman provinces of *bilad al-Sham*, or "geographical Syria," with Damascus, *al-Sham*, standing in for the whole. This area included what became the nation-states of Syria, Lebanon, Jordan, Israel, and the territory under the Palestinian Authority. I use *Syro-Lebanese* to indicate the intertwined histories of these two polities (Syria and Lebanon), and to acknowledge that while many immigrants to Southern California in the pre–World War II period came from what became the Republic of Lebanon, the term *Syrian* prevailed in the documents used for this book. The term *Lebanon* gained wider currency in the diaspora after the termination of the French Mandate (1923–1946).

4. *Los Angeles Times*, September, 2, 1940.

5. The totals are as follows: Lebanese, 19,757; Syrian 8,285; Jordanian, 2,852; Palestinian, 4,878. The other large national grouping is Egyptian at 16,555, as well as "Arab" at 10,476 persons. See 2017 American Community Survey, "People Reporting Ancestry—1 Year Estimates," Los Angeles County, available at Factfinder/census/gov. Thanks to Rita Stephan and Angela Buchanan for helping to secure these statistics.

Note that Arabic words in *Arab Routes* are transliterated according to the system found in the *International Journal of Middle East Studies*, with certain modifications. Aside from ayn (') and hamza ('), all diacritical marks have been omitted. In cases where a spelling is commonly found in either French or English, I have followed that usage: for example, "Beirut," not "Bayrut," and "Homs," not "Hims." I have transliterated individual and family names as the individuals themselves chose to do so; thus "Tamoush," not "Tahmush."

6. *Amairka* is the transliteration of the Arabic colloquial word for *America*. It connotes both North and South America, and it is used more often than the classical (*fusha*) *Amrika* in everyday speech. These tropes of newness and crisis can be found in the mainstream press as well as in the ethnic studies canon. Ronald Takaki's history *A Different Mirror* is an example of this slippage at play. In this impressive work of comparison and synthesis, he does not mention Arabs *in* America but does use the Middle East as a powerful metaphor of violence and disorder. See Takaki, *A Different Mirror: A History of Multicultural America* (Boston: Little Brown and Company, 1993), 4.

On the problem of situating Arabs exclusively in the Middle East and not as part of multiethnic America, see Therese Saliba, "Resisting Invisibility: Arab Americans in Academia and Activism," in *Arabs in America: Building a New Future,* ed. Michael W. Suleiman (Philadelphia: Temple University Press, 1999), 308; and Ella Shohat, "The Sephardic-Moorish Atlantic: Between Orientalism and Occidentalism," in *Between the Middle East and the Americas: The Cultural Politics of Diaspora,* ed. Shohat and Evelyn Alsultany (Ann Arbor: University of Michigan, 2013): 42–62. See also Amira Jarmakani's essay on the politics of invisibility within US feminist conferences, which reinscribe "the Arab as perpetually foreign." See "Arab American Feminisms: Mobilizing the Politics of Invisibility," in *Arab and Arab American Feminisms: Gender, Violence and Belonging,* ed. Abdulhadi, Alsultany, and Naber, 227–241 (Syracuse, NY: Syracuse University Press, 2011), 235. On the "newness" of Arab immigrants in California, see Mehdi Bozorgmehr, Claudia Der-Martirosian, and Georges Sabagh, "Middle Easterners: A New Kind of Immigrant," in *Ethnic Los Angeles,* ed. Roger Waldinger and Mehdi Bozorgmehr (New York: Russell Sage Foundation, 1996), 345–378.

7. With *imaginary* (in French, *imaginaire*), I am using Arjun Appadurai's definition, "a constructed landscape of collective aspirations." See his *Modernity*

at Large: Cultural Dimensions of Globalization (Minneapolis: University of Minnesota Press, 1996), 31.

8. Theresa Alfaro-Velcamp uses the helpful concept of "amplified Mexicanidad" to capture a "sense of feeling Mexican by Mexican nationals but remaining open to a range of individual and collective interpretations." See *So Far from Allah, So Close to Mexico: Middle Eastern Immigrants in Modern Mexico* (Austin: University of Texas Press, 2007), 18. For help thinking through Mexicanidad, see Laura Gutiérrez, *Performing Mexicanidad: Vendidas y Cabaretas on the Transnational Stage* (Austin: University of Texas Press, 2010).

9. The Arabic word *mahjar* is the noun of place derived from the verb *hajara* "to emigrate." See Hans Wehr, *A Dictionary of Modern Written Arabic*, ed. J. Milton Cowan (1961, repr., Beirut: Librairie du Liban, 1980), 157.

10. Representative work that propels this narrative includes Alixa Naff, *Becoming American: The Early Arab Immigrant Experience* (Carbondale: Southern Illinois University Press, 1985); Philip M. Kayal and Joseph M. Kayal, *The Syrian-Lebanese in America: A Study in Religion and Assimilation* (Boston: Twayne Publishers, 1975); Najib E. Saliba, *Emigration from Syria and the Syrian-Lebanese Community of Worcester, MA* (Ligonier, PA: Antakya Press, 1992); Adele L. Younis, *The Coming of the Arabic-Speaking People to the United States,* ed. Philip M. Kayyal (Staten Island, NY: Center for Migration Studies, 1995).

11. I prefer to use the term "migrant" because it better connotes ongoing movement and relocation which characterized the lives of those at the center of this book. However, I use "immigrant" when I am drawing on scholarship that also uses this term, or when I am describing government regulations, such as a tax imposed on "immigrants."

12. Scholars working on Californian immigrant communities have been especially adept at advancing this model of cultural adaptation. Representative work includes George J. Sánchez, *Becoming Mexican-American: Ethnicity, Culture, and Identity in Chicano Los Angeles, 1900–1945.* (New York: Oxford University Press, 1993); Mark Wild, "'So Many Children at Once and So Many Kinds': Schools and Ethno-Racial Boundaries in Early Twentieth-Century Los Angeles," in *Western Historical Quarterly* 33, no. 4 (Winter 2002), 453–476; and Dawn Bohulano Mabalon, *Little Manila Is in the Heart* (Durham, NC: Duke University Press, 2013).

13. There is a rich debate on definitions of *Latinidad* and *Latinidades*. I have found helpful Paul Allatson's summation that "Latinidad, and the less common Latinismo, are designations for panethnic Latino/a identifications, imaginaries, or community affiliations that encompass, but do not supersede, diminish, or destroy, national origin or historical minority identifications." See *Key Terms in Latino/a Cultural and Literary Studies* (Malden, MA: Blackwell Publishing, 2007), 138–139.

14. The declaration of intention was the first of a set of documents filed in the process to become an American citizen, also known as naturalization. After filing

these first papers, an immigrant eligible for citizenship would have to wait three years to file the petition for naturalization. If granted, this would be followed by a certificate of citizenship. The whole process took a minimum of five years. See "Declaration of Intention of Heilas [sic] Vitar," *Naturalization Records of the US District Court for the Southern District of California, Central Division (Los Angeles), 1887–1940*; microfilm roll 234; microfilm serial M1524; National Archives and Records Administration (NARA); Washington, DC; downloaded from Ancestry.com.

15. See Alfaro-Velcamp, *So Far from Allah,* Chapter 1. On multiracialism, particularly as it relates to indigenous migrant communities from Mexico, see Jonathon Fox, "Reframing Mexican Migration as a Multi-Ethnic Process," *Latino Studies* 4 (2006): 39–61.

16. For a discussion of step migration, see Leslie Page Moch, *Moving Europeans: Migration in Western Europe Since 1650* (Bloomington: Indiana University Press, 1992).

17. On this point, see Andrew Arsan's *Interlopers of Empire: The Lebanese Diaspora in Colonial French West Africa* (New York: Oxford University Press, 2014), 8–13.

18. Ann R. Gabbert, "El Paso, A Sight for Sore Eyes: Medical and Legal Aspects of Syrian Immigration, 1906–1907," *The Historian* 65, no. 1 (2002): 15–42; Velcamp, *So Far from Allah,* 37; Deirdre Maloney, *National Insecurities: Immigrants and US Deportation Policy Since 1882* (Chapel Hill: University of North Carolina Press, 2012), 117–119.

19. F.P. Sargent to T. Schmucker, February 11, 1907; correspondence contained in the "Seraphic Report 1906"; record group (RG) 85; INS Records #51423-1A; NARA.

20. See, for example, the work of Natalia Molina, *How Race Is Made in America: Immigration, Citizenship, and the Historical Power of Racial Scripts* (Berkeley: University of California Press, 2014); Natalia Molina, Daniel Martinez HoSang, Ramón A. Gutiérrez, *Relational Formations of Race: Theory, Method, Practice* (Berkeley: University of California Press, 2019); Nayan Shah, *Stranger Intimacy: Contesting Race, Sexuality, and the Law in the American West* (Berkeley: University of California Press, 2011); and John Rowe, ed., *Post-Nationalist American Studies* (Berkeley: University of California Press, 2000).

21. This tendency to bind the history of migrants within national spaces is evident in the canonical work in the field, *The Lebanese in the World,* edited by Albert Hourani and Nadim Shehadi. The anthology divides the Lebanese diaspora into three major geographical groups, America and Africa, as well as Australia. This paradigm makes it difficult to capture the ways in which the lives of migrants seeped across these borders. See *The Lebanese in the World: A Century of Emigration,* ed. Hourani and Shehadi (London: Centre for Lebanese Studies, I.B. Tauris, 1992).

22. See Arsan, *Interlopers of Empire*; John Towfik Karam, *Another Arabesque: Syrian-Lebanese Ethnicity in Neoliberal Brazil* (Philadelphia: Temple University Press, 2007); Stacy Farhenthold, *Between the Ottomans and the Entente: The First World War in the Syrian and Lebanese Diaspora, 1908–1925* (New York: Oxford University Press, 2019.

23. More recently, there has emerged an interest in exploring the "Pink Tide," or a set of solidarities between Latin America and the Middle East that organize around shared critiques of neoliberalism and American hegemony. See the special issue on the Latin East by Alejandro Velasco, Omar Dahi, Sinan Antoon, and Laura Weiss, "The Latin East," *NACLA Report on the Americas* 50, no. 1 (2018): 1–7.

24. To be sure, several excellent studies have adopted a transnational or diasporic approach to the study of Middle Eastern migrants. They have recognized the multiple connections that migrants have to home- and host-country (and problematized these distinctions), and emphasized the cross-border reach of nationalist organizations and networks of merchants. See, for example, Camila Pastor de María y Campos, "The Transnational Imagination," in *Palma Journal* 2, no. 1 (2009): 31–71; Arsan, *Interlopers of Empire*; Akram Fouad Khater, *Inventing Home: Emigration, Gender, and the Middle Class in Lebanon, 1870–1920* (Berkeley: University of California Press, 2001); Ilham Khouri-Makdisi, *The Eastern Mediterranean and the Making of Global Radicalism, 1860–1914* (Berkeley: University of California Press, 2010); Stacy Farhenthold, "Transnational Modes and Media: The Syrian Press in the Mahjar," *Mashriq and Mahjar* 1 (2013), 30–54; Jacob Norris, *Land of Progress: Palestine in the Age of Colonial Development, 1905–1948* (Oxford: Oxford University Press, 2013); Dalia Abdelhady, *The Lebanese Diaspora* (New York: New York University Press, 2011).

My goal is to push for an elaboration of the transnational that probes the layers of multiple migrations within and across nations. Too often transnational work forgets that *trans* denotes moving through space and across lines as well as changing the nature of something. As Aiwah Ong notes, "Besides suggesting new relations between nation-states and capital, transnationality also alludes to the transversal, the transactional, the transrelational, and the transgressive aspects of contemporary behavior and imagination that are incited, enabled, and regulated by the changing logics of states and capitalism." Quoted in David Thelen, "The Nation and Beyond: Transnational Approaches on United States History," *Journal of American History* 86, no. 3 (1999): 965–975, 968.

25. *Hollywood Monthly Magazine,* June and July 1951, 5.

26. Note that on the registration of her birth, her father is listed as white, but on his border-crossing card of 1927 into El Paso, his race is listed as Syrian. To complicate matters, he is classified as Mexican on the Ancestry.com website, not on the card itself. For the first document, see "Report of Birth for Bertha Maria

Touché (Sept. 30, 1931)," *Decimal Files, Compiled 1910–1949*; RG 59, General Records of the Department of State, 1763–2002; series ARC ID 2555709; series MLR no. A1 3001; series box no. 446; file no. 131; NARA; downloaded from Ancestry.com. For the second document, see "Border Crossing at El Paso, TX of Jose Jacobo Touche, Aug.19 1924," *Nonstatistical Manifests and Statistical Index Cards of Aliens Arriving at El Paso, Texas, 1905–1927*; NAI 2843448; RG title, *Records of the Immigration and Naturalization Service, 1787–2004*; RG 85; microfilm roll no. 119; NARA; downloaded from Ancestry.com.

27. Linda Basch, Nina Glick Schiller, and Cristina Szanton Blanc, *Nations Unbound: Transnational Projects, Postcolonial Predicaments, and Deterritorialized Nation-States* (Langhorne, PA: Gordon and Breach, 1994). The quote "transnationalism challenges concepts of citizenship and of nationhood itself" appears on the book's dust jacket.

28. Fox, "Reframing Mexican Migration," 42.

29. On Los Angeles and Pacific migrations, see Henry Yu, "Los Angeles and American Studies in a Pacific World of Migrations," *American Quarterly* 56, no. 3 (2005): 531–543.

30. I borrow this term "strange affinities" from Grace Hong and Roderick Ferguson, *The Gender and Sexual Politics of Comparative Racialization* (Durham, NC: Duke University Press, 2011).

31. I am drawn here to Natalia Molina's "relational notions of race." See *How Race Is Made in America*, 2–3. *Arab Routes* resonates not only with Arab American studies but with research on other ethnic communities such as Vivek Bald's work on the "lost histories" of South Asian working-class migrants in New Orleans and Harlem, Karen Leonard's work on Mexican Punjabis in California, and Neda Maghbouleh's book on Iranian American racialization "on the limits of whiteness." See Vivek Bald, *Bengali Harlem and the Lost Histories of South Asian America* (Cambridge, MA: Harvard University Press, 2013); Karen Leonard, *Making Ethnic Choices: California's Punjabi Mexican Americans* (Philadelphia: Temple University Press, 1994); Neda Maghbouleh, *The Limits of Whiteness: Iranian-Americans and the Everyday Politics of Race* (Stanford, CA: Stanford University Press, 2017).

32. Declaration of Intention of Nessim Hoha Levy; *Records of District Courts of the United States, 1685–2009*; NAI no. 594890; RG title 21 (sic); Riverside, CA: National Archives at Riverside; NARA; downloaded from Ancestry.com.

According to his grandson, Norman Levy, Nessim's original surname was Hamway (Hamoui?), but he used the nickname Hoha. Phone interview with Norman Levy, October 24, 2011.

33. Alessandro Portelli, "A Dialogical Relationship. An Approach to Oral History," published on the Shikshantar website; http://www.swaraj.org/shikshantar/expressions_portelli.pdf.

34. Steven Vertovec, "Conceiving and Researching Transnationalism," *Ethnic and Racial Studies* 22, no. 2 (1999): 447–462, 457.

35. James Clifford, *Routes: Travel and Translation in the Late Twentieth Century* (Cambridge, MA: Harvard University Press, 1997).

36. Alexandra Minna Stern, *Eugenic Nation: Faults and Frontiers of Better Breeding in Modern America*, 2nd ed. (Berkeley: University of California Press, 2016), 24. For thinking through the connections between gender, family, and migration, see Donna R. Gabaccia's classic work, *From the Other Side: Women, Gender, and Immigrant Life in the United States, 1820–1990* (Bloomington: Indiana University Press, 1995).

37. Robert Orsi, *The Madonna of 115th Street: Faith and Community in Italian Harlem* (New Haven, CT: Yale University Press, 1988).

38. Danny Thomas was born Amos Muzyad Yakhoob Kairouz to Syrian immigrants from Bsharri. In addition to his popularity as a film and television star, he spearheaded, with other philanthropic Syrians, the founding of St. Jude's Children's Research Hospital in Memphis, TN.

39. Joe Kadi, ed., *Food for Our Grandmothers: Writings by Arab-American and Arab-Canadian Feminists* (Boston: South End Press, 1994).

40. Carol Fadda-Conrey, *Contemporary Arab American Literature: Transnational Reconfigurations of Citizenship and Belonging* (New York: New York University Press, 2014); Nadine Naber, "Imperial Whiteness and the Diasporas of Empire," *American Quarterly* 66, no. 4 (2014): 1107–1115. Fadda now publishes under the name Carol W. N. Fadda.

41. Rabee Jaber, *Amerika* (Beirut: Dar al-Adab, 2010). The work was translated from Arabic to French by Simon Corthay and Charlotte Woillez and published as *Amerika* by Gallimard in 2013.

42. Jaber effectively breaks apart the chain migration thesis by having Marta "follow" her husband, find him, and sever connections to him. See Gualtieri, "Gendering the Chain Migration Thesis: Women and Syrian Transatlantic Migration," *Comparative Studies in South Asia, Africa, and the Middle East* 24, no. 1 (Spring 2004): 18–28.

CHAPTER I: THE SYRIAN PACIFIC

1. Author's interview with Vera Tamoush, La Brea, CA, November 21, 2011.

2. There are several different English transliterations of *Kobeh*. I use the one preferred by the Tamoush family. It appears on current government signage at the entrance to the town as Qobaa, a transliteration of the Arabic *al-Qab'*. It appears on Google Maps as Qabaa in the Jezzine district of Lebanon.

3. Border Crossing of Mansur or Manuel Nahra, 1913; *Nonstatistical Manifests and Statistical Index Cards of Aliens Arriving at Laredo, Texas, May 1903–November 1929;* NAI 2843448; RG title, *Records of the Immigration and*

Naturalization Service, 1787–2004; RG no. 85; microfilm roll no. 068; NARA; downloaded from Ancestry.com.

4. Declaration of Intention of Mansur Nahra, *Naturalization Records of the US District Court for the Southern District of California, Central Division (Los Angeles), 1887–1940*; microfilm roll 153; microfilm serial M1524; NARA; downloaded from Ancestry.com.

5. Entry for Mansur Nahra, Bureau of the Census, *Fourteenth Census of the United States, 1920– Population, Los Angeles,* enumeration district 244; NARA; downloaded from Ancestry.com. See also "Declaration of Intention of Antonio Nahra," *Naturalization Records of the US District Court for the Southern District of California, Central Division, 1887–1940, Los Angeles*; NAI no. 84; RG title M1524; NARA; downloaded from Ancestry.com.

6. For a discussion of step migration, see Leslie Page Moch, *Moving Europeans.*

7. Author's interview with Vera Tamoush, 2011. See also "Declaration of Intention of Mansur Nahra"; NARA. I am indebted to Vicki Tamoush for allowing me to read the personal papers of Mansur Nahra.

8. Author's interview with Vera Tamoush, 2011.

9. See the tables with distributions in Zidane Zeraoui, "Los Árabes en México: El Perfil de la Migración," in María Elena Ota Mishima, ed., *Destino México: Un estudio de las migraciones asiáticas a México, siglos XIX y XX* (México, D.F.: El Colegio de México, 1997), 257–304, 286. The Arab immigrant community was well distributed throughout the country; the states listed here are the ones with the larger percentages.

10. Petition for Naturalization of Adela Rico Organista; NAI no. 594890; RG no. 21; RG title *Records of District Courts of the United States, 1685–2009*; Riverside, CA: National Archives at Riverside; NARA; downloaded from Ancestry.com.

11. Petition for Naturalization of Jennie K. Hallal; NAI no. 594890; RG title 21 (sic); RG no. *Records of District Courts of the United States, 1685–2009* (sic); Riverside, CA: National Archives at Riverside; NARA.

12. According to Naturalization Petitions for the Southern District of California 1887–1949; RG M1524; NARA; available on Fold3.com.

13. Some preliminary work can be found in Sarah E. John, "Arabic-Speaking Immigrants to the El Paso Area, 1900–1935," in *Crossing the Waters: Arabic-Speaking Immigrants to the United States Before 1940,* ed. Eric Hoogland (Washington, DC: Smithsonian Institution Press, 1987).

14. See Myrna Zanetell, "Farah, Incorporated," Texas State Historical Association, Handbook of Texas Online; https://tshaonline.org/handbook/online /articles/dlfo2.

15. Author interview with Linda Gomez, Los Angeles, CA, May 30, 2012.

16. This number was arrived at by searching "Race/Nationality 'Syrian'" in *Border Crossings from Mexico to US, 1895–1964*; Records of the Immigration and

Naturalization Service; RG 85; NARA; on Ancestry.com. The number in 1913 was 22,000.

17. "Transcriptions of Katherine Sa'ade Farhat's Audio Tape of Aug. 8, 1971," from the personal collection of Kathy Saade Kenny. See Randa Tawil's description of attacks on Syrian and Chinese migrants in Chihuahua in "Racial Borderlines: Ameen Rihani, Mexico, and World War I," *Amerasia Journal* 44, no. 1 (2018): 85–104, 93. Syrians who were still Ottoman nationals also faced problems under the provisions of the US Trading with the Enemy Act of 1917, which forbade cross-border trading between US citizens and citizens of countries that were aligned with the Central Powers during World War I.

18. Quoted in "Transcriptions of Katherine Sa'ade Farhat," from Kathy Saade Kenny.

19. Quoted in Kathy Kenny, "The Power of Place: Katrina in Five Worlds," *Jerusalem Quarterly* 35, no. 5 (Autumn 2008): 5–30, 28. Katrina was able to retrieve only one of her three children, Fred, from her in-laws and had to wait until 1935 to receive Mary in New York. Her son George stayed in Palestine, enlisted in the British Army during World War II, and was eventually granted permission to enter the United States in 1946. See also Kathy Saade Kenny, *Katrina in Five Worlds*.

20. "KF letter to Patriarch from San Francisco 25 June 1937," Kathy Saade Kenny personal collection; and "Transcription of Katherine Sa'ade Farhat's Audio Tapes, Tape Made on May 30, 1975, Durango, Colorado," 10, from Kathy Saade Kenny's personal collection.

21. Kenny, "Power of Place," 29.

22. See Jeff Lesser's work on Phoenicianism in Brazil. In "(Re)Creating Ethnicity: Middle Eastern Immigration to Brazil," *Americas* 53, no. 1 (1996): 45–65.

23. Quoted in Rev. Methodios Shaloob, *Pacific Syrian-American Guide, 1937 Issue* (Santa Barbara, CA: Pacific Syrian-American Guide Publishing Co., 1937), 40.

24. On the lynching, see Sarah M.A. Gualtieri, *Between Arab and White: Race and Ethnicity in the Early Syrian American Diaspora* (Berkeley: University of California Press, 2009), Chapter 4.

25. Gualtieri, *Between Arab and White*, 37.

26. Its tone is very reminiscent of Philip Hitti's classic work, *The Syrians in America* (New York: George Doran, 1924), which extolled the virtues of the Syrians and emphasized their adaptability to the American environment.

27. Abraham M. Malouf, "The Syrian People in the United States as a Cornerstone in American Life," in Shaloob, *Pacific Syrian-American Guide*, 29–32.

28. *Pacific Syrian-American Guide*, 5.

29. République française, Ministère des Affaires étrangères, *Rapport à la Société des Nations sur la situation de la Syrie et du Liban, année 1931* (Paris: Imprimerie nationale, 1932), 31.

30. Ministère des Affaires étrangères, *Rapport année 1931*, 31.

31. Ministère des Affaires étrangères, *Rapport année 1932* (Paris: Imprimerie nationale, 1933), 31. See also Fahrenthold, *Between the Ottomans and the Entente*, on restrictions on passports.

32. See Suraya Khan's discussion of the Syrian Ladies Aid Society in "Political-Social Movements: Community-Based: United States: Early to Mid-20th Century," *Encyclopedia of Women and Islamic Cultures*, supplement 17, gen. ed. Suad Joseph (Leiden: Brill, 2018), https://referenceworks.brillonline.com/browse/encyclopedia-of-women-and-islamic-cultures.

33. See the translation of the flyer in Camila Pastor, *The Mexican Mahjar: Transnational Maronites, Jews, and Arabs Under the French Mandate* (Austin: University of Texas Press, 2017), 113.

34. Akram Khater has written on the importance of return migration to Lebanon and argues that despite the paucity and inconsistencies of the data, as many as one in four emigrants returned and became crucial participants in the building of the middle class. See *Inventing Home*, 110–112. According to the French Foreign Ministry (République française, Ministère des Affaires étrangères), the total number of emigrants (those leaving Syria and Lebanon) in 1929 was 7,941 with the following countries of destination receiving the largest number: Brazil, 2,026; Argentina, 2,258. The United States received only 635 persons. See *Rapport sur la situation de la Syrie et du Liban, Année 1929* (Paris: Imprimerie Nationale, 1930) 150.

35. Jacob Berman notes in his essay "Mahjar Legacies: A Reinterpretation" that "Gibran's reception as an 'Eastern' mystic . . . appealed to Bohemian artistic sensibilities." In Shohat and Alsultany, *Between the Middle East and the Americas*, 65–79, 72.

36. Rev. Methodios Shalhoob, *Pacific Syrian-American Lebanese-Palestinian Guide, 1942–43 Issue* (Santa Barbara, CA: Pacific Syrian-American Guide Publishing Co., n.d.) Shalhoob praises the president, p. 6; Governor Alfredo Chávez is quoted on p. 15.

37. Author's interview with Philip Tamoush, Redondo Beach, CA, March 17, 2016.

38. For a short history of the church, which opened in 1924, see http://stnicholasla.com/our-history/.

39. Samuel S. Mamey, ed., *Western Pacific Directory and Buyers Guide for 1954–1955: A Directory of Americans of Lebanese, Syrian, and Arabic-Speaking Origin in the Eleven Western States* (Los Angeles, CA: Saint Nicholas Orthodox Church, 1954), n.p. Author extends her gratitude to Robert Andrews for access to the guides.

40. The letter relating the death of Mike George is dated January 11, 1928; see Patriarch Howayek Files, "Letters to Bishop Abdallah Khuri 1925–1932 from America," Maronite Patriarchal Archive, Bkerki, Lebanon.

41. "Will Tells Tale of Success," *Los Angeles Times*, January 20, 1928, A9. His full name was Mike George Ghosn, originally from Batroun, Lebanon.

42. Maggie George's full-page "in memoriam" notice for her husband, Mike, appeared in the 1937 *Pacific Syrian-American Guide*, 20.

43. Mamey, *Western Pacific Directory*, 1.

44. Author's interview with Philip Tamoush.

45. Declaration of Intention of Antoine Vitar, *Naturalization Records of the US District Court for the Southern District of California, Central Division (Los Angeles), 1887–1940;* NAI no. 50; RG title M1524; NARA. Declaration of Intention of Heilas [sic] Vitar, *Naturalization Records of the US District Court for the Southern District of California, Central Division (Los Angeles), 1887–1940;* NAI no. 45; RG title: M1524; NARA. Both were downloaded from Ancestry.com.

46. Bureau of the Census, *Fifteenth Census of the United States, 1930, Los Angeles*; roll T626, enumeration district 19-795; NARA; downloaded from Ancestry.com.

47. Thomas Guglielmo, *White on Arrival: Italians, Race, Color, and Power in Chicago, 1890–1945* (New York: Oxford, 2003), 6.

48. In this regard, I am drawn to the useful category of "inbetweenness" employed by David Roediger (drawing on the work of John Higham and Robert Orsi) to get at the messiness of new immigrants' journey toward whiteness. See his *Working Toward Whiteness: How America's Immigrants Became White* (New York: Basic Books, 2005), 12–13.

49. See "That Syrian Case," *Los Angeles Times*, November 3, 1909.

50. This was section 2169 of the *Revised Statutes* (1878). The first naturalization law was passed in 1790 and provided that to be naturalized, an alien must be "a free white person." After the adoption of the Fourteenth Amendment, the act of 1870 extended naturalization "to aliens of African nativity and to persons of African descent." See Luella Gettys, *The Law of Citizenship in the United States* (Chicago: University of Chicago Press, 1934), 70; US House, *Citizenship of the United States, Expatriation, and Protection Abroad*, 59 Cong. 2 Sess. H. Doc. 326 (Washington, DC: Government Printing Office, 1906), 98–99.

51. Gualtieri, *Between Arab and White*, 58. On the Hall case, see Tomás Almaguer, *Racial Fault Lines: The Historical Origins of White Supremacy in California* (Berkeley: University of California Press, 2009; first published in 1994), 162–163.

52. Gualtieri, *Between Arab and White*, 75–77.

53. Entry for Seba Esmaloof, Bureau of the Census, *United States Census, 1910, Los Angeles Assembly District 74, Los Angeles, CA*; roll T624_83; page 9A; enumeration district 0064; FLH microfilm 1374096, NARA. Entry for Sails [probably Saib] George appears on page 9B. Both entries were downloaded from Ancestry.com.

54. See Molina, *How Race Is Made,* 99; Alan Kraut, *Silent Travelers: Germs, Genes, and the Immigrant Menace* (Baltimore: Johns Hopkins University Press, 1995).

55. "Seraphic Report 1906"; RG 85; INS Records #51423-1A; NARA.

56. See Deirdre M. Maloney, *National Insecurities: Immigrants and US Deportation Policy Since 1882* (Chapel Hill: University of North Carolina Press, 2012), 117–118; and "Seraphic Report 1906"; RG 85; INS Records #51423-1A; NARA. See also Rana Razek's perceptive analysis of disease conditions that were produced en route and often attributable to the abuses of labor contracts and indebtedness to middlemen, in "Trails and Fences: Syrian Migration Networks and Immigration Restriction, 1885–1911," *Amerasia Journal* 44, no. 1 (2018): 105–127.

57. Pastor, *The Mexican Mahjar,* 93.

58. Ramón E. Duarte, "Extranjeros periciosas ó Mexicanos? Middle Easterners and the Negotiation of National Identity in Mexico 1927–1937," MA thesis, New Mexico State University, Los Cruces, NM, 2009.

59. Duarte citing Alfaro-Velcamp in "Extranjeros periciosas," 93.

60. Duarte, "Extranjeros periciosas," 146–148 (translated from Spanish). Several excellent studies tell different, but complementary, stories about the Syrians in Mexico. Theresa Alfaro-Velcamp uses the "foreign citizen" concept to chart the incorporation of Middle Eastern immigrants into Mexican national identity, while Camila Pastor has focused on the cultivation of a hegemonic "Lebanese" Mexicanidad.

61. "Bayan 'an halat al-muwarana fi al-wilayat al-muttahida" (Report on the Status of the Maronites in the United States), by Father Youssef Eid, March 12, 1925, Patriarch Howayek Files, "Letters to Bishop Abdallah Khuri 1925–1932 from America," Maronite Patriarchal Archive, Bkerki, Lebanon.

62. Bureau of the Census, *Fifteenth Census of the United States, 1930, Los Angeles*; roll 166; page 13A; image 952.0; FHL microfilm 2339901; enumeration district 0795; NARA; downloaded from Ancestry.com. In 1909 a *Los Angeles Times* article described the chief Syrian "Colony" as being the section bounded by Main and Macy Streets, Alhambra Ave., and the Los Angeles River. See "Syrian Woman's Work," November 25, 1909.

63. Bureau of the Census, *Fifteenth Census of the US,* 1930; T626; NARA.

64. Declaration of Intention of Emilia Vitar (Furgo), 1943; NAI no. 618171; RG title 21 (sic); RG no. *Records of District Courts of the United States, 1685–2009* (sic); Riverside, CA: National Archives at Riverside; NARA; downloaded from Ancestry.com.

65. See for example the record for Amile Nahhas, October 9, 1931; *San Quentin 16 49722–52393*; Sacramento: CA: California State Archives; downloaded from Ancestry.com.

CHAPTER 2: MURDER AT THE SLEEPY LAGOON

An earlier version of this chapter was published in American Quarterly *71, no. 2 (June 2019): 425–448. Copyright © 2019 The American Studies Association.*

1. Climatological data shows a high of 95 degrees in Los Angeles on October 21, 1942. See "California," US Department of Commerce, Weather Bureau, *Climatological Data,* California, v. 45–47 (1942), 117.

2. The Sleepy Lagoon itself was a swimming hole, popular among Mexican American teenagers, located on the Williams Ranch in Montebello.

3. Carey McWilliams, *North from Mexico: The Spanish-Speaking People of the United States* (New York: Greenwood Press, 1990; first published in Philadelphia: J.B. Lippincott, 1949), 209.

4. See the nuanced interpretation in Eduardo Obregón Pagán, *Murder at the Sleepy Lagoon: Zoot Suits, Race, and Riot in Wartime LA* (Chapel Hill: University of North Carolina Press, 2003). On World War II shifts that were key to refashioning Southern California's racial hierarchy, see Laura Pulido, *Black, Brown, Yellow, and Left: Radical Activism in Los Angeles* (Berkeley: University of California Press, 2006), 34–35.

5. Mark A. Weitz, *The Sleepy Lagoon Murder Case: Race Discrimination and Mexican American Rights* (Lawrence, University Press of Kansas, 2010), 27.

6. Pagán, *Murder at the Sleepy Lagoon,* 210. See also Shana Bernstein, *Bridges of Reform: Interracial Civil Rights Activism in Twentieth-Century Los Angeles* (Oxford: Oxford University Press, 2011), 88–89.

7. George E. Shibley, "Sleepy Lagoon: The True Story," *New West,* January 15, 1979, in Alice McGrath Papers, box 6, folder 2, "Zoot Suit Play–reviews and ephemera," Special Collections, University of California Los Angeles (UCLA), Los Angeles, CA.

8. George Shibley interviewed by Paul Fitzgerald in *Forum Magazine* 6, no. 4 (July/August 1979), 5–10, Alice McGrath Papers, box 1, folder 17, UCLA Special Collections.

9. A review of key texts reveals a pattern of not accounting for Arab Americans in the social, cultural, and political realities of California. See Almaguer, *Racial Fault Lines*; William Deverell, ed., *A Companion to the American West* (Malden, MA: Blackwell Publishing 2004); and Takaki, *A Different Mirror.*

10. I am drawing here on *Beyond Alliances: The Jewish Role in Reshaping the Racial Landscape of Southern California,* ed. George Sánchez, Annual Review of the Casden Institute for the Study of the Jewish Role in American Life, vol. 9 (2012), xiii.

11. Shibley interview by Fitzgerald in *Forum,* UCLA Special Collections.

12. "George Shibley Has Given Many an Underdog His Day in Court," *Los Angeles Times,* January 16, 1986.

13. Pagán, *Murder at the Sleepy Lagoon*, 86. See also box 28, Sleepy Lagoon Defense Committee records, UCLA Special Collections. The film *The American Experience: Zoot Suit Riots*, directed by Joseph Tovares, first aired on PBS on March 1, 2002; http://www.pbs.org/wgbh/amex/zoot/eng_peopleevents/p_shibley.html, accessed September 25, 2016; "Attorney George Shibley, Defender of Sirhan, Dies," *Los Angeles Times*, July 5, 1989, 18.

14. Shibley interview by Fitzgerald in *Forum*, UCLA Special Collections.

15. William Shibley (son of George), phone conversation with author, June 15, 2016. In an email dated May 31, 2016, Barry Moreno, librarian at the Bob Hope Memorial Library at Ellis Island, sent William Shibley a profile that Moreno had written of Samuel Barbari. Shibley shared the email with me.

16. Bureau of the Census, *1920 Federal Census*, Manhattan Assembly District 22, New York, NY; roll T625-1226; page 38B; enumeration district 1482; NARA; downloaded from Ancestry.com.

17. Samuel, listed as a "chemist" and employer, produced a spray for citrus fruits, according to the Bureau of the Census, *1930 Federal Census, CA, Los Angeles, Long Beach*, ED 1149, sheet no. 22 B; NARA; downloaded from Ancestry.com.

18. "Two Brothers, Lead Orators," *Los Angeles Daily Times*, April 7, 1927.

19. Shalhoob, *Pacific Syrian-American Guide*.

20. Shibley, "Sleepy Lagoon: The True Story."

21. Shibley, interview by Fitzgerald, *Forum*, 6.

22. Shibley, interview by Fitzgerald, *Forum*, 5.

23. Shibley, interview by Fitzgerald, *Forum*, 9.

24. "Transcript of Trial," pages 750–751, SLDC Records 1942–1945, UCLA Special Collections, available online at http://www.oac.cdlib.org/findaid/ark:/13030/tf3b69n8z8/.

25. "Transcript of Trial," p. 751.

26. At the start of the trial, there were seven lawyers representing the defendants, only two of whom had significant trial experience. See Weitz, *The Sleepy Lagoon Murder Case*, 48.

27. Edward J. Escobar, *Race, Police, and the Making of a Political Identity: Mexican Americans and the Los Angeles Police Department, 1900–1945* (Berkeley: University of California Press, 1999), 210.

28. Alice McGrath Papers, box 1, folder 3, UCLA Special Collections.

29. Alice McGrath Papers, box 1, folder 3, UCLA Special Collections.

30. See Jack Shaheen, *Reel Bad Arabs: How Hollywood Vilifies a People* (Northampton, MA: Olive Branch Press, 3rd ed., 2014).

31. "Transcript of Trial," 797–798, SLDC.

32. "Transcript of Trial," 5422–5423, SLDC. Ruiz was born in San Juan de Los Lagos, Mexico.

33. McWilliams, *North from Mexico*, 209.

34. *American Experience: The Zoot Suit Riots*. See also Catherine S. Ramirez, *The Women in the Zoot Suit: Gender, Nationalism, and the Cultural Politics of Memory* (Durham, NC: Duke University Press, 2009).

35. "Transcript of Trial," 5942–5943, SLDC.

36. According to Alice McGrath: "3 convicted of 1st degree murder and sentenced to life; nine defendants found guilty of second degree murder and sentenced to five to life; five convicted of assault and released for time served in jail; five were acquitted." Alice McGrath to Kevin Starr, October 14, 2002. Alice McGrath Papers, box 3, folder 4, UCLA Special Collections.

37. Ben Margolis interview, tape no. 5, side two, July 1984, UCLA Oral History Collection (accessed http://www.oac.cdlib.org/view?docId=hb6c6010 vb;NAAN=13030&doc.view=frames&chunk.id=div00028&toc.depth=1&toc .id=&brand=oac4.

38. S. Guy Endore, *The Sleepy Lagoon Mystery* (Los Angeles: Sleepy Lagoon Defense Committee, 1944), 6. Alice McGrath Papers, box 1, folder 4, UCLA Special Collections. A 1972 reprint of this small book, issued by R and E Research Associates, is available in the University of Southern California library.

39. "Correspondence between McGrath and the defendants while in prison," Alice McGrath Papers, box 1, folder 5, UCLA Special Collections.

40. "Conviction of 12 Reversed in Sleepy Lagoon Murder," *Los Angeles Times,* October 5, 1944.

41. *People v. Zammora et al.*, Cr. 3719, District Court of Appeal, Second District, Division I, California, October 4, 1944, in 152 Pacific Reporter, 2d Series, Alice McGrath Papers, box 1, folder 2, UCLA Special Collections. The quote can be found on pages 201–202.

42. *People v. Zammora et al.*, Cr. 3719, District Court of Appeal,202.

43. Bernstein, *Bridges of Reform,* 61.

44. See Richard Griswold del Castillo, "The Los Angeles 'Zoot Suit Riots' Revisited: Mexican and Latin American Perspectives," *Mexican Studies/Estudios Mexicanos* 16, no. 2 (Summer 2000), 367–391.

45. Pagán does note that, "Had Shibley not laid down a pattern of objections and assignments throughout the proceedings, Ben Margolis would not have been able to argue for an appeal according to the rules of law." In *Murder at the Sleepy Lagoon,* 210.

46. Cited in Louis R. Torres and Jesús S. Treviño, "The Legacy of Sleepy Lagoon," in *Nuestro* (November 1977), 10, Alice McGrath Papers, box 6, folder 2, UCLA Special Collections.

47. Enlistment of George E. Shibley, March 11, 1943; *US World War II Army Enlistment Records, 1938–1946*; NARA; downloaded from Ancestry.com.

48. Shibley interview by Fitzgerald, *Forum*, 10.

49. Entry for Ann Kalustian, Bureau of the Census, *Sixteenth Census of the*

United States, 1940, Los Angeles; roll T627, page 17A, enumeration district 60–526; NARA; downloaded from Ancestry.com. See George Sánchez on the growth of mass culture in *Becoming Mexican American*, 177–187; and Anthony Macías on Mexican American "expressive culture," in *Mexican American Mojo: Popular Dance and Urban Culture in Los Angeles, 1935–1968* (Durham, NC: Duke University Press, 2008).

50. Author's interview with Sol and Lily Ajalat, July 30, 2016, Los Angeles, CA. Sol remembers hearing ethnic slurs at school. See also Shaheen, *Reel Bad Arabs*.

51. "An Open Letter," Mattachine Society Project, box 1, folder 14, "Citizens' Committee to Outlaw Entrapment," One Archive, University of Southern California, Los Angeles, CA.

52. Ben Margolis interview, UCLA Oral History Collection.

53. Bernstein, *Bridges of Reform*, 103.

54. *The Gazette and Daily* (York, PA), May 7, 1957, 21.

55. "Attorney Shibley Surrenders to Begin His Prison Term," *Los Angeles Times*, January 15, 1957.

56. "Parole Is Due Sunday for Attorney Shibley," *Long Beach Independent*, June 21, 1958.

57. Kevin Hillstrom, *The Zoot Suit Riots,* Defining Moments (Detroit: Omnigraphics, 2013), 150.

58. The Sirhan family moved first to East Jerusalem and then to Pasadena in 1957. See Salim Yaqub, *Imperfect Strangers* (Ithaca: Cornell University Press, 2016), 2.

59. Author's interview with Abdeen Jabara, May 3, 2017, via Skype.

60. See *People v. Sirhan*, 7 Cal. 3d, 710, June 16, 1972.

61. *Los Angeles Times*, June 8, 1968, 36.

62. According to Abdeen Jabara, "'of counsel' is a standard legal description that is used for a lawyer who is not counsel 'of record' but merely one who is advising one or all of the defense team." Jabara served in this capacity without pay. Email correspondence with author, April 27, 2019.

63. See the pamphlet prepared by the University of Southern California chapter of the Organization of Arab Students, with a foreword by Abdeen Jabara, "The Lost Significance of Sirhan's Case"; Mary Bisharat Collection, box 2, "Sirhan Folder," Arab American National Museum (AANM), Dearborn, MI.

64. Letter from Shibley to Sirhan, May 27, 1970; "Sirhan Sirhan" folder, box 1, Abdeen Jabara Papers, Bentley Historical Library (BHL), Ann Arbor, MI.

65. Letter from George Shibley to Mary Sirhan (Sirhan's mother), September 10, 1981; box 1, Abdeen Jabara Papers, BHL.

66. Letter from Mary Bisharat to Governor Edmund G. Brown Jr., November 15, 1977; Mary Bisharat Collection, box 3, AANM.

67. Luis Valdez, "Zoot Suit Play," first transcript draft, 1977, 36; Alice Mc-Grath Papers, box 3, folder 10, UCLA Special Collections.

68. Second transcript draft February 1978, 46; Alice McGrath Papers, box 3, folder 11, UCLA Special Collections.

69. Second transcript draft, February 1978, 46; Alice McGrath Papers, box 3, folder 11, UCLA Special Collections.

70. Final typescript draft, April 1978, 29; Alice McGrath Papers, box 3, folder 12, UCLA Special Collections.

71. Final draft of *Zoot Suit* revised, July 1978, 53; Alice McGrath Papers, box 3, folder 14, UCLA Special Collections.

72. Valdez to McGrath, February 2, 1978; box 3, folder 9, Alice McGrath Papers, UCLA Special Collections.

73. Alice McGrath Papers, box 3, folder 8, UCLA Special Collections.

74. Alice McGrath Papers, box 3, folder 8, UCLA Special Collections.

75. Shibley, "Sleepy Lagoon: The True Story."

76. McWilliams to Alice McGrath, January 15, 1979; Alice McGrath Papers, box 6, folder 20, UCLA Special Collections.

77. See also Carey McWilliams to Alice McGrath, December 20, 1978: "Dear Lady of Ventura: Its [sic] too bad about Shibley but I doubt that anything formal should be done about it. Maybe a letter to the station, copy to the local paper, and copy to UCLA for the archives. At least that is my quick reaction." Alice McGrath Papers, box 6, folder 20, UCLA Special Collections.

78. Rodriguez to McGrath, January 3, 1979; Alice McGrath Papers, box 3, folder 8, UCLA Special Collections.

79. Carlos Larralde, "Josefina Fierro and the Sleepy Lagoon Crusade, 1942–1945," *Southern California Quarterly* 92, no. 2 (Summer 2010): 117–160.

80. Cited in Larralde, "Josefina Fierro and the Sleepy Lagoon Crusade," 151.

81. Carlos M. Haro, introductory remarks at "The Sleepy Lagoon Case, Constitutional Rights, and the Struggle for Democracy" symposium, May 20, 2005, Chicano Studies Research Center, UCLA Special Collections.

82. See, for example, the forum organized by Laura Pulido and David Lloyd, "From La Frontera to Gaza: Chicano-Palestinian Connections," *American Quarterly* 62, no. 4, December 2010, 791–794.

83. "The Funeral Procession of Nagi Daifullah," in Chavez, Cesar, 1927–1993, Huerta, Dolores, 1930–, United Farm Workers Photographs, Walter P. Reuther Library, Archives of Labor and Urban Affairs, Wayne State University, Detroit, MI; http://reuther.wayne.edu/node/292.

84. I borrow this term "coordinates" from Alex Lubin's *Geographies of Liberation: The Making of an Afro-Arab Political Imaginary* (Chapel Hill: University of North Carolina Press, 2014), 17.

85. *Zoot Suit*, act 1, scene 6.

86. See Evelyn Alsultany, "Arabs and Muslims in the Media After 9/11: Representative Strategies for a 'Postrace Era,'" *American Quarterly* 65, no. 1 (March 2013): 161–169. On imperative patriotism, see Steven Salaita, "Ethnic Identity and Imperative Patriotism: Arab Americans Before and After 9/11," *College Literature* 32, no. 2 (Spring 2005): 146–168; and Melani McAlister, *Epic Encounters: Culture, Media, and US Interests in the Middle East, 1945–2000* (Berkeley: University of California Press, 2001).

87. "Zoot Suit at the Taper: An LA Revival Perfectly Timed," *Los Angeles Times*, February 12, 2017.

88. I borrow the term *worldmaking* from Dorinne Kondo, *Race, Performance, and the Work of Creativity* (Durham, NC: Duke University Press, 2018).

CHAPTER 3: MEETING AT THE MAHRAJAN

1. Benjamin Griffith, "Danny Thomas," *St. James Encyclopedia of Popular Culture*, ed. Thomas Riggs, vol. 5 (Detroit: St. James Press, 2013; 2nd ed.), 100–101.

2. Thomas notes in his memoir that two of the show's writers, Frank Tarloff and Mac Bnoff, were blacklisted and used pseudonyms in their correspondence with him around the show. See Danny Thomas and Bill Davidson, *Make Room for Danny* (New York: G.P Putnam's Sons, 1991), 211.

3. Lynn Spiegel, *Make Room for TV: Television and the Family Ideal in Post-War America* (Chicago: University of Chicago Press, 1992), 2–3.

4. Thomas and Davidson, *Make Room for Danny*, 193.

5. Uncle Tanoose was played by Hans Conried; see Thomas and Davidson, *Make Room for Danny*, 20.

6. ALSAC–St. Jude Children's Research Hospital, *From His Promise: A History of ALSAC and St. Jude Children's Research Hospital* (Memphis, TN: Guild Bindery Press, 1996), 6. See also Thomas and Davidson, *Make Room for Danny*, 13.

7. Lindsay Jones, "The Rise of a Fundraising Powerhouse," *Memphis: The City Magazine*, February 1, 2012. Jones writes that ALSAC is the fifteenth largest charity in the US. See also ALSAC–St. Jude, *From His Promise*, 20.

8. "Timeline: From Dream to Reality: 1960s," St. Jude's Children's Research Hospital; https://www.stjude.org/about-st-jude/history/timeline.html#1960.

9. Mervyn Rothstein, "Danny Thomas, 79, the TV Star of 'Make Room for Daddy,' Dies," *New York Times*, February 7, 1991; http://www.nytimes.com /1991/02/07/obituaries/danny-thomas-79-the-tv-star-of-make-room-for-daddy-dies .html.

10. "Frank Lackteen, (1895–1968)," IMDb; https://www.imdb.com/name /nm0480156/.

11. "Frank Samuel Lackteen," Villains and Supporting Players; http://www.b -westerns.com/villan37.htm; and "Muhammad Yaqtin: The Journey of an Obscure Actor from Lebanon to Hollywood (in Arabic)," *al-Sharq al-awsat*, July 18, 2013.

12. *Life Magazine,* January 10, 1944, 77.

13. See Michael Malek Najjar, *Arab American Drama, Film, and Performance: A Critical Study, 1908 to the Present* (Jefferson, NC: MacFarland, 2015).

14. Two massively popular biblical epics were released in the 1950s, *Ben Hur* and *The Ten Commandments,* both of which helped propel the image of US power as "benevolent supremacy." See Melani McAlister, *Epic Encounters,* 45–46.

15. *The Danny Thomas Show,* season 5, episode 3, "Kathy Is Approved."

16. Throughout this chapter I use the term *expressive culture* to mean participation in popular music, dance styles, and fashion. See Anthony Macías, *Mexican American Mojo.*

17. Sally Howell, "Cultural Interventions: Arab American Aesthetics Between the Transnational and the Ethnic," *Diaspora: A Journal of Transnational Studies* 9, no. 1 (Spring 2000), 61.

18. Louise Beavers played housekeeper Lee in six episodes in 1953–1954. See "Louise Beavers (1902–1962)" IMDb; https://www.imdb.com/name/nm0064792/?ref_=tt_cl_t6.

19. *Make Room for Daddy,* season 2, episode 7, "Hollywood Trip."

20. Mervyn Rothstein, "Danny Thomas" (obituary), *New York Times,* February 7, 1991.

21. Thomas and Davidson, *Make Room for Danny,* 21.

22. CD liner notes by Anne K. Rasmussen, "The Music of Arab Americans: A Retrospective Collection," Rounder Records CD 1133, Cambridge, MA, 1997.

23. *Hollywood Monthly Magazine,* October 1951. In 1952 *Hollywood Monthly Magazine* was chosen as the official organ of the Hollywood Foreign Correspondents Association.

24. Evelyn Alsultany, *Arabs and Muslims in the Media: Race and Representation After 9/11* (New York: New York University Press, 2012), 7–10.

25. McAlister, *Epic Encounters,* "Introduction," 11.

26. Matthew Jaber Stiffler, "Consuming Orientalism: Public Foodways of Arab American Christians," *Mashriq and Mahjar* 4 (2014): 111–138.

27. *Los Angeles Times,* September 2, 1940.

28. *Los Angeles Times,* September 2, 1940.

29. From Orsi, *Madonna of 115th St.,* 2.

30. Younis, *The Coming of the Arabic-Speaking Peoples to the US,* 212.

31. Stanley Rashid, "Cultural Traditions of Early Arab Immigrants to New York," in *A Community of Many Worlds: Arab Americans in New York City,* ed. Kathleen Benson and Philip M. Kayal (New York: Museum of the City of New York, 2002), 78.

32. A few articles and dissertations, including the excellent one by Matthew Stiffler, address contemporary food festivals, but there is still no published comprehensive attempt to theorize mahrajans as an important component of ethnic

identity. See Stanley Rashid, "Cultural Traditions," and Matthew W. Stiffler, "Authentic Arabs, Authentic Christians: Antiochian Orthodox and the Mobilization of Cultural Identity" (PhD diss., University of Michigan, 2010).

33. Edward W. Said, *The Politics of Dispossession: The Struggle for Palestinian Self-Determination, 1969–1994* (New York: Pantheon, 1994), 53.

34. Anne K. Rasmussen, "Individuality and Social Change in the Music of Arab-Americans" (PhD diss., University of California, Los Angeles, 1991), 2.

35. *Hollywood Monthly Magazine*, October 1951.

36. *Hollywood Monthly Magazine*, October 1951.

37. Author interview with Joe Farrage by phone from Newport Beach, CA, August 1, 2017. This group interview was conducted at his daughter's house in Newport Beach, with Farrage participating by phone.

38. Rasmussen, "Individuality and Social Change," 155.

39. *Hollywood Monthly Magazine*, October 1951.

40. *Hollywood Monthly Magazine*, June–July 1951.

41. *Hollywood Monthly Magazine*, February 1952.

42. *National Herald*, August 1957, 12. The National Herald was the official publication of the National Association of Federations of Syrian and Lebanese American Clubs.

43. *Hollywood Monthly Magazine*, January 1952.

44. *Hollywood Monthly Magazine*, October 1951.

45. Paul D. Garrett and Kathleen A. Purpura, *Frank Maria: A Search for Justice and Peace in the Middle East* (Bloomington, IN: Author House, 2007), 90. For more on Truman's actions, see "Recognition of the State of Israel," on the Harry S. Truman Presidential Library and Museum website, https://www.trumanlibrary.org/whistlestop/study_collections/israel/large/index.php?action=bg.

46. "A Solution for Palestine," *Federation Herald* 9, no. 2 (February 1953), 6. This publication is available at the Arab American National Museum Archives in Dearborn, MI.

47. Its activities on the question of Palestine might be described as "moderate" within the diverse range of political ideologies in the Arab American community, before a shift among some to a more "radical" approach detailed by historian Pam Pennock. See Pamela E. Pennock, *The Rise of the Arab American Left: Activists, Allies, and Their Fight Against Imperialism and Racism, 1960s-1980s* (Chapel Hill: University of North Carolina Press, 2017).

48. Pennock, *Rise of the Arab American Left*, 7.

49. *Federation Herald*, August 1953.

50. ALSAC–St. Jude, *From His Promise*, 18.

51. Entry for La Vonne Maloof, Bureau of the Census, *Sixteenth Census of the United States, 1940*; Census Place: Indianapolis, Indiana; roll m-t0627-01126; page 9B; enumeration district 96–162; NARA; downloaded from Ancestry.com.

52. Garrett and Purpura, *Frank Maria*, 97.

53. Interview by author by phone with Jamie Farr, October 30, 2017; interview with Paula Anter Rodriguez and others, Newport Beach, CA, August 1, 2017.

54. Anne K. Rasmussen, "'An Evening in the Orient:' The Middle Eastern Nightclub in America," *Asian Music* 23, no. 2 (1992), 81.

55. See Feiruz Aram, "Great Moments at the Fez," The Best of Habibi, Fall 1994; http://thebestofhabibi.com/vol-13-no-4-fall-1994/lou-shelby.

56. See Jamila Salimpour, "Antoinette Awayshak and 'La Belle Epoch'," The Best of Habibi, Summer 1994; http://thebestofhabibi.com/vol-13-no-3 -summer-1994/antoinette-awayshak/.

57. See Salimpour, "Antoinette Awayshak and 'La Belle Epoch'."

58. George Sánchez, "What's Good for Boyle Heights Is Good for the Jews: Creating Multiracialism on the East Side in the 1950s," *American Quarterly* 56, no. 3 (2004): 631–666.

59. Michael Rogin, "'Blackface, White Noise,' The Jewish Jazz Singer Finds His Voice," *Critical Inquiry* 18, no. 3 (1992): 417–453.

60. What he calls "a newly consolidated status as Caucasians" in Matthew Frye Jacobson, *Whiteness of a Different Color: European Immigrants and the Alchemy of Race* (Cambridge, MA: Harvard University Press, 1998), 272. See also Mae Ngai, *Impossible Subjects: Illegal Aliens and the Making of Modern America* (Princeton, NJ: Princeton University Press, 2004), Chapter 1.

61. Spiegel, *Make Room for TV,* 154.

62. Theresa Alfaro-Velcamp argues that the use of culturally familiar Mexican actors to play immigrants actually had the effect of humanizing the characters and of expanding notions of Mexican national identity, "to allow ethnic others to join the Mexican nation." See "'Reelizing' Arab and Jewish Ethnicity in Mexican Film," *The Americas* 63, no. 2 (October 2006): 280.

63. Kevin Smullin Brown, "The Lebanese of Mexico: Identifications in Aspects of Literature and Literary Culture," PhD thesis, University College London, 2010.

64. "En los cuarenta . . . en esa época los judíos en los países latinoamericanos eran los desendientes de quienes mataron Cristo." Smullin Brown, "The Lebanese of Mexico," 120.

65. Smullin Brown, "The Lebanese of Mexico," 127.

66. Thomas had proposed the name, "Aiding Leukemia Stricken American Children," as an early formulation of ALSAC, but it became in 1957 the American Lebanese Syrian Associated Charities. See *From His Promise,* 19.

The St. Jude website briefly discusses the importance of the hospital being integrated, which also required hotels that were housing St. Jude families to be integrated; see https://www.stjude.org/about-st-jude/history/timeline.html.

67. Gregory Orfalea, *The Arab Americans: A History* (Northampton, MA: Olive Branch Press, 2006), 126.

68. Orfalea, *The Arab Americans*, 128.

69. See Helen Hatab Samhan, "Not Quite White: Racial Classification and the Arab American Experience," in *Arabs in America*, ed. Michael W. Suleiman, 209–226.

70. Author's interview with Sol and Lily Ajalat, Los Angeles, CA, July 30, 2016.

71. Jamie Farr with Robert Blair Kaiser, *Just Farr Fun* (Clearwater, FL: Eubanks/Donizetti Inc., 1994), 16, 103; and interview with author, October 30, 2017.

72. *Just Farr Fun*, 155.

73. *Just Farr Fun*, 153.

74. I am aware of the criticism of Farr by Jack Shaheen in his film *Reel Bad Arabs*. Shaheen points to Farr's portrayal of an oil-rich "sheik" in *Cannonball Run* as being part of a denigrating repertoire of Gulf Arabs. The 2006 film features narration by Shaheen and is directed by Jeremy Earp and Sut Jhally; see https://www.imdb.com/title/tt0948465/.

75. Mathew Frye Jacobson, *Roots Too: White Ethnic Revival in Post-Civil Rights America* (Cambridge, MA: Harvard University Press, 2006), 4.

CHAPTER 4: FRAGMENTS OF THE PAST, IDENTITIES OF THE PRESENT

1. "Najeeb E. Halaby, Former Airline Executive, Dies at 87," *New York Times*, July 3, 2003; https://www.nytimes.com/2003/07/03/us/najeeb-e-halaby-former-airline-executive-dies-at-87.html; Queen Noor, *Leap of Faith: Memoirs of an Unexpected Life* (London: Phoenix, 2003), 11–12.

2. Queen Noor, *Leap of Faith*, 9.

3. "Hussein Weds American, Makes Her His Queen," *Los Angeles Times*, June 15, 1978.

4. *Faces of America with Henry Louis Gates, Jr.*, episode 2, "Becoming American"; https://www.pbs.org/wnet/facesofamerica/. Lisa Halaby's father and grandfather were both named Najeeb.

5. *Leap of Faith*, 32.

6. Suad Joseph, "Against the Grain of the Nation—The Arab-." In *Arabs in America*, ed. Michael W. Suleiman, 257–271.

7. Naber, *Arab America*, 6.

8. Naber, *Arab America*, 8.

9. Carol Fadda-Conrey, *Contemporary Arab American Literature*, 67. (The author is now publishing under the name Carol W. N. Fadda.)

10. See for example, Nabeel Abraham's essay "To Palestine and Back," in *Arab Detroit: From Margin to Mainstream*, ed. Nabeel Abraham and Andrew Shryock (Detroit: Wayne State University Press, 2000). He writes: "I began to grow comfortable with a semimarginal place in American society as a hyphenated American, as an 'Arab-American,'" 456.

11. Kadi's anthology, *Food for Our Grandmothers*, is a groundbreaking text in the field, the first to use the figure of the grandmother as a symbol of cohesion for the various essays. See also Michelle Hartman, "Grandmothers, Grape Leaves, and Kahlil Gibran: Writing Race in Anthologies of Arab American Literature," in *Race and Arab Americans Before and After 9/11: From Invisible Citizens to Visible Subjects*, ed. N. Naber and A. Jamal (Syracuse, NY: Syracuse University Press, 2008), 170–203; Rachel Norman, "Eating the Matriarch: Locating Identity in the Arab American Female Body," *Amerasia Journal* 44, no. 1 (2018): 128–145; Fadda, *Arab-American Literature*.

12. See Andrew Flinn, "Archival Activism: Independent and Community-led Archives, Radical Public History, and the Heritage Professions," *InterActions: UCLA Journal of Education and Information Series* 7, no. 2 (2011); https://eschol arship.org/uc/item/9pt2490x.

13. Interviewees agreed to have their names published.

14. Kathy Kenny talk at https://vimeo.com/29249575.

15. Pauline Homsi Vinson, "Voice, Narrative, and Political Critique," in *Etel Adnan: Critical Essays on the Arab-American Writer and Artist*, ed. Lisa Suheir Majaj and Amal Amireh (Jefferson, NC: McFarland, 2001), 193.

16. Author's interview with Kathy Saade Kenny, via Skype, April 17, 2017, from Los Angeles, CA, to Nayarit, Mexico.

17. Author's interview with Kathy Saade Kenny, April 17, 2017.

18. Author's interview with Kathy Saade Kenny, April 17, 2017.

19. Author's interview with Kathy Saade Kenny, April 17, 2017.

20. The Oslo Accord (1993) and Oslo II or "Interim Agreement" (1995) consisted of an exchange of letters and agreed-upon proposals between the government of Israel and the Palestine Liberation Organization (PLO). The 1993 and 1995 agreements were intended to ease the dispute between the two sides. In historian Charles D. Smith's words, however, the 1993 accord in particular was "fraught with obstacles, with each side holding radically different conceptions of what its terms signified." See Smith, *Palestine and the Arab-Israeli Conflict*, 6th ed. (Boston: Bedford/St. Martin's, 2007), 450.

21. Naber, *Arab America*, 53.

22. Author's interview with Kathy Saade Kenny, April 17, 2017.

23. Email correspondence with author.

24. Kathy Saade Kenny, interview with Shirin Sadeghi on New America Media, March 2011; http://newamericamedia.org/2011/05/index.php.

25. "Big Service Flag for Labor," *Los Angeles Evening Herald*, January 2, 1918.

26. Author's interview with Vicki Tamoush, Los Angeles, CA, May 26, 2017.

27. Jeff Karoub, "Ellis Island Exhibit Revives New York's Lost Little Syria," *Morning Call*, October 22, 2016; https://www.mcall.com/travel/mc-travel-little -syria-new-york-20161022-story.html.

28. Kitry Krause, "Enemies: These Jews and Palestinians Meet at Least Once a Month to Share Dinner and Discuss Their Differences. It's a Start," *Chicago Reader,* March 22, 1990.

29. Krause, "Enemies."

30. Krause, "Enemies."

31. Author's interview with Vicki Tamoush, Los Angeles, CA, May 26, 2017.

32. Author's interview with Vicki Tamoush, Los Angeles, CA, May 26, 2017. The importance of bearing witness is a recurring theme in women-of-color feminist writing on Palestine. Interviewed after her visit to Gaza in 2009 with Code Pink, poet Alice Walker said: "It's totally important that people come to visit [Gaza] and to see for themselves." See also Alice Walker's *Overcoming Speechlessness: A Poet Encounters the Horror in Rwanda, Eastern Congo, and Palestine/Israel* (New York: Seven Stories Press, 2010); interview available at https://www.democracynow.org/2010/4/13/poet_and_author_alice_walker_speaking_in_gaza. See also Keith P. Feldman's discussion of June Jordan breaking the "quasi-mandated silence" on critiquing Israel's invasion of Lebanon in 1982, in *Shadow Over Palestine: The Imperial Life of Race in America* (Minneapolis: University of Minnesota Press, 2015), 207–208.

33. Author's interviews in Los Angeles, CA, with Carole Shammas, January 19, 2017, and Diane Shammas, February 27, 2017.

34. Shammas also became the first president of the World Lebanese Union in 1980. See the obituary: "Nickolas N. Shammas, 87: Auto Dealer," *Los Angeles Times,* July 2, 2003.

35. Code Pink is a grassroots activist organization that spearheaded delegations to Gaza after the Israeli blockade. Begun in 2007, the blockade severely restricted the movement of people and goods in and out of the territory.

36. Abdulhadi, Alsultany, and Naber, *Arab and Arab American Feminisms,* xxx.

37. See Evelyn Shakir, *Bint Arab: Arab and Arab American Women in the United States* (Westport, CT: Praeger, 1997).

38. "From 'Becoming American' to Transnational Alliances: Feminist Methodologies and Transformations in Arab American Studies" (paper presented at the Arab American Studies Conference, Dearborn, MI, April 4, 2014), 13. I thank Therese Saliba for sharing this unpublished essay with me.

39. Author's interview by Skype with Therese Saliba, November 20, 2017; and Saliba, "Sittee (Or Phantom Appearances of a Lebanese Grandmother)," in *Food for Our Grandmothers,* 9.

40. Therese Saliba, "Forgotten Land," *Berkeley Fiction Review* 6 (1985–86): 21–24.

41. Saliba, "Sittee (Or Phantom Appearances)," 8.

42. Saliba, "Sittee (Or Phantom Appearances)," 8.

43. Saliba, "Sittee (Or Phantom Appearances)," 14.

44. Kadi, Introduction in *Food for Our Grandmothers,* xx. See also Nadine Naber, "Class Equality, Gender Justice, and Living in Harmony with Mother Earth: An Interview with Joe Kadi," in *Arab and Arab American Feminisms,* ed. Abdulhadi, Alsultany, and Naber, 242–247.

45. Victoria Saliba, interview by Alixa Naff, Los Angeles, CA, 1962, transcript, series 4-A-2, Naff Arab American Collection, National Museum of American History, Archives Center, Smithsonian Institution, Behring Center, Washington, DC.

46. "From 'Becoming American' to Transnational Alliances: Feminist Methodologies and Transformations in Arab American Studies," 13.

CHAPTER 5: PALIMPSESTS IN ICONIC CALIFORNIA

1. I thank Sara Crown of Santa Monica History Museum for her help in reproducing these photographs.

2. Entry for Elias Khoury Rayheb, *Federal Naturalization Records, 1843–1999*; NAI no. 594890; RG title 21 (sic); RG no. *Records of District Courts of the United States, 1685–20* (sic); Riverside, CA: National Archives at Riverside; NARA. The passenger manifest, however, has him arriving from Buenos Aires in 1936 (two years earlier); see *New York Passenger and Crew Lists Including Castle Garden and Ellis Island, 1820–1957*; microfilm publication M237, 675 rolls; NAI 6256867; *Records of the US Customs Service*; RG 36; NARA; downloaded from Ancestry.com.

3. Draft registration card for Abraham Auad; RG *Records of the Selective Service System 147*; box 67; National Archives in St. Louis, MO; downloaded from Ancestry.com.

4. Entry for Leo Khoury, *Sixteenth Census of the United States 1940, Santa Monica, Los Angeles, California*; roll m-t0627-00256; page *61A*; enumeration district 19-752; downloaded from Ancestry.com. The citation on Ancestry.com has Auad mistakenly entered as "Anad" and his native language as "Jewish." This appears to be a transposing of a supplemental question asked of another resident, Gloria Nina Smith, and then erroneously added to the entry for Abraham Auad. The City Directory lists Auad as a "waiter" at Leo Khoury's café.

5. *New York Passenger and Crew Lists Including Castle Garden and Ellis Island, 1820–1957* lists the year as 1939 and arrival at New York, NY; microfilm serial T715, 1897–1957; microfilm roll 6414; line 1; page 41; downloaded from Ancestry.com.

6. Elias Sady, *Sixth Issue (1948–1950) of the Directory of California* (n.p.: 1950?), 173. The directory, compiled and published by Archpriest Elias Sady provided "names and addresses of American Arabic-speaking people and their families from Syria, Lebanon, Palestine and the Levant." See also Mamey, *Western Pacific Directory and Buyers Guide,* 209.

7. Author's interview with Edythe (Edie) Nassief, Los Angeles, CA, September 19, 2016.

8. Joseph R. Haiek, ed., *Arab American Almanac,* 6th ed. (Los Angeles: News Circle Publishing, 2010), 48.

9. Declaration of Intention of George Sulayman Shishim; *Naturalization Records in the Superior Court of Los Angeles, California, 1876–1915;* microfilm roll 17; microfilm serial M1614; NARA; downloaded from Ancestry.com.

10. Petition for Citizenship of George Sulayman Shishim; *Naturalization Records in the Superior Court of Los Angeles, California, 1876–1915;* microfilm roll 17; microfilm serial M1614; NARA; downloaded from Ancestry.com.

11. See Gualtieri, *Between Arab and White,* Chapter 2.

12. Haiek, *Arab American Almanac,* 48.

13. See Kevin Starr, *Americans and the California Dream, 1850–1915* (New York: Oxford University Press, 1986).

14. The historiography on these groups is very extensive. I cite here only a few of the major texts: Josh Sides, *LA City Limits: African American Los Angeles from the Great Depression to the Present* (Berkeley: University of California Press, 2003); Nayan Shah, *Contagious Divides: Epidemics and Race in San Francisco's Chinatown* (Berkeley: University of California Press, 2001); Natalia Molina, *How Race Is Made in America;* Ana Elizabeth Rosas, *Abrazando el Espíritu: Bracero Families Confront the US-Mexican Border* (Berkeley: University of California Press, 2014).

15. *Amerika* is the transliteration of the Arabic *Amairka* in the French translation published by Gallimard. The phrase "du monde entier" (from the whole world) appears on the front matter to signal that the book is part of the publisher's foreign literature collection.

16. David Joseph Wrisley argues that Kafka's *Amerika* is an important intertext for Jaber. See his "Metafiction Meets Migration: Art from the Archives in Rabee Jaber's *Amerika,*" *Mashriq and Mahjar* 2 (2013): 99–119.

17. Jaber, *Amerika (Arabic),* 13. I use both the French and Arabic versions in this chapter. Translations into English are my own.

18. *Amerika* (Arabic), 21.

19. "Assise sur une natte au pied du mûrier," 23.

20. *Amerika* (French), 24.

21. One reviewer in Arabic calls this disclaimer "a game." Wrisley calls it a "playful wink." See "Metafiction Meets Migration," 104.

22. *Kasha* is an Arabization of the Portuguese word "caixa" meaning box.

23. *Amerika* (French), 78.

24. Konrad Bercovici, "Around the World in New York—The Syrian Quarter," *Century Magazine* 108 (July 1924), 348; "A Picturesque Colony: Syrians Settled in the First Ward," *New York Tribune,* October 2, 1892.

25. Jaber, *Amerika*, 123. "Savez-vous, cher lecteur, qu'une partie de Damas ou de Constantinople a été transportée telle quelle—par la mer—jusqu'en Amérique?"

26. *Amerika* (French), 159. Compare with Naff, *Becoming American*, 162.

27. Wrisley, using a term coined by Linda Hutcheon, "Metafiction Meets Migration," 105.

28. *Amerika* (French), 77.

29. *Amerika* (French), 133.

30. "Il était jaune, abattu." *Amerika*, 174.

31. Early mahjar writer 'Afifa Karam wrote extensively about this issue in the Arabic-language press. See Sarah M.A. Gualtieri, "From Lebanon to Louisiana: 'Afifa Karam and Arab Diasporic Feminism," in *Arab American Women*, ed. Suad Joseph (collection manuscript under review; Syracuse, NY: Syracuse University Press).

32. *Amerika* (French), 477.

33. *Amerika* (French), 478.

34. *Amerika* (Arabic), 395. In French (478): "La kacha fit son retour durant la Grande Dépression, mais ce fut un pâle retour, chiche, inconsistent."

35. *Amerika* (Arabic), 397.

36. *Amerika* (Arabic), 496.

37. Therí Pickens, "Modern Family: Circuits of Transmission Between Arabs and Blacks," *Comparative Literature* 68, no. 2 (2018), 136.

38. Naff, *Becoming American*, 176.

39. Todd Fine, "Remembering Alixa Naff: The 'Mother' of Arab American Studies," Arab American Institute; http://www.aaiusa.org/remembering-alixa -naff-the-mother-of-arab-american-studies.

40. "Beyond the Label, Arab American Faces, Places and Traces: Arab American Association Conference in Honor of Alixa Naff (1919–2013)." See the conference program on the Arab American Studies Association website, https:// arabamstudies.wordpress.com/conferences/past-conferences/.

41. Alixa Naff, "Growing Up in Detroit: An Immigrant Grocer's Daughter," in *Arab Detroit: From Margin to Mainstream*, 107.

42. Naff, "Growing Up in Detroit," 139, 140.

43. Naff, "Growing Up in Detroit," 108.

44. Fine, "Remembering Alixa Naff."

45. Naff, "Growing Up in Detroit," 111.

46. See also Devon Akmon's opening remarks at the Arab American National Museum lifetime achievement award, https://www.youtube.com/watch?v =eFdkiBBCFDY; and the video posted by Clay Farris Naff (Alixa Naff's nephew) in which her brother Tom talks about Alixa going to London "with us," and touring through Europe in the Volkswagen beetle, first with a woman, then with a man, before going on to Syria.

47. Alixa Naff, "In Search of Arab Heritage in the US," *Arab Perspectives* 6 (1985): 25–28. See also Charlotte Karem Albrecht's article, in which she conceives of Naff's oral-history gathering as an "oppositional strategy" to counter elite-bias in Arab American historiography. "Narrating an Arab American History: The Peddling Thesis," *Arab Studies Quarterly* 37, no. 1 (2015), 105.

48. Entry for Dr. A.S. Abdun-Nur, Los Angeles, California, City Directory, 1924, p. 168; Ancestry.com. Interview with Therese Saliba, via Skype, Nov. 20, 2017.

49. Naff, *Becoming American*, 307.

50. Saliba, "From 'Becoming American' to Transnational Alliances," 13.

51. Victoria Saliba, interview by Alixa Naff, Los Angeles, CA, 1962, transcript, series 4-A-2, Naff Arab American Collection, National Museum of American History, Archives Center, Smithsonian Institution, Behring Center, Washington, DC.

52. Victoria Saliba, interview by Alixa Naff.

53. "Translator's Note," to Faris Naff, "The Story of My Life: From the Age of 12 Until the End of My Days," unpublished manuscript, box 27, folder 9, Naff Arab American Collection.

54. Alixa Naff, "In Search of Arab Heritage," 27.

55. Wrisley, "Metafiction Meets Migration," 99.

56. *Amerika* (French), 507.

CONCLUSION: MESTIZAJE IN
ARAB AMERICAN FAMILIES

1. Although Los Angeles has the largest number of Arab Americans, Dearborn has the largest percentage. It is estimated that Dearborn's population is more than 30 percent Arab. For a discussion of the statistical challenges involved in counting the Arab American population in the United States, see Kim Schopmeyer, "Arab Detroit After 9/11: A Changing Demographic Portrait," in *Arab Detroit 9/11: Life in the Terror Decade,* ed. Nabeel Abraham, Sally Howell, and Andrew Shryock (Detroit: Wayne State University Press, 2011), 29–63.

2. Gary Nabhan, "Camel Whisperers: Desert Nomads Crossing Paths," *Journal of Arizona History* 49, no. 2 (2008), 99; "Camels in Arizona and in the West," *Arizona Days and Ways Magazine,* March 6, 1968, 40. In newspaper articles for the *Arizona Republic,* author Roscoe G. Willson draws on the rumor that one of the camel drivers, the "Syrian Elias," fathered the future president of Mexico, Plutarco Calles, who thus ended up with the name "El Turco." See Roscoe G. Willson, "Arizona Days," *Arizona Republic,* September 14, 1958, 15; and Jurgen Buchenau, *Plutarco Elias Calles and the Mexican Revolution* (Denver: Rowman and Littlefield, 2006).

3. Orfalea, *The Arab Americans*, 49. The most comprehensive treatment can be found in Gary Nabham's article, "Camel Whisperers."

4. Evan Taparata, "More American than Apple Pie, Muslims Have Been Migrating to US for Centuries," Public Radio International, April 4, 2016; https://www.pri.org/stories/2016-04-04/more-american-apple-pie-muslims-have-been-migrating-us-centuries.

5. See Steve Frangos, "Philip Tedro: A Greek Legend of the American West," *Greek-American Review* (posted October 2006, updated November 26, 2007), available at http://www.helleniccomserve.com/philiptedro.html. See the "first Syrian" claim on this PRI Radio page, https://www.pri.org/stories/2017-05-12/one-americas-first-syrian-immigrants-helped-conquer-west-camels. A trailer for Turkish American director Mert Turkoglu's documentary on his life is available at https://vimeo.com/249878811.

6. Arizona Department of Health Services, Arizona Death Records; downloaded from Ancestry.com. Serna is listed as Gertrude Serna Tidro, died May 6, 1936, age seventy-six, with a question mark beside her age. The same record lists her place of birth as Hermosillo, Mexico, daughter of Fernando Serna and Maria Espinoza. However, the 1910 Census lists her age as forty-five, meaning that she would have been born in 1865, making her fifteen years old in 1880. "Entry for Gertrude T. Tedro, *1910 Census*, Tucson Ward, Pima, AZ; roll T624_41; page 5A; enumeration district 0105; FHL microfilm 1374054; available on Ancestry.com.

7. Based on the remarks of an acquaintance of Hi Jolly, Fred Kuehn, as mentioned in Harland D. Fowler, citing Roscoe Willson, in *Three Caravans to Yuma: The Untold Story of Bactrian Camels in Western America* (Glendale, CA: Arthur H. Clark, 1980), 133.

8. Roscoe G. Willson, "Hi Jolly Closed an Era," *Arizona Republic,* April 3, 1966.

9. See for example the front matter of Linda K. Jacobs's exhaustive study of the Syrian community in fin de siècle New York. Jacobs, *Strangers in the West: The Syrian Colony of New York City, 1880–1990* (New York: Kalimah Press, 2015).

10. See Gualtieri, "From Lebanon to Louisiana."

11. Nabhan, "Camel Whisperers," 112.

12. Gualtieri, *Between Arab and White*, 137.

13. *Arizona Republic*, December 5, 1958, 15.

14. The definition of *mestizaje* varies greatly. I use it here to draw on a discourse of mixture and cultural hybridity. See Lourdes Martínez-Echazábel, "Mestizaje and the Discourse of National/Cultural Identity in Latin America, 1845–1959," *Latin American Perspectives* 25, no. 3 (1998), 21–42.

15. I take this term "epistemological inequalities" from Adriana Estill's review of Paul Allatson's book *Key Terms in Latino/a Cultural and Literary Studies* in *Latino Studies* 7 (2009): 397–399.

16. Alexandra Minna Stern, "Eugenics and Racial Classification in Modern Mexican America," in *Race and Classification: The Case of Mexican America,* ed. Ilona Katzew and Susan Deans-Smith (Stanford, CA: Stanford University Press, 2009), 172.

17. On minor archives, see Gil Hochberg, "Archival Afterlives in a Conflict Zone: Animating the Past in Jumana Manna's Cinematic Fables of Pre-1948 Palestine," *Comparative Studies in South Asia, Africa, and the Middle East* 38, no. 1 (2018): 30–42.

18. "Le garçon traqua son regard jusqu'à ce que la pointe de la flèche atteigne son maître." Jaber, *Amerika* (French), 170.

19. Rudolph Vecoli, "Problems in Comparative Studies of International Emigrant Communities," in *The Lebanese in the World,* 721. For a discussion of the Arbeely family, including the family's surprising trajectory out of New York to Tennessee, Georgia, and California (where Yusuf Arbeely died in 1894), see Linda K. Jacobs, *Strangers in the West,* 31–33; and Akram Khater, "Arbeely Family: Pioneers to America and Founders of the First Arabic-Language Newspaper," Moise A. Khayrallah Center for Lebanese Diaspora Studies, North Carolina State University, November 30, 2016; https://lebanesestudies.news.chass.ncsu.edu/2016/11/30/arbeely-family-pioneers-to-america-and-founders-of-the-first-arabic-language-newspaper/. Khater writes that "they paved the way for subsequent immigrants and planted the seed for creating a community in America."

20. Linda K. Jacobs, "The Disappointed Counsel: Nageeb J. Arbeely," *Jerusalem Quarterly* 71 (2017): 69–80; and Jacobs, "The 'First Syrian Immigrant Family,'" available at Kalimah Press, December 2, 2015; http://kalimahpress.com/blog/the-first-syrian-immigrant-family/. There are several different transliterations of Yusuf's name. I have used the one closest to the transliteration system found in the *International Journal of Middle East Studies.*

21. "Emigrants from Syria," *New York Times,* August 23, 1878; Ibrahim 'Arbili, "Al-Haditha," (The Event), *Al-Kalima* 9, no. 8 (1913): 151–161.

22. "Emigrants from Syria," *New York Times.*

23. Entry for Amelia Arbeely, *1880 Federal Census*; Census Place: Maryville, Blount, Tennessee; roll 1245; page 147D; enumeration district 194; downloaded from Ancestry.com. Mary is actually listed on this schedule, taken on June 19, 1880, but her gravestone in Maryville, Blount County, TN, reads that she died on June 9, 1880, at age forty-eight.

24. Jacobs, "The Disappointed Counsel," 72.

25. "Dr. Arbeely's Death: The Romantic History of the Noted Scholar's Life," *Los Angeles Times,* August 14, 1894.

26. Fowler, *Three Caravans to Yuma*, 133.

27. Entry for Kalixto Tabet, *Fifteenth Census of the United States 1930*; Census place: Punta, Torrance, New Mexico; page 1B; enumeration district 0005; FHL microfilm 2341135; downloaded from Ancestry.com.

28. Monika Ghattas, *Los Árabes of New Mexico: Compadres from a Distant Land* (Santa Fe, NM: Sunstone Press, 2012), 57.

29. Membership card for Lola Tabet, *Cadet Nurse Corps Files, Compiled 1943—1948, Documenting the Period 1942–1948*; Box #074; NARA; downloaded from Ancestry.com.

30. "The Last Camp of Hi Jolly," Historical Marker Database, June 16, 2016; https://www.hmdb.org/marker.asp?marker=32201.

31. "Winding Up the Camel Experiment That Drove the Wild West Crazy," *Montana Standard,* May 31, 1936.

32. Quoted in Wendy Roth, *Race Migrations: Latinos and the Cultural Transformation of Race* (Stanford, CA: Stanford University Press, 2012), 9.

33. See for example, Orfalea, *The Arab Americans*; Michael W. Suleiman, "Introduction," *Arabs in America*, 1.

34. The wave model is a rough typology that describes and differentiates these periods from one another not only in terms of size but also in terms of class and religion. The *first wave* is typically thought of as a sojourner period in which predominantly Christian migrants from peasant backgrounds labored, primarily in peddling, before making a decision to settle permanently in *Amairka*. The *second wave* is narrated as one propelled by family reunification and high rates of assimilation; while the *third* is often marked as a period of politicization, even "awakening," as new migrants, infused by the politics of Arab nationalism, interfaced with communities and worked synergistically with the civil rights movement of the 1960s and 1970s to advance Arab American causes. Naff famously argued in *Becoming American* that "If political and economic events had not reactivated Arab immigration and an interest in Arab culture, Syrian-Americans might have Americanized themselves out of existence" (330). Orfalea uses the language of "awakening" to describe the period between 1972 and 1981 in *The Arab Americans*, 213.

35. The Porfiriato is named after Mexican President Porfirio Díaz and demarcates the period from 1876 to 1911, when Mexico had an open-door policy, albeit one that favored European immigrants. See Alfaro-Velcamp, *So Far from Allah*, 55–61. The *Estado Novo* describes the period in Brazil associated with the rule of President Getúlio Vargas (1937–1945), who, Jeff Lesser notes, was a "populist, a nationalist, and a proto-fascist." See Lesser, "From Pedlars to Proprietors: Lebanese, Syrian and Jewish Immigrants in Brazil," in Hourani and Shehadi, *The Lebanese in the World*, 394.

36. Pastor, *The Mexican Mahjar,* 6; Lily Pearl Balloffet, "From the Pampa to the Mashriq: Arab-Argentine Philanthropy Networks," *Mashriq and Mahjar* 4, no. 1 (2017): 4–28.

37. On this point see Sarah M.A. Gualtieri and Pauline Homsi Vinson, "Introduction," in *Amerasia Journal* 44, no. 1 (2018): vii–xxi.

38. Molly Hennessy-Fiske, "A New Ellis Island on the Border; Texans Open Homes and Hearts to Help Asylum Seekers in Brownsville and Mexico," *Los Angeles Times,* November 22, 2018.

39. Aaron Montes, "A Refuge for Immigrants in El Paso Is the 'Ellis Island of the Southwest Border,'" *Los Angeles Times,* August 25, 2018.

40. Mae M. Ngai, "How Grandma Got Legal," *New York Times,* May 16, 2006.

41. Marian L. Smith, "Women and Naturalization," *Genealogy Notes* 30, no. 2 (Summer 1998); https://www.archives.gov/publications/prologue/1998 /summer/women-and-naturalization-1.html.

42. Ngai, "How Grandma Got Legal."

43. Bill Hutchison, Jordyn Phelps, and Matt Gutman, "Trump Admits He Nas 'No Proof' of 'Middle Easterners' in Caravan, 'but There Could Well Be,'" ABC News, October 23, 2018; https://abcnews.go.com/US /trump-admits-proof-middle-easterners-caravan/story?id=58686056.

44. She also left her daughter, Mary, but was able to secure her passage to New York with the aid of the Red Cross in 1935.

45. Kenny, "The Power of Place," 35.

46. Border crossing card for George Farhat; *Manifests of Alien Arrivals at Naco, Arizona, May 24, 1908–ca. December 1952*; NAI 2843448; RG title *Records of the Immigration and Naturalization Service, 1787–2004*; RG no. 85; microfilm roll no. 02; NARA; downloaded from Ancestry.com.

47. Petition for Naturalization of George Solomon Farhat; NAI no. 594890; RG no. 21; RG title *Records of District Courts of the United States, 1685–2009*; Riverside, CA: National Archives at Riverside; NARA; downloaded from Ancestry.com.

BIBLIOGRAPHY

ARCHIVES

Abdeen Jabara Papers: 1956–1994. Bentley Historical Library, Ann Arbor, MI.

Arab American National Museum, Dearborn, MI.

California State Archives, Sacramento, CA.

Faris and Yamna Naff Arab-American Collection. National Museum of American
History. Archives Center. Smithsonian Institution, Behring Center, Washington, DC.

Huntington Library. San Marino, CA.

Maronite Patriarchal Archive, Bkerki, Lebanon.

National Archives and Records Administration (NARA). NARA houses census,
immigration, naturalization, and other government materials at its headquarters in Washington, DC, and regional centers. Some of these materials
are also available on Ancestry.com.

One Archive, University of Southern California, Los Angeles, CA.

Ministère des Affaires étrangères, Série E. Levant, 1918–1940. Archives Diplo-
matiques, Paris.

St. Nicholas Antiochian Orthodox Christian Cathedral, Los Angeles, CA.

Special Collections. University of California Los Angeles, Los Angeles, CA.

United Farm Workers Photographs, Walter P. Reuther Library, Archives of Labor
and Urban Affairs, Wayne State University, Detroit, MI.

PUBLISHED SOURCES

Abdelhady, Dalia. *The Lebanese Diaspora*. New York: New York University Press, 2011.

Abdulhadi, Rabab, Evelyn Alsultany, and Nadine Naber, eds. *Arab and Arab American Feminisms: Gender, Violence and Belonging*. Syracuse, NY: Syracuse University Press, 2011.

Abraham, Nabeel. "To Palestine and Back: Quest for Place." In *Arab Detroit: From Margin to Mainstream*, edited by Abraham and Shryock, 425–462.

Abraham, Nabeel, and Andrew Shryock, eds. *Arab Detroit: From Margin to Mainstream*. Detroit: Wayne State University Press, 2000.

Albrecht, Charlotte Karem. "Narrating an Arab American History: The Peddling Thesis." *Arab Studies Quarterly* 37, no. 1 (2015): 100–117.

Alfaro-Velcamp, Theresa. "'Reelizing' Arab and Jewish Ethnicity in Mexican Film." *The Americas* 63, no. 2 (October 2006): 261–280.

———. *So Far from Allah, So Close to Mexico: Middle Eastern Immigrants in Modern Mexico*. Austin: University of Texas Press, 2007.

Allatson, Paul. *Key Terms in Latino/a Cultural and Literary Studies*. Malden, MA: Blackwell Publishing, 2007.

Almaguer, Tomás. *Racial Fault Lines: The Historical Origins of White Supremacy in California*. Berkeley: University of California Press, 2009. First published in 1994.

ALSAC–St. Jude Children's Research Hospital. *From His Promise: A History of ALSAC and St. Jude Children's Research Hospital*. Memphis, TN: Guild Bindery Press, 1996.

Alsultany, Evelyn. "Arabs and Muslims in the Media After 9/11: Representational Strategies for a 'Postrace Era.'" *American Quarterly* 65, no. 1 (March 2013): 161–169.

———. *Arabs and Muslims in the Media: Race and Representation After 9/11*. New York: New York University Press, 2012.

Appadurai, Arjun. *Modernity at Large: Cultural Dimensions of Globalization*. Minneapolis: University of Minnesota Press, 1996.

'Arbili, Ibrahim. "Al-Haditha," (The Event). *Al-Kalima* 9, no. 8 (1913): 151–161.

Arsan, Andrew. *Interlopers of Empire: The Lebanese Diaspora in Colonial French West Africa*. New York: Oxford University Press, 2014.

Bald, Vivek. *Bengali Harlem and the Lost Histories of South Asian America*. Cambridge, MA: Harvard University Press, 2013.

Balloffet, Lily Pearl. "From the Pampa to the Mashriq: Arab-Argentine Philanthropy Networks." *Mashriq and Mahjar* 4, no. 1 (2017): 4–28.

Basch, Linda, Nina Glick Schiller, and Cristina Szanton Blanc. *Nations Unbound: Transnational Projects, Postcolonial Predicaments, and Deterritorialized Nation-States*. Langhorne, PA: Routledge, 1994.

Bayoumi, Moustafa. *How Does It Feel to Be a Problem: Being Young and Arab in America.* New York: Penguin Books, 2009.

Berman, Jacob. "Mahjar Legacies: A Reinterpretation." In Shohat and Alsultany, *Between the Middle East and the Americas,* 65–79.

Bernstein, Shana. *Bridges of Reform: Interracial Civil Rights Activism in Twentieth-Century Los Angeles.* Oxford: Oxford University Press, 2011.

Bozorgmehr, Mehdi, Claudia Der-Martirosian, and Georges Sabagh. "Middle Easterners: A New Kind of Immigrant." In *Ethnic Los Angeles,* ed. Roger Waldinger and Mehdi Bozorgmehr, 345–378.

Buchenau, Jurgen. *Plutarco Elias Calles and the Mexican Revolution.* Denver: Rowman and Littlefield, 2006.

Clifford, James. *Routes: Travel and Translation in the Late Twentieth Century.* Cambridge, MA: Harvard University Press, 1997.

de Maria y Campos, Camila Pastor. "Inscribing Difference: Maronites, Jews, and Arabs in Mexican Public Culture and French Imperial Practice." *Latin American and Caribbean Ethnic Studies* 6, no. 2 (July 2011): 169–187.

———. "The Transnational Imagination." *Palma Journal* 2, no. 1 (2009): 31–71.

Deverell, William, ed. *A Companion to the American West.* Malden, MA: Blackwell Publishing 2004.

Endore, S. Guy. *The Sleepy Lagoon Mystery.* Los Angeles: Sleepy Lagoon Defense Committee, 1944. Reprinted San Francisco, CA: R and E Research Associates, 1972.

Escobar, Edward J. *Race, Police, and the Making of a Political Identity: Mexican Americans and the Los Angeles Police Department, 1900–1945.* Berkeley: University of California Press, 1999.

Estill, Adriana. Review of *Key Terms in Latino/a Cultural and Literary Studies* by Paul Allatson. *Latino Studies* 7, (2009): 397–399.

Fadda-Conrey, Carol. *Contemporary Arab American Literature: Transnational Reconfigurations of Citizenship and Belonging.* New York: New York University Press, 2014.

Fahrenthold, Stacy. "Transnational Modes and Media: The Syrian Press in the Mahjar." *Mashriq and Mahjar* 1 (2013): 30–54.

———. *Between the Ottomans and the Entente: The First World War in the Syrian and Lebanese Diaspora, 1908–1925.* New York: Oxford University Press, 2019.

Farr, Jamie, with Robert Blair Kaiser. *Just Farr Fun.* Clearwater, FL: Eubanks/Donizetti Inc., 1994.

Feldman, Keith P. *Shadow over Palestine: The Imperial Life of Race in America.* Minneapolis: University of Minnesota Press, 2015.

Fine, Todd. "Remembering Alixa Naff: The 'Mother' of Arab American Studies." Arab American Institute. http://www.aaiusa.org/remembering-alixa-naff -the-mother-of-arab-american-studies.

Fitzgerald, Paul. "George Shibley." *Forum Magazine,* 6, no. 4 (July/August 1979): 5–10.

Flinn, Andrew. "Archival Activism: Independent and Community-Led Archives, Radical Public History, and the Heritage Professions." *InterActions: UCLA Journal of Education and Information Series* 7, no. 2 (2011). https://escholarship.org/uc/item/9pt2490x.

Fowler, Harlan D. *Three Caravans to Yuma: The Untold Story of Bactrian Camels in Western America.* Glendale, CA: Arthur H. Clark, 1980.

Fox, Jonathon. "Reframing Mexican Migration as a Multi-Ethnic Process." *Latino Studies* 4 (2006): 39–61.

Frangos, Steve. "Philip Tedro: A Greek Legend of the American West." *Greek-American Review,* posted October 2006, updated November 26, 2007. http://www.helleniccomserve.com/philiptedro.html.

Gabaccia, Donna R. *From the Other Side: Women, Gender, and Immigrant Life in the United States, 1820–1990.* Bloomington: Indiana University Press, 1995.

Gabbert, Ann R. "El Paso, A Sight for Sore Eyes: Medical and Legal Aspects of Syrian Immigration, 1906–1907." *The Historian* 65, no. 1 (2002): 15–42.

Garrett, Paul D., and Kathleen A. Pupura. *Frank Maria: A Search for Justice and Peace in the Middle East.* Bloomington, IN: AuthorHouse, 2007.

Gettys, Luella. *The Law of Citizenship in the United States.* Chicago: University of Chicago Press, 1934.

Ghattas, Monika. *Los Árabes of New Mexico: Compadres from a Distant Land.* Santa Fe, NM: Sunstone Press, 2012.

Griffith, Benjamin. "Danny Thomas." In *St. James Encyclopedia of Popular Culture,* edited by Thomas Riggs, 100–101. 2nd ed. Detroit: St. James Press, 2013.

Griswold del Castillo, Richard. "The Los Angeles 'Zoot Suit Riots' Revisited: Mexican and Latin American Perspectives." *Mexican Studies/Estudios Mexicanos* 16, no. 2 (Summer 2000): 367–391.

Gualtieri, Sarah M. A. *Between Arab and White: Race and Ethnicity in the Early Syrian American Diaspora.* Berkeley: University of California Press, 2009.

———. "From Lebanon to Louisiana: 'Afifa Karam and Arab Diasporic Feminism." In *Arab American Women,* edited by Suad Joseph. Collection manuscript under review. Syracuse, NY: Syracuse University Press.

———. "Gendering the Chain Migration Thesis: Women and Syrian Transatlantic Migration." *Comparative Studies in South Asia, Africa, and the Middle East* 24, no. 1 (Spring 2004): 18–28.

Gualtieri, Sarah M. A., and Pauline Homsi Vinson. "Introduction." *Amerasia Journal* 44, no. 1 (2018): vii–xxi.

Guglielmo, Thomas. *White on Arrival: Italians, Race, Color, and Power in Chicago, 1890–1945.* New York: Oxford University Press, 2003.

Gutiérrez, Laura G. *Performing Mexicanidad: Vendidas y Cabaretas on the Transnational Stage.* Austin: University of Texas Press, 2010.

Haiek, Joseph R., ed. *Arab American Almanac,* 6th ed. Los Angeles, CA: News Circle Publishing, 2010.

Hall, Stuart, and Bill Schwarz. *Familiar Stranger: A Life Between Two Islands.* Durham, NC: Duke University Press, 2017.

Hartman, Michelle. "Grandmothers, Grape Leaves, and Kahlil Gibran: Writing Race in Anthologies of Arab American Literature." In *Race and Arab Americans Before and After 9/11: From Invisible Citizens to Visible Subjects,* edited by N. Naber and A. Jamal, 170–203. Syracuse, NY: Syracuse University Press, 2008.

Hillstrom, Kevin. *Defining Moments: The Zoot Suit Riots.* Defining Moments. Detroit: Omnigraphics, 2013.

Hitti, Philip. *The Syrians in America.* New York: George Doran, 1924.

Hochberg, Gil. "Archival Afterlives in a Conflict Zone: Animating the Past in Jumana Manna's Cinematic Fables of Pre-1948 Palestine." *Comparative Studies in South Asia, Africa, and the Middle East* 38, no. 1 (2018): 30–42.

Hong, Grace, and Roderick Ferguson. *The Gender and Sexual Politics of Comparative Racialization.* Durham, NC: Duke University Press, 2011.

HoSang, Daniel Martinez. *Racial Propositions: Ballot Initiatives and the Makings of Postwar California.* Berkeley: University of California Press, 2010.

Hourani, Albert, and Nadim Shehadi, eds. *The Lebanese in the World: A Century of Emigration.* London: Centre for Lebanese Studies, I.B. Tauris, 1992.

Howell, Sally. "Cultural Interventions: Arab American Aesthetics Between the Transnational and the Ethnic." *Diaspora: A Journal of Transnational Studies* 9, no. 1 (Spring 2000): 59–82.

Jaber, Rabee. *Amerika.* Beirut: Dar al-Adab, 2010.

———. *Amerika.* Translated from Lebanese Arabic to French by Simon Corthay and Charlotte Woillez. Paris: Gallimard, 2013.

Jacobs, Linda K. *Strangers in the West: The Syrian Colony of New York City, 1880–1990.* New York: Kalimah Press, 2015.

———. "The Disappointed Counsel: Nageeb J. Arbeely." *Jerusalem Quarterly* 71 (2017): 69–80.

———. "The 'First Syrian Immigrant Family.'" Kalimah Press, December 2, 2015. http://kalimahpress.com/blog/the-first-syrian-immigrant-family/.

Jacobson, Matthew Frye. *Whiteness of a Different Color: European Immigrants and the Alchemy of Race.* Cambridge, MA: Harvard University Press, 1998.

———. *Roots Too: White Ethnic Revival in Post-Civil Rights America.* Cambridge, MA: Harvard University, 2006.

Jarmakani, Amira. "Arab American Feminisms: Mobilizing the Politics of Invisibility." In Abdulhadi, Alsultany, and Naber, *Arab and Arab American Feminisms,* 227–241.

John, Sarah E. "Arabic-Speaking Immigrants to the El Paso Area, 1900–1935."
In *Crossing the Waters: Arabic-Speaking Immigrants to the United States Before
1940*, edited by Eric Hoogland, 105–118. Washington, DC: Smithsonian
Institution Press, 1987.

Joseph, Suad. "Against the Grain of the Nation—The Arab-." In *Arabs in America*,
edited by Suleiman, 257–271.

Kadi, Joe, ed. *Food for Our Grandmothers: Writings by Arab-American and Arab-
Canadian Feminists*. Boston: South End Press, 1994.

Karam, John Towfik. *Another Arabesque: Syrian-Lebanese Ethnicity in Neoliberal
Brazil*. Philadelphia: Temple University Press, 2007.

Katzew, Ilona, and Susan Deans-Smith, ed. *Race and Classification: The Case of
Mexican America*. Stanford, CA: Stanford University Press, 2009.

Kayal, Philip M., and Joseph M. Kayal. *The Syrian-Lebanese in America: A Study
in Religion and Assimilation*. Boston: Twayne Publishers, 1975.

Kenny, Kathy. "The Power of Place: Katrina in Five Worlds." *Jerusalem Quarterly*
35, no. 5 (Autumn 2008): 5–30.

Kenny, Kathy Saade. *Katrina in Five Worlds: A Palestinian Woman's Story*. 3rd ed.
n.p.: Five Worlds Press, 2010.

Khan, Suraya. "Political-Social Movements: Community-Based: United States: Early
to Mid-20th Century." *Encyclopedia of Women and Islamic Cultures*. Supplement
17. General editor Suad Joseph. Leiden: Brill, 2018. https://referenceworks
.brillonline.com/browse/encyclopedia-of-women-and-islamic-cultures.

Khater, Akram. "Arbeely Family: Pioneers to America and Founders of the
First Arabic-Language Newspaper." Moise A. Khayrallah Center for Lebanese Diaspora Studies, North Carolina State University, November 30,
2016. https://lebanesestudies.news.chass.ncsu.edu/2016/11/30/arbeely
-family-pioneers-to-america-and-founders-of-the-first-arabic-language
-newspaper/.

Khater, Akram Fouad. *Inventing Home: Emigration, Gender, and the Middle Class
in Lebanon, 1870–1920*. Berkeley: University of California Press, 2001.

Khouri-Makdisi, Ilham. *The Eastern Mediterranean and the Making of Global Radicalism, 1860–1914*. Berkeley: University of California Press, 2010.

Kondo, Dorinne. *Worldmaking: Race, Performance, and the Work of Creativity*.
Durham, NC: Duke University Press, 2018.

Kraut, Alan. *Silent Travelers: Germs, Genes, and the Immigrant Menace*. Baltimore:
Johns Hopkins University Press, 1995.

Larralde, Carlos. "Josefina Fierro and the Sleepy Lagoon Crusade, 1942–1945."
Southern California Quarterly 92, no. 2 (Summer 2010): 117–160.

Leonard, Karen. *Making Ethnic Choices: California's Punjabi Mexican Americans*.
Philadelphia: Temple University Press, 1994.

Lesser, Jeff. "From Pedlars to Proprietors: Lebanese, Syrian and Jewish Immigrants in Brazil." In *The Lebanese in the World*, edited by Hourani and Shehadi, 393–410.

———. "(Re)Creating Ethnicity: Middle Eastern Immigration to Brazil." *Americas* 53, no. 1 (1996): 45–65.

"Louise Beavers (1902–1962)." IMDb. https://www.imdb.com/name/nm0064792/?ref_=tt_cl_t6.

Lubin, Alex. *Geographies of Liberation: The Making of an Afro-Arab Political Imaginary.* Chapel Hill: University of North Carolina Press, 2014.

Mabalon, Dawn Bohulano. *Little Manila Is in the Heart.* Durham, NC: Duke University Press, 2013.

Macías, Anthony. *Mexican American Mojo: Popular Dance and Urban Culture in Los Angeles, 1935–1968.* Durham, NC: Duke University Press, 2008.

Maghbouleh, Neda. *The Limits of Whiteness: Iranian-Americans and the Everyday Politics of Race.* Stanford, CA: Stanford University Press, 2017.

Maloney, Deirdre. M. *National Insecurities: Immigrants and US Deportation Policy Since 1882.* Chapel Hill: University of North Carolina Press, 2012.

Mamey, Samuel S., ed. *Western Pacific Directory and Buyers Guide for 1954–1955: A Directory of Americans of Lebanese, Syrian, and Arabic-Speaking Origin in the Eleven Western States.* Los Angeles, CA: Saint Nicholas Orthodox Church, 1954.

Martínez-Echazábel, Lourdes. "Mestizaje and the Discourse of National/Cultural Identity in Latin America, 1845–1959." *Latin American Perspectives* 25, no. 3 (1998): 21–42.

McAlister, Melani. *Epic Encounters: Culture, Media, and US Interests in the Middle East, 1945–2000.* Berkeley: University of California Press, 2001.

McWilliams, Carey. *North from Mexico: The Spanish-Speaking People of the United States.* New York: Greenwood Press, 1990. First published in Philadelphia: J.B. Lippincott, 1949.

Mishima, María Elena Ota, ed. *Destino México: Un estudio de las migraciones asiáticas a México, siglos XIX y XX.* México, D.F.: El Colegio de México, 1997.

Moch, Leslie Page. *Moving Europeans: Migration in Western Europe Since 1650.* Bloomington: Indiana University Press, 1992.

Molina, Natalia. *How Race Is Made in America: Immigration, Citizenship, and the Historical Power of Racial Scripts.* Berkeley: University of California Press, 2014.

Molina, Natalia, Daniel Martinez HoSang, Ramón A. Gutiérrez, *Relational Formations of Race: Theory, Method, Practice.* Berkeley: University of California Press, 2019.

Naber, Nadine. *Arab America: Gender, Cultural Politics, Activism.* New York: New York University Press, 2012.

———. "Imperial Whiteness and the Diasporas of Empire." *American Quarterly* 66, no. 4 (2014): 1107–1115.

———. "Class Equality, Gender Justice, and Living in Harmony with Mother Earth: An Interview with Joe Kadi." In *Arab and Arab American Feminisms,* 242–247.

Nabhan, Gary. "Camel Whisperers: Desert Nomads Crossing Paths." *Journal of Arizona History* 49, no. 2 (2008), 95–118.

Naff, Alixa. *Becoming American: The Early Arab Immigrant Experience.* Carbondale: Southern Illinois Press, 1985.

———. "Growing Up in Detroit: An Immigrant Grocer's Daughter." In *Arab Detroit: From Margin to Mainstream,* edited by Abraham and Shryock, 107–148.

———. "In Search of Arab Heritage in the US." *Arab Perspectives* 6 (September–November 1985): 25–28.

Najjar, Michael Malek. *Arab American Drama, Film, and Performance: A Critical Study, 1908 to the Present.* Jefferson, NC: MacFarland, 2015.

Ngai, Mae. *Impossible Subjects: Illegal Aliens and the Making of Modern America.* Princeton, NJ: Princeton University Press, 2004.

Noor, Queen. *Leap of Faith: Memoirs of an Unexpected Life.* London: Phoenix, 2003.

Norman, Rachel. "Eating the Matriarch: Locating Identity in the Arab American Female Body." *Amerasia Journal* 44, no. 1 (2018): 128–145.

Norris, Jacob. *Land of Progress: Palestine in the Age of Colonial Development, 1905–1948.* Oxford: Oxford University Press, 2013.

Orfalea, Gregory. *The Arab Americans: A History.* Northampton, MA: Olive Branch Press, 2006.

Orsi, Robert. *The Madonna of 115th Street: Faith and Community in Italian Harlem.* New Haven, CT: Yale University Press, 1988.

Pagán, Eduardo Obregón. *Murder at the Sleepy Lagoon: Zoot Suits, Race, and Riot in Wartime LA.* Chapel Hill: University of North Carolina Press, 2003.

Pastor, Camila. *The Mexican Mahjar: Transnational Maronites, Jews, and Arabs Under the French Mandate.* Austin: University of Texas Press, 2017.

Pennock, Pamela. *The Rise of the Arab American Left: Activists, Allies, and Their Fight Against Imperialism and Racism, 1960s–1980s.* Chapel Hill: University of North Carolina Press, 2017.

Pickens, Therí. "Modern Family: Circuits of Transmission Between Arabs and Black." *Comparative Literature* 68, no. 2 (2018): 130–140.

Portelli, Alessandro. "A Dialogical Relationship. An Approach to Oral History." Shikshantar. http://www.swaraj.org/shikshantar/expressions_portelli.pdf.

Pulido, Laura. *Black, Brown, Yellow, and Left: Radical Activism in Los Angeles.* Berkeley: University of California Press, 2006.

————, and David Lloyd. "From La Frontera to Gaza: Chicano-Palestinian Connections." *American Quarterly* 62, no. 4 (December 2010): 791–794.

Ramírez, Catherine S. *The Women in the Zoot Suit: Gender, Nationalism, and the Cultural Politics of Memory.* Durham, NC: Duke University Press, 2009.

Rashid, Stanley. "Cultural Traditions of Early Arab Immigrants to New York." In *A Community of Many Worlds: Arab Americans in New York City,* edited by Kathleen Benson and Philip M. Kayal, 74–82. New York: Museum of the City of New York, 2002.

Rasmussen, Anne K. "'An Evening in the Orient:' The Middle Eastern Nightclub in America." *Asian Music* 23, no. 2 (1992): 63–88.

————. "The Music of Arab Americans: A Retrospective Collection." Liner notes. Rounder Records CD 1133, Cambridge, MA, 1997.

Razek, Rana. "Trails and Fences: Syrian Migration Networks and Immigration Restriction, 1885–1911." *Amerasia Journal* 44, no. 1 (2018): 105–127.

République française. Ministère des Affaires étrangères. *Rapport à la Société des Nations sur la situation de la Syrie et du Liban, année 1931.* Paris: Imprimerie Nationale, 1932.

————. *Rapport à la Société des Nations sur la situation de la Syrie et du Liban, année 1932.* Paris: Imprimerie Nationale, 1933.

Roediger, David. *Working Toward Whiteness: How America's Immigrants Became White.* New York: Basic Books, 2005.

Rogin, Michael. "'Blackface, White Noise,' The Jewish Jazz Singer Finds His Voice." *Critical Inquiry* 18, no. 3 (1992): 417–453.

Rosas, Ana Elizabeth. *Abrazando el Espíritu: Bracero Families Confront the US-Mexican Border.* Berkeley: University of California Press, 2014.

Roth, Wendy. *Race Migrations: Latinos and the Cultural Transformation of Race.* Stanford, CA: Stanford University Press, 2012.

Rowe, John, ed. *Post-Nationalist American Studies.* Berkeley: University of California Press, 2000.

Sady, Elias. *1948–1950 Syrian Directory of California.* N.p.: Elias Sady, 1950(?).

Said, Edward W. *The Politics of Dispossession: The Struggle for Palestinian Self-Determination, 1969–1994.* New York: Pantheon, 1994.

Salaita, Steven. "Ethnic Identity and Imperative Patriotism: Arab Americans Before and After 9/11," *College Literature* 32, no. 2 (Spring 2005): 146–168.

Saliba, Najib E. *Emigration from Syria and the Syrian-Lebanese Community of Worcester, MA.* Ligonier, PA: Antakya Press, 1992.

Saliba, Therese. "Forgotten Land." *Berkeley Fiction Review* 6 (1985–86): 21–24.

————. "From 'Becoming American' to Transnational Alliances: Feminist Methodologies and Transformations in Arab American Studies." Paper presented at Arab American Studies Conference, Dearborn, MI, April 4, 2014.

———. "Resisting Invisibility: Arab Americans in Academia and Activism." In *Arabs in America,* edited by Suleiman, 304–319.

Samhan, Helen Hatab. "Not Quite White: Racial Classification and the Arab American Experience." In *Arabs in America,* edited by Suleiman, 209–226. Philadelphia: Temple University Press, 1999.

Sánchez, George J. *Becoming Mexican-American: Ethnicity, Culture, and Identity in Chicano Los Angeles, 1900–1945.* New York: Oxford University Press, 1993.

———, ed. *Beyond Alliances: The Jewish Role in Reshaping the Racial Landscape of Southern California.* Annual Review of the Casden Institute for the Study of the Jewish Role in American Life, vol. 9. West Lafayette, IN: Purdue University Press, 2012.

———. "What's Good for Boyle Heights Is Good for the Jews: Creating Multiracialism on the East Side in the 1950s." *American Quarterly* 56, no.3 (2004): 631–666.

Schopmeyer, Kim. "Arab Detroit After 9/11: A Changing Demographic Portrait." In *Arab Detroit 9/11: Life in the Terror Decade,* edited by Nabeel Abraham, Sally Howell, and Andrew Shryock, 29–63. Detroit: Wayne State University Press, 2011.

Shah, Nayan. *Contagious Divides: Epidemics and Race in San Francisco's Chinatown.* Berkeley: University of California Press, 2001.

———. *Stranger Intimacy: Contesting Race, Sexuality, and the Law in the American West.* Berkeley: University of California Press, 2011.

Shaheen, Jack. *Reel Bad Arabs: How Hollywood Vilifies a People.* Northampton, MA: Olive Branch Press, 3rd. ed., 2014.

Shakir, Evelyn. *Bint Arab: Arab and Arab American Women in the United States.* Westport, CT: Praeger, 1997.

Shalhoob, Rev. Methodios. *Pacific Syrian-American Guide, 1937 Issue.* Santa Barbara, CA: Pacific Syrian-American Guide Publishing Co., 1937.

———. *Pacific Syrian-American Lebanese-Palestinian Guide, 1942–1943 Issue.* Santa Barbara, CA: Pacific Syrian-American Guide Publishing Co., n.d. (A copy of this guide is available in the Special Collections department at the Huntington Library, San Marino, CA.)

Shibley, George E. "Sleepy Lagoon: The True Story." *New West,* January 15, 1979.

Shohat, Ella. "The Sephardic-Moorish Atlantic: Between Orientalism and Occidentalism." In Shohat and Alsultany, *Between the Middle East and the Americas: The Cultural Politics of Diaspora,* 42–62.

Shohat, Ella Habiba, and Evelyn Azeeza Alsultany, eds. *Between the Middle East and the Americas: The Cultural Politics of Diaspora.* Ann Arbor: University of Michigan Press, 2013.

Sides, Josh. *LA City Limits: African American Los Angeles from the Great Depression to the Present.* Berkeley: University of California Press, 2003.

Smith, Charles D. *Palestine and the Arab-Israeli Conflict: A History with Documents.* 6th ed. Boston: Bedford/St. Martin's, 2007.

Smith, Marian L. "Women and Naturalization." *Genealogy Notes* 30, no. 2 (Summer 1998). https://www.archives.gov/publications/prologue/1998/summer/women-and-naturalization-1.html.

Spiegel, Lynn. *Make Room for TV: Television and the Family Ideal in Post-War America.* Chicago: University of Chicago Press, 1992.

Starr, Kevin. *Americans and the California Dream, 1850–1915.* New York: Oxford University Press, 1986.

Stern, Alexandra Minna. *Eugenic Nation: Faults and Frontiers of Better Breeding in Modern America.* 2nd ed. Berkeley: University of California Press, 2016.

———. "Eugenics and Racial Classification in Modern Mexican America." In *Race and Classification: The Case of Mexican America,* edited by Ilona Katzew and Susan Deans-Smith.

Stiffler, Matthew Jaber. "Consuming Orientalism: Public Foodways of Arab American Christians." *Mashriq and Mahjar* 4 (2014): 111–138.

Suleiman, Michael W., ed. *Arabs in America: Building a New Future.* Philadelphia: Temple University Press: 1999.

Takaki, Ronald. *A Different Mirror: A History of Multicultural America.* Boston: Little Brown and Company, 1993.

Taparata, Evan. "More American than Apple Pie, Muslims Have Been Migrating to US for Centuries." Public Radio International, April 4, 2016. https://www.pri.org/stories/2016-04-04/more-american-apple-pie-muslims-have-been-migrating-us-centuries.

Tawil, Randa. "Racial Borderlines: Ameen Rihani, Mexico, and World War I." *Amerasia Journal* 44, no. 1 (2018): 85–104.

Thelen, David. "The Nation and Beyond: Transnational Approaches on United States History." *Journal of American History* 86, no. 3 (1999): 965–975.

Thomas, Danny, and Bill Davidson. *Make Room for Danny.* New York: G.P. Putnam's Sons, 1991.

Torres, Louis R., and Jesús S. Treviño. "The Legacy of Sleepy Lagoon." *Nuestro,* November 1977.

US Department of Commerce. Weather Bureau. *Climatological Data.* California, v. 45–47. 1942.

Vecoli, Rudolph. "Problems in Comparative Studies of International Emigrant Communities." In *The Lebanese in the World,* edited by Hourani and Shehadi, 716–724.

Velasco, Alejandro, Omar Dahi, Sinan Antoon, and Laura Weiss. "The Latin East." *NACLA Report on the Americas* 50, no. 1 (2018): 1–7.

Vertovec, Steven. "Conceiving and Researching Transnationalism." *Ethnic and Racial Studies* 22, no. 2 (1999) 447–462.

Vinson, Pauline Homsi. "Voice, Narrative, and Political Critique." In *Etel Adnan: Critical Essays on the Arab-American Writer and Artist*, edited by Lisa Suheir Majaj and Amal Amireh, 176–196. Jefferson, NC: McFarland, 2001.

Waldinger, Roger, and Mehdi Bozorgmehr, eds. *Ethnic Los Angeles*. New York: Russell Sage Foundation, 1996.

Walker, Alice. *Overcoming Speechlessness: A Poet Encounters the Horror in Rwanda, Eastern Congo, and Palestine/Israel*. New York: Seven Stories Press, 2010.

Wehr, Hans. *A Dictionary of Modern Written Arabic*. Edited by J. Milton Cowan. 1961. Reprint, Beirut: Librairie du Liban, 1980.

Weitz, Mark A. *The Sleepy Lagoon Murder Case: Race Discrimination and Mexican-American Rights*. Lawrence: University Press of Kansas, 2010.

Wild, Mark. "So Many Children at Once and So Many Kinds: Schools and Ethno-Racial Boundaries in Early Twentieth-Century Los Angeles." *Western Historical Quarterly* 33, no. 4 (Winter 2002): 453–476.

Wrisley, David Joseph. "Metafiction Meets Migration: Art from the Archives in Rabee Jaber's *Amerika*." *Mashriq and Mahjar* 2 (2013): 99–119.

Yaqub, Salim. *Imperfect Strangers: Americans, Arabs, and U.S.–Middle East Relations in the 1970s*. Ithaca: Cornell University Press, 2016.

Younis, Adele. *The Coming of the Arabic-Speaking Peoples to the United States*, ed. Philip Kayal. Staten Island, NY: Center for Migration Studies, 1995.

Yu, Henry. "Los Angeles and American Studies in a Pacific World of Migrations." *American Quarterly* 56, no. 3 (2005): 531–543.

Zanetell, Myrna. "Farah, Incorporated." Texas State Historical Association. Handbook of Texas Online. https://tshaonline.org/handbook/online/articles/dlf02.

Zeraoui, Zidane. "Los Árabes en México: El Perfil de la Migración." In *Destino México*, edited by Mishima, 257–304.

THESES AND DISSERTATIONS

Duarte, Ramón E. "Extranjeros periciosas ó Mexicanos? Middle Easterners and the Negotiation of National Identity in Mexico 1927–1937." MA thesis, New Mexico State University, Los Cruces, NM, 2009.

Rasmussen, Anne K. "Individuality and Social Change in the Music of Arab-Americans." PhD diss., University of California, Los Angeles, 1991.

Smullin Brown, Kevin. "The Lebanese of Mexico: Identifications in Aspects of Literature and Literary Culture." MA thesis., University College London, 2010.

Stiffler, Matthew W. "Authentic Arabs, Authentic Christians: Antiochian Orthodox and the Mobilization of Cultural Identity." PhD diss., University of Michigan, 2010.

INDEX

Abdun-Nur, Assad, 129
Abraham, Nabeel, 176n10
activism. *See* politics and activism
Adnan, Etel, 97
Ajalat, Lily and Sol, 89
Albrecht, Charlotte Karem, 181n47
Alfaro-Velcamp, Theresa, 157n8,
 166n60, 175n62
Allatson, Paul, 157n13, 184n15
ALSAC (American Lebanese Syrian As-
 sociated Charities), 69, 74, 83, 88,
 175n66
Alsultany, Evelyn, 76
Alvarez, Luis, 65
Alvidiez family, 38
Amairka, as term, 11, 156n6
The American Experience: Zoot Suit Riots
 (film), 168n13
Amerika (Jaber), 119–25, 132, 138,
 140, 147, 180nn15–16
Amir, Amira, 80

Ansara, James M., 82–83
Appadurai, Arjun, 156n7
Arab American Arab Society of Orange
 County, 118
Arab American migrants: and frame-
 works of analyzing migratory
 movement, 7–10, 145–48, 185n34;
 in Mexico, 19–23, 24, 29, 36–38;
 population statistics, 2, 156n5,
 182n1; and presentist frame of
 analysis, 43–44, 65–66; representation in literature, 119–25, 132,
 138, 140, 147; representation in
 oral histories, 128–31, 182n47; in
 traditional historical narrative, 3–5,
 9, 140–42, 158n21. *See also* Arab-
 Latino/a interaction; culture;
 national identity; racial and ethnic
 identity
Arab American National Museum,
 133–34

disease, 7–8, 36, 166n56
Doumanian Mutual Aid Society, 129
Drake, Eddie and George, 113
Duarte, Ramón, 37

Eastern Federation (National Associa-
    tion of Syrian and Lebanese Amer-
    ican Federations), 82–83, 84,
    174n47
Ellis Island, 3–4, 7, 147–48
El Paso, Texas, 23–24
Endore, Guy, 50–51
entertainment industry, 68–69, 70–74,
    86–90
Ernest Hidalgo dance troupe, 81
Escobedo, Elizabeth, 49
Esmaloof family, 37–38
Estado Novo, 146, 185n35
Estill, Adriana, 184n15
ethnicity. See racial and ethnic identity
eugenics, 36
expressive culture, as term, 173n16

Fadda-Conrey, Carol, 17
family histories. See archival activism
Farah, Mansour, 23
Farhat, George, 149–50
Farhat, Suleiman, 24–25, 138
Farr, Jamie, 89–90, 176n4
Farrage, Joe, 79
Federation Herald (magazine), 82–83
Feldman, Keith P., 178n32
Fernández Bustamante, Adolfo, 88
festivals. See mahrajans
The Fez (nightclub), 85
Fierro de Bright, Josefina, 51, 64
Fitzgerald, Paul, 44, 46, 47
Food for Our Grandmothers (Kadi),
    107–8, 109, 177n11
The Fortieth Door (film), 70
Fox, Jonathon, 10
Fricke, Charles W., 41–42, 47–48, 50,
    51–52
Fuleihan, George, 80

Garcia family, 38
Gates, Henry Louis, Jr., 93, 108
gay rights, 56
Gelbart, Larry, 89
gender, womanhood, 106–7. See also
    marriage
George, Maggie, 32, 165n42
George, Mike, 31–32, 164nn41–42
George family, 37–38
Ghannaji, Emily, 80
Gibran, Kahlil, 29, 164n35
Gomez, Linda, 23
grandmothers, as literary trope, 95–96,
    177n11. See also archival activism
Great Depression, 28–29
The Greatest Story Ever Told (film), 89
Greenfield, Alice (McGrath), 44, 51,
    53, 61–63, 64, 169n36
Griffith, D. W., 85
Gualtieri, Sarah M. A., 163n24,
    181n31, 186n37, 190
Guglielmo, Thomas, 33
Gulf War (1990–1991), 99

Haddad, Agnes Necebia, 9
Haddad, Bashara and Nicholas, 113
Hadj Ali, 136; in historiography, 133–
    35; marriage, 135–39, 136, 142–
    43; memorializing of, 144–45
haflats (social gatherings), 82
Halaby, Lisa Najeeb (Queen Noor al-
    Hussein of Jordan), 91, 92–94,
    108–9
Halaby, Najeeb, 91–92
Hallal, Mansur, 102
Hallal, Rafiq (Rufie), 22
Hallal, Shafiqa, 101–3, 102
Hanna, Byron C., 115
Hanna, Julia, 79
Haro, Carlos M., 64–65
Hayworth, Rita, 51, 70
Helú, José, 88
Higham, John, 165n48
Hi Jolly. See Hadj Ali

Stanford Studies in
COMPARATIVE RACE AND ETHNICITY

Published in collaboration with the Center for Comparative Studies in
Race and Ethnicity, Stanford University

SERIES EDITORS
Hazel Rose Markus
Paula M. L. Moya

South Central Is Home: Race and the Power
of Community Investment in Los Angeles
Abigail Rosas
2019

The Border and the Line: Race, Literature, and Los Angeles
Dean J. Franco
2019

Black Power and Palestine: Transnational Countries of Color
Michael R. Fischbach
2018

Race and Upward Mobility: Seeking, Gatekeeping,
and Other Class Strategies in Postwar America
Elda María Román
2017

The Emotional Politics of Racism: How Feelings Trump Facts in an Era of Colorblindness
Paula Ioanide
2015

Beneath the Surface of White Supremacy: Denaturalizing US Racisms Past and Present
Moon-Kie Jung
2015

Race on the Move: Brazilian Migrants and the Global Reconstruction of Race
Tiffany D. Joseph
2015

The Ethnic Project: Transforming Racial Fiction into Racial Factions
Vilna Bashi Treitler
2013

On Making Sense: Queer Race Narratives of Intelligibility
Ernesto Javier Martínez
2012

The authorized representative in the EU for product safety and compliance is:
Mare Nostrum Group
B.V Doelen 72
4831 GR Breda
The Netherlands

www.ingramcontent.com/pod-product-compliance
Lightning Source LLC
Chambersburg PA
CBHW030818270326
41928CB00007B/794